THE FACE OF POETRY

The publisher gratefully acknowledges the following individuals and organizations for their generous support of this book:

BENEFACTORS

Anonymous

Alafi Family Foundation

Center for the Art of Translation

Fishman Family Foundation

Jacqueline Leventhal

Monte and Ruthellen Toole

CHAIRMAN'S CIRCLE OF THE UNIVERSITY OF CALIFORNIA PRESS FOUNDATION

Anonymous

Jeanne and Michael Adams

Jacqueline and Clarence Avant

Carol and John Field

Jean Gold Friedman

Sukey and Gilbert Garcetti /
    Roth Family Foundation

Ann Given Harmsen
    and Bill Harmsen

Adele M. Hayutin

Barbara S. Isgur

Beth and Fred Karren

Lata Krishnan and Ajay Shah

Eric Lax and Karen Sulzberger

John Lescroart and Lisa Sawyer

James and Carlin Naify

Loren and Frances Rothschild

Meryl Selig

Ralph and Shirley Shapiro

The Sidney Stern Memorial Trust

Susan Stone

John and Donna Sussman

Judith and William Timken

Peter Booth Wiley and Valerie Barth

THE FACE OF POETRY

PORTRAITS MARGARETTA K. MITCHELL   EDITOR ZACK ROGOW   FOREWORD ROBERT HASS

UNIVERSITY OF CALIFORNIA PRESS

Berkeley   Los Angeles   London

University of California Press, one of the most distinguished university presses in the United States, enriches lives around the world by advancing scholarship in the humanities, social sciences, and natural sciences. Its activities are supported by the UC Press Foundation and by philanthropic contributions from individuals and institutions. For more information, visit www.ucpress.edu.

University of California Press
Berkeley and Los Angeles, California

University of California Press, Ltd.
London, England

For acknowledgment of permissions for previously published poems and for tracks on compact disc, please see credits, page 344

Library of Congress Cataloging-in-Publication Data

The face of poetry / portraits by Margaretta K. Mitchell ; edited by Zack
    Rogow ; foreword by Robert Hass.
        p.   cm.
    Includes index.
    ISBN 0-520-24603-9 (alk. paper). — ISBN 0-520-24604-7
 (pbk. : alk. paper)
     1. American poetry—20th century.   2. Poets, American—
 20th century—Portraits.   3. American poetry—21st century.
 4. Poets, American—21st century—Portraits.   5. Oral interpretation
 of poetry—History.   I. Rogow, Zack.

PS615.F24   2005
811'.508—dc22   2005040867

Manufactured in Canada

14   13   12   11   10   09   08   07   06   05
10   9   8   7   6   5   4   3   2   1

The paper used in this publication meets the minimum requirements of ANSI/NISO Z39.48-1992 (R 1997) (*Permanence of Paper*).

CONTENTS

FOREWORD

This anthology is based on a poetry reading series at the University of California at Berkeley that went by the name of Lunch Poems. *Lunch Poems* is also the title of a book by Frank O'Hara, published by City Lights Books in 1964. He was forty years old, and he died two years later. He was the comet of his generation, or the kingfisher—a trace of phosphor in the air. By the time of his death he had already come to stand for freedom, spontaneity, and playfulness in poetry. An earlier book of his had been called *Meditations in an Emergency*. In the days when his presence was being felt most intensely, all the young poets knew his short essay "Personism: a Manifesto," which was both a poetic manifesto and a send-up of poetic manifestoes. It read, in part: "You just go on nerve. If someone's chasing you down the street with a knife you just run, you don't turn around and shout, 'Give it up! I was a track star for Mineola Prep.'" It also had this to say: "Nobody should experience anything they don't need to, if they don't need poetry bully for them. I like the movies too. And after all, only Whitman and Crane and Williams, of the American poets, are better than the movies."

The reading series borrowed its name from the book mainly because it was conceived as a noontime event on the Berkeley campus: poems for people who wanted poems for lunch. It was probably also trying to borrow some of the glamour of O'Hara's generosity and casualness and wit. Free poems for lunch, this conjuring of O'Hara seemed to say—practically as good as a free lunch. The readings occurred in a comfortable old reading room in the campus's main library. They were scheduled for the first Thursday of the month during the academic year, because the organizers thought that would be an easy way for people to remember when they happened. The first reading of each year featured members of the university community reading poems they liked. The chancellor of the university, who was Chinese-American, read a poem that had been written on the wall of an internment facility by a detained Chinese immigrant early in the twentieth century. The coach of the rowing crew read E. E. Cummings. A biochemistry professor read Emily Dickinson. A writer from the journalism school who had recently written a book about war crimes read W. H. Auden's great elegy for William Butler Yeats. The last reading of the year featured students reading their own poems. In between were the readings that are remembered here, a very broad range of mostly American poets reading their poems to a lunchtime crowd of between fifty and seven hundred people, depending on the poet and the weather and the season.

The series was initiated in the mid-1990s, and Margaretta Mitchell made portraits of the poets from the very beginning. Because the organizers of the series had different, sometimes conflicting, interests in poetry, and because they wanted to represent a wide range of voices, this anthology, drawn from almost a decade of readings, is a snapshot; it evokes the variety and intensity of American poetry at the end of the twentieth and the beginning of the twenty-first century and shows us some of poetry's faces. The range of poetries collected here reflects something of the spirit of the opening sentence of Walt Whitman's "Democratic Vistas," which remarks that "the greatest lessons of Nature through the universe are perhaps the lessons of variety and freedom."

A nice thing about the idea of freedom proposed by O'Hara's *Lunch Poems* was that it had to do, first of all, with the presumption that a poem written at lunchtime belongs to the part of the day and of the mind that the company doesn't own. Poetry is always free in that fundamental sense. When the person you live with says to you, "Will you get me a glass of water while you're up?," the appropriate response is to get the person a glass of water. When a poet says the same thing in a poem, you don't have to do anything. The appropriate thing to do with that particular verbal presentation is to think about it—perhaps considering it a sort of haiku on the nature of human relationship or, if you are in another frame of mind, on contingency and obligation; in either case you are allowed to make what you want of the symbolic values in a glass of water, whether of clarity, or transparency, or the quenching of thirst. The point of poetry must be to store and pass on to others the whole range of human thought and feeling. It does that by allowing its auditor or reader simply to think freely about language and the world conjured by language, to take pleasure in them, at whatever level of the attentive or the idling mind, rather than to take orders from them.

For the listener, who must always be at least partly listening to herself or himself listening, a poetry reading is presumably an occasion for the kind of freedom reverie provides. Reading poetry to yourself, as *The Face of Poetry* invites us to do, usually requires a more active state of mind, and you're usually under a greater obligation to the meaning of the words, though really you can read a poem any way you want. Ralph Waldo Emerson said—or if he didn't say, he implied—that if a book was any good, you probably wouldn't finish it because it would do what a good book does and stimulate your own thoughts. I suppose that we all read poems that way some of the time, for the lines that cause us to set the book aside. But the best reading of poetry is deeply attentive and absorptive, rapt and analytic at the same time.

Listening to other people—it's a human quality that seems to be part of what we mean by "consciousness"—we have this capacity to become them, to leap to the center of the other's speech and, momentarily, inhabit it. We also have the ability to stand aside and assess what other people say to us. The deepest, most intimate reading of poetry requires both capacities. And that requirement is its freedom. The other kind of freedom, the freedom not to pay attention, is all too available to us. The freedom that comes from deep attention presumes listening all the way into what is being said and how it's being said. The person who says to a friend "I know just what you mean" before the other has completed his thought is not listening; he's leapt too quickly into the moment of identification to hear what might be different, even if only slightly, in another person's experience—and hearing what other people are saying is one of the only ways we ever get outside ourselves. In poetry, as in the other arts, we get to experience what it's like to think someone else's thoughts, feel someone else's feelings. Or we inhabit what it's like to make something—a mark, a gesture, a construction—out of words, out of the intimacy of language and the freight of meanings and feelings that it bears. That requires attention. This is also among the freedoms that poetry has to offer.

These plural freedoms are connected, as Walt Whitman observed, to the variety of human experience. And it's neither an easy nor an assured thing that the variousness of lives will produce that variety in art. It's quite possible that, if we listen deeply into a poem, we end by hearing only what we expected. We hear that we were right to think that we could have completed the thought before it got completely said. Jane Austen is supposed to have written under poems she didn't like: "How true!" Uninteresting poetry tells us exactly what we already know. I believe it was the Russian formalist critic Boris Eichenbaum who said that the function of art "is to make the grass grass and the stone stone by freeing us from the automatism of perception." Style itself can become a kind of automatism. Poetry can get in the way of poetry. What sears us into seeing in one generation can lull us into being too comfortable to really see in the next.

American modernism, for example, became sometimes condensed, difficult, and antilyrical, sometimes full of learned references, because poets felt they had to break out of comfortable late-Victorian ideas about poetry to get to poetry. By the mid-1950s restive younger poets were rebelling against some aspects of modernism, especially its impersonality and high-mindedness, and that rebellion took such forms as a more personal and intimate subject matter or a more spontaneous and playful style—in effect, a return to romanticism. By the 1980s the personal poetry of the 1960s, with its surprising frankness and directness, had begun to seem merely chatty and self-involved; it seemed to have neglected the inventiveness of the art, and a new generation found its way, in turn, back toward modernist difficulty, toward a variety of poetries akin to abstract expressionism in painting or

Russian constructivism in sculpture. Once the daringly difficult began to sound academic, the darlingly personal emerged. Once the personal began to resemble television talk shows, a daringly impersonal postmodernism emerged. This is one of several cycles of innovation and renovation to play out in American poetry in the last fifty years or so. These turnings, which keep the freshness of art fresh, are there in the history of any art, and they are among the things this anthology reflects.

The Lunch Poems reading series was initiated in the mid-1990s. The original organizers, Zack Rogow and Natalie Gerber, wanted to bring to campus poets they were enthusiastic about. They were also interested, as I remember, in poets who read their poems well. They wanted an audience. As an anthology, *The Face of Poetry* therefore reflects the reading series and its moment in interesting ways. It begins with a figure, not an American, whose career spanned much of the twentieth century. Czeslaw Milosz was born in Lithuania in 1911. He spent World War II in Poland, went into exile in France in 1950, and moved to Berkeley to teach in 1960. He came to be read by an American audience after he won the Nobel Prize for Literature in 1980. His work begins this book both because the poems are arranged in chronological order by the author's date of birth and because a poetry series at Berkeley necessarily included a reading from the university's Nobel laureate. On the spring day when he read, he was a vigorous man in his late eighties, erect, his eyes glittering with amusement at the number of students who filled the room and spilled into the galleries in the library's second floor arcade to get a glimpse of him. Their parents had not yet been born when he had watched the Russian Revolution sweep across his grandparents' Lithuanian farm. And now, almost a century later and half a world away, he was reading his poems in a language not his own to a room full of young Californians whose ethnic stories must have encompassed most of the peoples of the earth. It was a sweet moment, and he was perhaps the only person in the room to feel fully the strangeness of it.

It is an oddity, therefore, but a very interesting oddity that one of the early poems in this book of late twentieth-century and early twenty-first-century American poems is a translation of a 1936 Polish poem written in Vilnius (then Wilno), Lithuania, when the violent storm of the Second World War, in which forty-five million people would perish, was gathering force. "Slow River" sounds at first like a pastoral poem in the Polish romantic tradition, and then a voice, in a mode much closer to French symbolist poetry, filled with premonitory dread, with images of a picnic interrupted by or ending among crematoria, erupts into the poem. This is a curious poem with which to begin, but it reminds us, in a voice from outside our own tradition, outside our time, of the world we have inherited. The other Milosz poems—"Bypassing Rue Descartes," with its reflections on the revolutionary and ideological struggles of the twentieth century, and "A Song on the End of the World," with its evocation, in the midst of catastrophe, of the living and always perishable present—are also part of the entry to this book.

After that, the anthology gives us a glimpse of some of the central American poets who came of age just after the Second World War. This was the period when a new generation began to respond to and define itself against the modernists of the first half of the century and to take their idiom in unexpected directions. My Berkeley colleague Charles Altieri, in his magisterial book on the new poetry of the 1950s and 1960s, *Enlarging the Temple,* has described one of the central impulses of that work as a revival of romanticism. Interestingly, he identifies two strands in English romantic poetry that reappear in American poetry after 1950. To simplify (probably to oversimplify) the matter, one strand is a Coleridgean poetics that insists on the creative power of the mind and its free play with the world of things it finds itself inhabiting. The other is a Wordsworthian poetics that seeks to take its form from—and find its inspiration and its meaning in—nature, or perhaps in the nature of things. If this is so, John Ashbery can stand very well for the Coleridgean impulse and Galway Kinnell for the Wordsworthian impulse in American poetry of the last half century.

Poets hate to be pigeonholed, of course. And these characterizations don't really convey the complex skeins of influence and invention that form any artist's style. John Ashbery drew on the modernists, particularly Wallace Stevens and Gertrude Stein, but he also took a great deal from French poetry, from the abstract expressionist painters who were his contemporaries in New York, and from his love of eccentric traditions of all kinds in both literature and painting. And Galway Kinnell seemed formed partly by his reading of Walt Whitman and William Carlos Williams but also by poets he has translated, such as François Villon, Rainer Maria Rilke, and the contemporary French poet Yves Bonnefoy. The range and depth of these two poets and their work of almost fifty years is glimpsed in the poems collected here, sipped. The same could be said of the two slightly younger members of that generation. Gary Snyder took a great deal from the idioms of both Ezra Pound and William Carlos Williams, forging from them and from the influence of classical Chinese and Japanese poets a completely fresh and original poetry rooted in the landscapes of the Pacific coast. Linda Pastan took from William Carlos Williams what was to be one of the central impulses of American poetry in those years, an almost daily practice of the short informal lyric and a steady attention to a discovered shapeliness in her subjects and to the pulse of everyday life. Snyder's early work was associated with the Beat generation and Pastan's with the emergence of a feminist poetry in the 1970s, but they too in their actual poems resist categories.

The four of them can stand for the sense of renewal and for the range of stylistic pos-sibilities in American poetry in the 1950s and 1960s, and one enters through these poets into the center of the anthology, which is divided about equally between poets born in the 1940s, who came of age as artists in the 1970s and 1980s, and poets born in the 1950s, who came of age in the 1980s and 1990s. I won't try to characterize them here—readers can do that for themselves—except to notice what Lunch Poems as a reading series set out to convey: the intensity and variety of experiences, styles, kinds, and subject matters in the poetry of the last thirty years.

About this variety there is a good deal one might say, and a few salient facts. Consider the American modernist in the 1910s. Robert Frost, Wallace Stevens, T. S. Eliot, and E. E. Cummings went to Harvard, and Gertrude Stein went to Radcliffe. Theirs (except for Stein) was the culture of New England, with its Puritan origins. Ezra Pound and William Carlos Williams went to the University of Pennsylvania, and Marianne Moore and Hilda Doolit-tle went to nearby Bryn Mawr. Theirs was the culture of the middle Atlantic states, with its Quaker and Presbyterian and German pietist admixture. These poets went to college at a time when only one to two percent of Americans had any higher education. Among the poets of the 1950s generation, John Ashbery, Frank O'Hara, Robert Creeley, Kenneth Koch, and Donald Hall went to Harvard, and Adrienne Rich and Linda Pastan went to Radcliffe. Allen Ginsberg, Jack Kerouac, and John Hollander went to Columbia, and Galway Kinnell and William Merwin went to Princeton. Immediately after the war about ten percent of the population had some college education, and a handful of Ivy League schools were still pro-ducing most of the poets. But things were beginning to change, as the G.I. Bill, a federal program to give veterans access to colleges and universities, began to democratize higher education in America.

Today more than a third of Americans have some postsecondary education, and this fact is reflected in the poets included in this book. They are from all over the country, and they went to colleges both large and small. There are poets here of mixed Scotch-Irish and African descent and of Mexican and Apache descent. There are poets like Lyn Hejinian, who revived and reframed the poetry of Gertrude Stein in the 1980s and gave a new di-rection to the American avant-garde; poets like Sekou Sundiata, who could reach back to the poems of Sterling Brown and reinvent a performed poetry accompanied by live jazz, blues, and reggae and tip a hat to the young rappers whom he teaches. In fact, most of these poets have made their livings at one time or another teaching poetry in universities and colleges. That is another of the changes that mark these generations of poets. The older poets, those born around 1940, graduated at a time when there were very few creative writing courses in American universities. Most of the poets born after 1950, on the other hand, took undergraduate writing courses and went on to graduate programs in creative writing, and universities have become the principal place where poetic traditions are transmitted from one generation to another. No doubt this situation will change again, but at the moment American higher education provides a place where aspiring writers study poetry and poets make a living teaching it, and that is surely one of the reasons for the explosion in the publication of poetry in the last twenty years.

All of this, of course, is sociology. Margaretta Mitchell's art gives faces to the social facts and gives us a series of striking portraits of individual artists to set against the poems. Between the poems and the faces looking out from the photographs a new space grows up, born of the conversation between poetry and photography. The poems themselves return us to the fact of reading. Poems have their own faces. When the poems matter, so does the culture that produces them, and so does the social history of this art form in a given time and place, and the poems matter if they come to life inside readers.

Robert Hass
Berkeley, April 2005

ACKNOWLEDGMENTS

We would like to thank all those who helped make this book possible and to acknowledge the inspiration of the poets who read at the Lunch Poems Reading Series at the University of California, Berkeley.

Thanks to Lunch Poems in all its parts. Thanks to Robert Hass for his fine foreword and for his leadership in the series. Our gratitude to Alex Warren for hosting the readings in the Morrison Library. Many thanks to all the wonderful Lunch Poems volunteers who worked on the thousands of details of putting together this anthology—Susan Amateau, Liz Jameyson, Karinna Pacheco, Jill E. Thomas, and Maianna Voge. Special thanks to Olivia Friedman for her mighty effort to obtain all the reprint permissions, Holly Fox for listening to so many of the readings to find the poems for the CD, Padma Rajaoui and Elena Balashova for moving this project forward in so many ways, Joseph Bush for driving the poets, and Laura Wetherington for keeping the LPRS ship afloat. And thanks to Vic Wong for his database wizardry in keeping track of the poems and the permissions.

Thanks to those who suggested poems, including Elena Balashova, Anne Barrows, Natalie Gerber, and Bill Zavatsky.

To Photo Lab for ongoing proofing and to Jason Langer for his masterful printing of the final gelatin silver prints for both book and exhibition.

To Marion Abbott Bundy for expert editorial advice on Margaretta Mitchell's introduction.

To Jose Zavaleta for his masterful mastering of the CD and his tireless work in tracking down the tracks. To Obie Greenberg and Jim Richards of UC Berkeley's Educational Technology Services and Gina Hotta at the Berkeley Language Center, University of California, for their help on the CD. Thanks to Steve Dickison and The Poetry Center and American Poetry Archives at San Francisco State University for permission to use recordings of Jorie Graham, Ntozake Shange, and Sekou Sundiata for the CD.

To Sim Warkov special thanks from Margaretta for help along this eight-year journey. And to Colette Patt special gratitude from Zack for her support and advice on this project.

For sponsorship of *The Face of Poetry* project (both book and exhibition) we are grateful for ideas and efforts from Roger Wicker, Tom Jimison, Andrea McLaughlin, Anne Saldich, and Elizabeth Pigford; for support received from the following contributors to *The Face of Poetry*: Monte and Ruthellen Toole, Betty Fishman of The Fishman Family Fund, The Center for the Art of Translation, Jacqueline Leventhal, Ginger Alafi of the Alafi Family Fund,

Sim Warkov, Russell Ellis; and for in-kind contributions of film and photographic chemistry from Tom Kunhardt of Eastman Kodak Company and photographic paper from Tim Bruno of Agfa Photo USA.

Particular thanks to Laura Cerruti of the University of California Press for her recognition of the value of portraits as companions to poems and for her wise and unflagging editorial attention to *The Face of Poetry* and thanks to Rachel Berchten, also of the University of California Press, for shepherding the book through the editorial and production process.

Margaretta K. Mitchell and Zack Rogow

EDITOR'S INTRODUCTION

A poetry renaissance is happening in the United States. From the explosion in creative writing programs and workshops to the poetry slams and open mikes in every city to the reading groups venturing beyond prose for the first time to verse on countless web sites, poetry is suddenly everywhere.

This poetry rebirth has been building slowly over decades, beginning with the excitement of the Beat Generation's pass-the-wine-jug readings in the 1950s that featured writers like Gary Snyder, Allen Ginsberg, and Lawrence Ferlinghetti. The renaissance grew with the confessional poets of the late 1950s and early 1960s, including writers such as Sylvia Plath, Anne Sexton, and Robert Lowell, who wore their personal secrets in their poems as openly as political buttons. It exploded in the Black Arts Movement in the late 1960s and early 1970s in the work of African American writers like June Jordan and Ntozake Shange who celebrated the music of Black English. This poetry rebirth flourished in the writings of the female personal-as-political poets of the 1970s and 1980s, including Adrienne Rich, who told the truth about their lives as women. It includes a rediscovery of the experimental strain in American verse beginning with the rise of the Language poets in the 1970s. It gained momentum as poets from all these movements dug into elementary schools to teach kids to write poems not long after they learned how to write their ABCs.

The rebirth of American poetry is now incredibly diverse. Writers come from every region and are of every race, age, ethnicity, and religion in the United States.

The styles that these poets are writing in are also enormously varied. They include poetry where the language is shaped by the cadences and dynamics of jazz, as in the work in this anthology by Sekou Sundiata and Cornelius Eady. The styles include confessional poetry, where the poet writes a narrative of personal experience in order to take on larger issues. Examples in this book are poems by Linda McCarriston and Sharon Olds. Another style involves poetry rooted in stand-up comedy and performance, including the wildly humorous poems of Billy Collins and Bill Zavatsky. Contemporary poetry styles also include verbal collage, where the poet pieces together contrasting elements from many contexts. Work in that category includes some of the poems in this anthology by John Ashbery, Lyn Hejinian, Robert Hass, Brenda Hillman, Harryette Mullen, and Mary Ruefle. Some contemporary American poets are also returning to formal poetry, revamping traditional structures such as the sonnet, villanelle, and ghazal, as well as making up their own forms. Poets in the anthology who write in this mode include Marilyn Hacker and Agha Shahid Ali.

One exciting thing about this variety of styles is that these schools are now mingling. Individual poets can now pull from all these styles. This mixing of schools is producing a crop of lively hybrids.

One of the main places this poetry rebirth has surfaced is the Lunch Poems Reading Series at the University of California, Berkeley. The series began on September 5, 1996. Robert Hass, Natalie Gerber, and I invited ten campus notables to read their favorite poems at the first Lunch Poems event. We had no clue how many people might turn out for this strange happening. We even asked the campus chancellor, Chang-Lin Tien, to read poems. He was an engineer by profession, and we didn't know how he would respond to this invitation. We also asked a computer scientist, an Olympic swimmer, a geologist, an actor, a biologist, and an anthropologist, among others, to read poetry at midday, an activity usually confined to literati in late-night cafes. The event was boosted by the fact that Robert Hass was then a very active and visible U.S. poet laureate.

The turnout surpassed our most crazed hopes. A standing-room-only crowd crushed into the Morrison Library, enthusiastically welcomed by its director, Alex Warren. There were literally people hanging off the balcony. I prayed that there wouldn't be a fire or an earthquake. Chancellor Tien gave a bilingual reading of an anonymous poem by a Chinese immigrant detained at Angel Island, just as his own admission to the United States had been delayed when he first came to this country:

> *Why should one complain*
> *If detained and imprisoned here?*
> *From ancient times heroes*
> *Were often the first to face adversity.*

Then Margaret Wilkerson rocked the room with a performance of "When Malindy Sings" by the great African American poet Paul Laurence Dunbar, a poem her mother had read to her as a child while combing out her hair.

It was these personal stories of how the poems inhabited the readers' lives that made the event so compelling. Poetry was kickin' in the Morrison Library that day!

But this had to be a fluke. That many people just don't show up for poetry readings, do they? And in broad daylight? So we were more than curious to see what would happen the next month, when our first featured reader, Mark Doty, came from Iowa to inaugurate the next phase of Lunch Poems.

To our amazement, the audience turned out again, even standing on tiptoe in the back to catch a glimpse. Mark Doty didn't disappoint, giving a mesmerizing, torch-song reading of his hymn to perfume and to drag culture:

> *Now,*
> *you call me*
> *Evening in Paris, call me Shalimar,*
>
> *call me Crêpe de Chine.*

The applause at the end of his set was the longest sustained ovation I'd heard in thirty years of attending poetry events.

Overnight, Lunch Poems became a phenomenon, and the Lunch Poems events have continued to pack in audiences, and many of the readings are now available on demand on the Internet (http://lunchpoems.berkeley.edu) and through the University of California's satellite and cable TV network, UCTV.

Part of the electricity of Lunch Poems is that the series is not the possession of any one school of poetry. Too often literary series become inbred, with all the openness of a middle school clique. Small groups of poets come together to laugh a bit too loudly at friends' jokes. Lunch Poems escaped this fate, partly because Robert Hass and I often had very different taste in poetry. Between the two of us, we invited poets from all camps. I think that the audience has responded to that inclusive impulse by turning out in large numbers and by listeners challenging themselves to hear poets they might not have chosen on their own.

Among the earliest fans of Lunch Poems was the remarkable portrait photographer Margaretta (Gretta) K. Mitchell. Gretta came up with the idea of inviting the poets to her studio after the readings (and after we'd given them a good meal!). The publicity photos the poets were sending us were often blurred snapshots taken with throwaway cameras. We realized that most of these poets had never been well photographed. Gretta began working her magic in her studio and has given unstintingly of her time. With a decade of devotion to this project, she has assembled a historic portfolio of U.S. poets, the largest of its kind by a professional photographer. Gretta's photos are not just pictures. She studies the poets and their work. Her portraits are interpretations of the poets. Gretta's photos have an excitement similar to what the audience feel when they hear the poets live at Lunch Poems.

Gretta's portfolio of portraits got fuller and fuller as the tenth anniversary of the founding of Lunch Poems approached. She had accumulated quite a few photos, and she encouraged me to select my favorite poems from the series. It seemed like time to take inventory of where the series had been. That's when Gretta suggested we combine the photos and poems into this anthology.

It's an almost impossible task for an editor to choose a few pages to represent a poet's whole lifetime of work. I had the amazing experience of hearing all these poets read, which helped me immensely in my selection. If a poem made me give a soft involuntary moan of sympathy, it was in. If I burst out laughing or applauded so loudly that I hurt my hands, it was in. That might be another way of saying that my personal bias leans toward accessibility. At times this meant selecting work from a particular book or period in a poet's career. With Jorie Graham and John Ashbery, for instance, their earlier poems provide the best doorway to their work.

In introducing each poet, I've tried to find the fingerprint, what makes that writer distinctive. Influenced by Gretta's example, I've sometimes attempted a portrait of the writer. If there is a good story about the poet's appearance at Lunch Poems, I tell it.

In writing about a particular poem, my goal is to open doors, point out clues. I also try to provide useful background information. I hope that I haven't boxed in the reader with an explanation of what a poem is "about" or what it "says." I prefer for the reader to have room to explore the poem individually.

I have included many wonderful poets and poems in this anthology, but there are gaps. Lunch Poems can only feature six poets a year. Many fine writers have not yet been asked to read. Others have declined because of the need to travel to the West Coast or the drain on their creative time. Still others have read in the series but were shy of the camera. Despite these absences, it has been a thrilling experience to collect the huge bouquet of poems and photos in these pages.

Zack Rogow

PHOTOGRAPHER'S INTRODUCTION

In Celebration of Portraits and Poets

I was inspired to create this portrait collection in 1997 when I met Zack Rogow at a family portrait session in San Francisco. With great enthusiasm he told me about the new project he was working on at the University of California, Berkeley: the Lunch Poems Reading Series. As a lover of poetry, I am always interested in hearing and seeing poets, so I responded in kind, announcing boldly that I would begin my portrait project right away. Surely it would become a book. Eight years later, our book is in hand.

Given the diversity of the Lunch Poems Reading Series, I sought a consistent approach, but one in which the eventual assembly of faces would not fall into the format of a school yearbook. I decided to photograph the poets close up in black and white, with a simple studio backdrop, in order to concentrate on the faces and create a graphic vocabulary for the accompanying poems. This was not the place for journalistic grab-shots of poets caught open-mouthed at the microphone during their readings. To make a memorable portrait, I needed time with each poet to make more revealing images. I wanted to focus on facial expression and, whenever appropriate, gesture. Hands can talk, animating the face and evoking the poet's performance.

In preparation for each portrait, I read selections of the poet's work and then attended the reading, where I observed the poet as presenter. I treasured the direct experience of hearing a poet speak while I "listened" for the messages of gesture and persona. For each poet, I prepared the studio set ahead of time, but it was not until after the reading that I refined my artistic approach. As the poet connected with the audience, I attempted to intercept that connecting energy and bring it back to the studio. From then on, everything I did was intuitive. A drift of lighting might suggest a quality I saw in the writer's work, the contrast or absence of light and shadow contribute to the mood. Each face presented a fresh design challenge; each personality, another mystery to unravel and a unique biography to imbed in the image. Rather than imposing a style on the subject, the personality and creativity of the poet dictated the aesthetics of the portrait.

A portrait, like a poem, is an event—a distillation of experience. While prose can expand endlessly, poetry concentrates words. In this way a photographic portrait is like a poem. In a photograph, expression is confined by time and space. Intuition and insight are the tools of the trade for both poet and photographer. Both proceed with minimal support to make a connection emotionally and symbolically with the viewer or reader. A sympathetic portrait is more than a document and different from other kinds of pictures of people. It can become an experience of consciousness, not unlike the shorthand of poetry, or dance, where the slightest gesture tells all. The startled rise in the arch of an eyebrow can say so much. Oddly enough, the artistic challenge of a portrait is often invisible, a kind of magic, a product of intuition, an entanglement of life experience and memories: an encounter, a conversation without words. In such a dialogue, listening and speaking become visual.

I want to honor the physical realities of this world with a clear-eyed naturalism. Memory matters to me, and I believe that we photograph to remember, to be intimate with the world. A portrait photograph is particular. It stands for a moment in a life, it interprets humanity for the ongoing generations. I know that in the far future, people will see these poets and know them through my eyes. In that slice of reality, a person was there across from the lens, from the camera, from the photographer.

Portraits belong to the historical river of realism. They become the face of history, the signature of a culture, the "look" of an era. When I study the faces of the Fayum portraits, those first- and second-century encaustic paintings from Egypt that are so real in contrast to their mummy shrouds, I feel that I know these people and can imagine their world. I bring that awareness to the faces of these individual and diverse poets, carefully chosen to form a collection and to bear witness to this generation in American literature, at a time when the voice of the poet is reawakening as a cultural force, calling on everyone to participate.

Like many readers of poetry, I have a fascination with personality. When I pick up a book, I always look for the picture on the dust jacket. I find it compelling to read the face for clues to the mind of the author whose words I am about to read. Maybe I am just curious. I want to "know" the person whose words move me in much the same way as I want to see my favorite dancer offstage. The sensitive artist in any medium connects us with ourselves. This is the connection I seek in these photographs.

Working toward that goal, I try never to draw attention to myself. Neither am I interested in imposing a style on my subjects. Rather, I want them to be at center stage. In order to express their essential character, I become a window, not a mirror, a contrast among photographers drawn by John Szarkowski in his seminal work *Looking at Photographs: 100 Pictures from the Collection of the Museum of Modern Art* (1973). I do my best to leave my ego at the door of the studio. There is an art to disappearing into the portrait. It is the director's role. Acting as medium for a character to reveal itself is reminiscent of the theatrical partnership of director and actor.

Indeed, making a portrait involves the work of not one but two people: the subject and the photographer. However, as in the theater, eventually, three participate in the process.

When the viewer or audience enters the picture, both figuratively and literally, the photograph lives on its own, changing its meaning as culture changes.

Each portrait has a tale to tell. Unfortunately, there is not enough room here for the story of each portrait, but I have tried to represent them all by recounting some special moments. These few anecdotes convey the tone of my experiences with these remarkable personalities.

Czeslaw Milosz, accompanied by his wife, Carol, entered without fanfare. As the poet settled into the chair, Carol took me aside to tell me that his hearing aids were being remade and that she would sit close by and speak directly into his ear every time I had something to tell him.

At the reading, I had envisioned Milosz the poet as a monolithic stone, a solid rock of granite. I knew that I would photograph him from the front—square to the lens. No exploration of light from one side or another. Like a sculpture of Buddha, he was simply there, I told him. Carol repeated my thought in his ear. After a few extended moments of silence, he spoke: "If I am granite, then my wife is a diamond." His eyelids opened wide and his eyebrows arched up high; a smile rippled up to his eyes, and he added, "No, she is an emerald." The connections were electric, his charm sparkled and dazzled, like a silent bright snow caught by sunlight, melting from the warmth of the rock itself.

It was an honor to capture the sweet side of this genius, a true gentleman, elegantly outfitted in a blend of blues and browns, an ageless man who appreciated women, this woman in particular.

There is no doubt that a person with eyes intensely focused on you can have an unnerving effect. So it is in a photograph. Gary Snyder's sly hawk eye riveted me—I might have been hapless prey. However, his slight edge of a smile reminded me that Snyder is a man of nature, not a character whom viewers might imagine keeps a rifle across his lap. In the 1960s, looking for grounding, many of us discovered him, and we took his words as seriously as we did those of Thoreau. Now he has seen it all, and the knowing and the seeing unite in his expressive, weathered face.

Ishmael Reed finely tunes his antennae to everything around him, even society's secrets. From the 1960s on, he has brilliantly distilled the black experience into a myriad of forms, commanding, cajoling, and, with a juicy bite of satire, pointing to what we should know. In our session, I could see that his mind overflows with delight in the formation of ideas. He writes to bring the world to his door, where, conscious of himself as an icon, he is proud to stand up for his hometown, Oakland, California, where he champions the possibility and the necessity of racial and cultural diversity.

In conversation with Fanny Howe, I felt as comfortable as I would with an old friend, bouncing views of our creative lives off each other. Eloquent in her observations about challenges, frustrations and sacrifice, she allowed herself to be real. I was touched by the humanity of her gesture. It seemed as if her whole life story rested under the roof her hands formed as they sheltered her brow.

I knew Maxine Hong Kingston not only from her work but also from our mutual experience as survivors of the firestorm of 1991, which devastated her house and left my own a picturesque ruin. I had just finished reading her latest book, *The Fifth Book of Peace,* and still identified her with the image of a woman warrior, so I was not prepared for the woman before me dressed in pink: a lovely cashmere sweater graced by a necklace of elegantly carved pale pink quartz. Her polka dot skirt and cowboy boots playfully completed the picture. This scrim of pink gave way as she told stories from her life as a daughter, mother, and wife. New facets of her personality kept appearing like a kaleidoscope, and I watched her expressions shift. "This is a woman of paradox," I thought, while I listened to her stories.

My time with Robert Pinsky was a reunion of sorts. We had known each other through a salon lunch group, organized by the composer Charles Shere, that took place years ago, when Pinsky taught at Berkeley. I had been in awe of him then and have continued to admire his work since. He read masterfully and with an intensity of focus coming from his feet that had him on his toes most of the time. Later, in front of the camera, he relaxed and was charming, the way I imagined he would be as an actor in a movie.

Magic was in the air the day that Billy Collins read his poems. For starters the audience was stuffed into a larger space on the campus, the Zellerbach Playhouse, and it was obvious from the buzz in the crowd that this poet has charisma.

I already knew this because our schedule placed the portrait before the reading. I had seen him perform in the studio space where he explored his many selves. Captivated, I knew that it would be almost impossible to confine his expressive nature to one image.

A man with secrets tucked behind his steady open gaze, he is awake to the everyday moment while seeing far beyond it. In conversation he projects intimacy, but with the slightly distant courtliness that seems to come from another century. A charming, self-deprecating humor popped up when I asked him if he knew that he was to read in a spacious theater setting to allow for the expected crowd of fans. "Well," he said, "I hope they won't regret it!" We talked of dogs, cats, illness, poems, gardens and vegetables, all jumbling into the easy conversation of old friends by the time the portrait was completed. What a delightful surprise and yet a perfectly natural gesture when he pulled a camera from his pocket and took my picture.

No one exudes generosity of spirit like Robert Hass. He is like a mountain stream under sun and shadow, always refreshing, always taking a new turn, always offering another view. Each of his introductions for the Lunch Poems Reading Series was illuminating, thoroughly considered, and spoken with conviction. His own presence as a poet felt large, open and thoughtful, confident and close, simple and straightforward, embracing all the world of poets as his family.

When Sharon Olds came to read, it was her first visit to her hometown, Berkeley, in a long time, apparently a very emotional event for her. Cordial, but lost in her own thoughts, she warmed up to the portrait as I gave her time to relax. If I retain an image of her from that day, dressed in a black kimono-like garment lined with white along the neckline, it would be that of a Zen Buddhist priest.

Bill Zavatsky is a man who can make you laugh out loud. The zany quality of his words spill over to his person, which made my time with him a complete delight. He attacked the task of posing with enthusiasm and put on a show worthy of the best comedy today. And yet he was completely himself. Loving jazz, he could not resist giving me a private concert, until he discovered the sour note on my untuned piano. Graciously, he worked around it and made even that detail into something humorous, exclaiming, "We all have a bent note in our personality that we need to work around to make music!"

Though I consistently used a studio setting for the project, I did not always work with artificial light. For the portrait of Linda McCarriston, I chose an image flooded with natural light from a dramatic sunset—a perfect fit for this intrepid woman, who has triumphed against the odds and taken herself to the Alaskan wild, moving from Vermont across the continent with dog, cat, and horse in tow. For me, the intimate view of Linda looking candidly into the lens conveys her complexity: humor interlaced with wincing pain from her life, and beauty shining forth through her Irish, French, and Native American features.

From Yusef Komunyakaa's commanding presence, I took away a mythic vision of an African chieftain. To convey this sense of ancient ritual, I sliced with a knife into the backdrop paper, then illuminated it from behind, to simulate royal scarifications. This came to me as I envisioned the power of his words and the nobility of his gaze.

A few days later, I received a call from Komunyakaa's editor at Farrar, Straus & Giroux asking me to send them a copy of the photograph: "Komunyakaa wants to use your portrait in his forthcoming book, *Talking Dirty to the Gods*." "But," I replied in great confusion, "I haven't even developed the film yet." The editor smoothly replied, "But Yusef told me that he knew that the portrait would be wonderful." I had imagined him as king, but maybe psychic was more accurate.

Heather McHugh protested that she had never had a good picture of herself. She saw getting one taken as impossible. I suggested that perhaps her glasses had presented problems, limiting certain angles of the face because of distracting reflections. I moved beyond the spectacles to find the quick wit waiting beneath: a mischievous glance signaling a playful personality.

As Ntozake Shange stepped into my front hall the morning after her reading, she announced broadly that she had a terrible headache, that she was really exhausted, and that it would be impossible to get a good photograph. I dug out an aspirin and a tall glass of water and said, "Well, you're here, let's make pictures anyway." I focused on her fabulous hair, which was intricately patterned with beads and braids. Her personality, which I knew from her reading the night before, was even more theatrical. As we worked together, she looked increasingly better and calm. She grew more peppy and responsive; her face more relaxed and expressive. Toward the end of our session, I wanted to coax out the spirited creature I had seen deliver that dramatic reading, so I commented, "What I find truly impressive are your perfectly crafted nails." With that her hands shot up, her smile blazed, and, bingo, she was on fire! It was the last frame in the camera.

I watched a joyous glow emanate from Sekou Sundiata when he was on stage at Berkeley's Greek Theater, music flowing around the spoken word under the night sky. Constantly in motion, his hands framed the poetry with style, casual, yet aware of the effect of even a tilt of his head. As a director, I found it gratifying that he was willing to create a mini-performance for the camera.

I had heard that David St. John was not only a fine poet but also a great and magnanimous teacher. I understood what that combination meant when I saw how easily he presented himself, without a shred of self-consciousness. During our time together, he was completely attentive to the nuances of what I was doing. He gave himself over to the portrait as he must do for his students in workshops, listening with the whole of himself and then commenting with remarkable sensitivity. He asked to see some of the portraits. "So many of these poets are old friends," he said, "yet you've captured some element of each that I've never seen before."

If there were a diva among poets, it would be Jorie Graham. Blessed with a beautiful face, sultry in tone but imperious in symmetry, she appeared to me like a force of nature, visually represented by her torrential streams of hair and the expressions that moved across her face like so many summer storms. From the moment she arrived, Jorie was completely involved in the process of seeing and being seen, giving me a portrait photographer's dream session. We made so many sensational versions of her that I still am not sure if I chose the right one. I expect that all those other personae will appear and reappear in her poetic future.

The pleasure he demonstrated in posing for the camera made my time with Agha Shahid Ali especially smooth. A long poem about his mother, which evoked my own feelings both for my mother and for being a mother myself, stuck in my mind as we began. During the portrait session, when I told him how much it meant to me to hear him read it, he recited some lines with a flourish, looked off into space, and said with stark conviction, "She should never have died."

There are moments in everyday life when a simple scene of birds in the backyard becomes spellbinding because of a poet's vision. Brigit Pegeen Kelly has that kind of vision that transforms the ordinary into the extraordinary. Her shamanistic power is contained by a modest demeanor, quiet and clear, rooted in nature.

Few people have the natural knack for connecting with the audience as does Jimmy Santiago Baca. He arrived with his entourage of musician friends and followers, who had made his reading into quite a show. His presentation displayed a remarkably sophisticated sense of the political. In the portrait session, I was drawn into the entourage as he projected a passionate, down-to-earth sensuality, comfortably sharing intimate details from his life, at home with himself while fearlessly connecting with the lens and the world.

Magic seems to be left in the wake of so many of my encounters with these poets. Mary Ruefle's quirky humor belies the intensity of her X-ray eyes. I wish I could bottle and sell whatever I did to touch off a delightful series of facial expressions ready like puppets to pop up and tell their secrets. Spotting the ancestral dollhouse (which belonged to my mother and then came to me), she wanted to investigate every room and all the furniture. A week later, a tiny note arrived addressed to the Little People, followed by the announcement that the Little People were named Victor and Viola Mint. At Christmas, gifts arrived for the family. Victor appreciated the fine wine, and the Mint children adored the scooter. In her accompanying note, Mary admonished them not to mix the two.

As a maker of visual memories, I am haunted by the relentless trek of time passing. Over the years, I have been driven to devote myself and my camera to recording families and children, my own and others, as they change, to capturing moments on film before they pass, to recording the face of my beloved before he died.

When Mark Doty read his poem "The Embrace," I felt an instant connection. He had lost his life partner; I had recently lost my husband of thirty-seven years. We were both still raw, and his poem struck a nerve. The poem admits a photograph's power to evoke memories, while at the same time revealing that the photograph of his lover is not enough.

A photograph cannot bring the person back. But it may be all we have. We have felt the loss, yearned for art to heal, to provide solace, and yet we face the reality of our inadequacy to recall the memories vividly enough even in dreams. Perhaps only love remains.

Looking into the translucence of this man's pale blue eyes, I felt the sensitivity of his words. Mark showed me how in writing such a poem, a deeply felt aesthetic experience can in its stark truth make life more bearable.

Intensity radiates from the shaved dome and dark eyes of Frank Paino. During the reading I was swept back into a lush and dark sensibility I associate with literature from the end of the nineteenth century, yet when he and his sister Gerrie arrived for the portrait, I had the feeling that they were standing (spiritually) at the edge of a new age. Later in our portrait time, we shared ideas and enthusiasms as if we were opening trunks of memorabilia stored in the family attic. I asked him about his experience of changing gender and he answered simply and without hesitation, "I am the same person."

In the first decade of the twenty-first century, the significance of portraiture is being rediscovered. We confront it on a daily basis. We recall the many portraits proliferating in the pages of newspapers after every major natural disaster. We have studied with sadness the rows of photos of those fallen and lost in the tragic attacks of 9/11 appearing in page after page of the *New York Times,* especially the hundreds of firemen facing forward like a graduating class. We continue to note the silent showing on television of the next soldier to die in Iraq.

Like poetry, photography can be soul work. All over the world, there are people who are afraid to be photographed for fear that the soul will be sacrificed to the black box. In a sense, this fear is real, because whoever takes the photograph is in control and may, in fact, be using the subject for his or her own purposes or obsession, which might be malevolent, or simply egotistical. There are as many ways to work as a photographer as there are different personalities. For me, a portrait is always an intimate experience. I am not interested in tricks or manipulation. I always seek clarity and connection with the inner core of the person I am photographing. The subject can become objectified, surrendered to the narcissistic taker, or the portrait experience can be enhancing, a dance of two in rhythm, making music together. Then the portrait will last and speak for both subject and artist, as well as for the mysterious power of the art of portraiture.

Margaretta K. Mitchell

THE FACE OF POETRY

CZESLAW MILOSZ

Czeslaw Milosz (1911–2004) is one of the major figures in world literature of the past hundred years. Born in Lithuania, he wrote poetry for close to a century. Milosz wrote in his native Polish but lived in exile in the United States starting in 1951 after defecting from the Polish government that consolidated Communist rule during that time. He began teaching at the University of California, Berkeley, in 1960, as professor of Slavic languages and literature. After he retired from his professorship, he divided his time between California and Poland. In 1980, he won the Nobel Prize for Literature. His many poetry books in English include *Czeslaw Milosz: The Collected Poems, 1931–1987* (1988) and the more recent *Road-Side Dog* (1998). He is also the author of numerous books of prose, including *To Begin Where I Am: Selected Essays* (2001) and *A Treatise on Poetry* (2001). Milosz also edited *A Book of Luminous Things: An International Anthology of Poetry* (1996).

"Bypassing Rue Descartes," one of Milosz's best-known poems, deals with world politics. Milosz commented on this poem that his native Lithuania was one of the last places in Europe to be Christianized. Many pagan superstitions remained there in his youth, including the belief that killing a water snake led to bad luck. This poem contrasts the backward world of the "barbarian" provinces with the seekers of the modern "universal" who flocked to Paris. Milosz evokes a hierarchical, patriarchal world of barefoot female servants. But if they are oblivious to the very local customs and tastes even of the city of Paris, those who aim to impose a universal order as a remedy for this oppression end up as murderers. "Bypassing Rue Descartes" describes a tragedy—the tragedy of recent history.

"A Song on the End of the World" was written during the Warsaw Ghetto Uprising (April 19–May 16, 1943) when Jews engaged in a desperate effort to fight deportation to the Nazi death camps. In Polish, the poem sounds like a song, with rhyme and softly sibilant consonants. Milosz witnessed a city indifferent to the massacre of the rebels, who fought with makeshift weapons against the much more numerous and better-equipped German army.

His poem "Slow River" begins on a pastoral note, with a lovely spring in deep colors. But quickly the poem steers toward the ominous when the speaker addresses an innocent who seems eager for evil. The poem sprouts omens of doom, such as husbands taking bread from their pregnant wives. "Slow River" was written before the Nazis invaded Poland in 1939, and before the Communists came to power after World War II, but it seems incredibly prophetic in its sense of impending violence. Milosz's long view looks toward a true spring.

BYPASSING RUE DESCARTES

Bypassing rue Descartes
I descended toward the Seine, shy, a traveler,
A young barbarian just come to the capital of the world.

We were many, from Jassy and Koloshvar, Wilno and Bucharest, Saigon and Marrakesh,
Ashamed to remember the customs of our homes,
About which nobody here should ever be told:
The clapping for servants, barefooted girls hurry in,
Dividing food with incantations,
Choral prayers recited by master and household together.

I had left the cloudy provinces behind,
I entered the universal, dazzled and desiring.

Soon enough, many from Jassy and Koloshvar, or Saigon or Marrakesh
Would be killed because they wanted to abolish the customs of their homes.

Soon enough, their peers were seizing power
In order to kill in the name of the universal, beautiful ideas.

Meanwhile the city behaved in accordance with its nature,
Rustling with throaty laughter in the dark,
Baking long breads and pouring wine into clay pitchers,
Buying fish, lemons, and garlic at street markets,
Indifferent as it was to honor and shame and greatness and glory,
Because that had been done already and had transformed itself
Into monuments representing nobody knows whom,
Into arias hardly audible and into turns of speech.

Again I lean on the rough granite of the embankment,
As if I had returned from travels through the underworlds
And suddenly saw in the light the reeling wheel of the seasons
Where empires have fallen and those once living are now dead.

There is no capital of the world, neither here nor anywhere else,
And the abolished customs are restored to their small fame
And now I know that the time of human generations is not like the time of the earth.

As to my heavy sins, I remember one most vividly:
How, one day, walking on a forest path along a stream,
I pushed a rock down onto a water snake coiled in the grass.

And what I have met with in life was the just punishment
Which reaches, sooner or later, the breaker of a taboo.

Translated from the Polish by Renata Gorczynski and Robert Hass

A SONG ON THE END OF THE WORLD

On the day the world ends
A bee circles a clover,
A fisherman mends a glimmering net.
Happy porpoises jump in the sea,
By the rainspout young sparrows are playing
And the snake is gold-skinned as it should always be.

On the day the world ends
Women walk through the fields under their umbrellas,
A drunkard grows sleepy at the edge of a lawn,
Vegetable peddlers shout in the street
And a yellow-sailed boat comes nearer the island,
The voice of a violin lasts in the air
And leads into a starry night.

And those who expected lightning and thunder
Are disappointed.
And those who expected signs and archangels' trumps
Do not believe it is happening now.
As long as the sun and the moon are above,
As long as the bumblebee visits a rose,
As long as rosy infants are born
No one believes it is happening now.

Only a white-haired old man, who would be a prophet
Yet is not a prophet, for he's much too busy,
Repeats while he binds his tomatoes:
There will be no other end of the world,
There will be no other end of the world.

WARSAW, 1944

Translated by Anthony Milosz

SLOW RIVER

There has not been for a long time a spring
as beautiful as this one; the grass, just before mowing,
is thick and wet with dew. At night bird cries
come up from the edge of the marsh, a crimson shoal
lies in the east till the morning hours.
In such a season, every voice becomes for us
a shout of triumph. Glory, pain and glory
to the grass, to the clouds, to the green oak wood.
The gates of the earth torn open, the key
to the earth revealed. A star is greeting the day.
Then why do your eyes hold an impure gleam
like the eyes of those who have not tasted
evil and long only for crime? Why does this heat
and depth of hatred radiate
from your narrowed eyes? To you the rule,
for you clouds in golden rings
play a music, maples by the road exalt you.
The invisible rein on every living thing
leads to your hand—pull, and they all
turn a half-circle under the canopy
called cirrus. And your tasks? A wooded mountain

awaits you, the place for cities in the air,
a valley where wheat should grow, a table, a white page
on which, maybe, a long poem could be started,
joy and toil. And the road bolts like an animal,
it falls away so quickly, leaving a trail of dust,
that there is scarcely a sight to prepare a nod for,
the hand's grip already weakened, a sigh, and the storm is over.
And then they carry the malefactor through the fields,
rocking his gray head, and above the seashore
on a tree-lined avenue, they put him down
where the wind from the bay furls banners
and schoolchildren run on the gravel paths,
singing their songs.

—"So that neighing in the gardens, drinking on the green,
so that, not knowing whether they are happy or just weary,
they take bread from the hands of their pregnant wives.
They bow their heads to nothing in their lives.
My brothers, avid for pleasure, smiling, beery,
have the world for a granary, a house of joy."

—"Ah, dark rabble at their vernal feasts
and crematoria rising like white cliffs
and smoke seeping from the dead wasps' nests.
In a stammer of mandolins, a dust-cloud of scythes,
on heaps of food and mosses stomped ash-gray,
the new sun rises on another day."

For a long time there has not been a spring
as beautiful as this one to the voyager.
The expanse of water seems to him dense
as the blood of hemlock. And a fleet of sails
speeding in the dark, like the last
vibration of a pure note. He saw
human figures scattered on the sands

under the light of planets, falling from the vault
of heaven, and when a wave grew silent, it was silent,
the foam smelled of iodine? heliotrope?
They sang on the dunes, Maria, Maria,
resting a spattered hand on the saddle
and he didn't know if this was the new sign
that promises salvation, but kills first.
Three times must the wheel of blindness
turn, before I look without fear at the power
sleeping in my own hand, and recognize spring,
the sky, the seas, and the dark, massed land.
Three times will the liars have conquered
before the great truth appears alive
and in the splendor of one moment
stand spring and the sky, the seas, the lands.

WILNO, 1936

Translated by Renata Gorczynski

JOHN ASHBERY

John Ashbery (b. 1927), born and raised in Rochester, New York, is a major figure in U.S. literature. Ashbery has developed a unique structure and texture for his poems. He creates word collages without seams, as if an artist had figured out how to paste images on paper while making the edges between the elements disappear. He has an exquisite ability to describe difficult-to-capture moments. Ashbery adds to this materials from popular culture, daily life, philosophy, and art history in a way that is both meditative and extremely funny. His knowledge of art is voluminous—he worked as a critic and editor for *ARTnews* magazine.

The chatty, prosy tone of his poems allows Ashbery to sneak up on the reader with surprising insights. His poetry reflects on the making of poetry. His language talks about the limits of language. His self meditates on the variety, opacity, and strangeness of the self.

Ashbery's more than twenty books of poems have gleaned for him almost every honor open to an American poet. His collection *Self-Portrait in a Convex Mirror* (1975) won the triple crown of U.S. poetry in 1975: the Pulitzer Prize, the National Book Award, and the National Book Critics Circle Award. He was the first English-language poet to win the prestigious Grand Prix des Biennales Internationales de Poésie.

"Some Trees" is the title poem from his first book. The poem's logic is elaborate, maybe too dense to unravel. But is that the point? The poem is a puzzle of oxymorons, the poet "Arranging by chance" what he sees and thinks. The poem ducks in and out of the observed world to the realm of literature and art till they can't be told apart. But by their presence and their beauty, the trees in the poem affirm the connection between the speaker and the person he is addressing.

"Scheherazade" comes from the book *Self-Portrait in a Convex Mirror.* Like the heroine of *1001 Arabian Nights,* for whom the poem is named, Ashbery dazzles with words. The poem playfully and continuously flirts with narrative but never quite gives itself to story, just as Scheherazade puts off her execution by not coming to the end of her train of tales.

His poem "Melodic Trains," from the book *Houseboat Days,* is a wonderful account of a rail trip. Ashbery has sifted this journey so completely into reflection that the reader is always in doubt whether the voyage exists as an account of an actual event or as a fantasy/metaphor/self-parody.

SOME TREES

These are amazing: each
Joining a neighbor, as though speech
Were a still performance.
Arranging by chance

To meet as far this morning
From the world as agreeing
With it, you and I
Are suddenly what the trees try

To tell us we are:
That their merely being there
Means something; that soon
We may touch, love, explain.

And glad not to have invented
Such comeliness, we are surrounded:
A silence already filled with noises,
A canvas on which emerges

A chorus of smiles, a winter morning.
Placed in a puzzling light, and moving,
Our days put on such reticence
These accents seem their own defense.

SCHEHERAZADE

Unsupported by reason's enigma
Water collects in squared stone catch basins.
The land is dry. Under it moves
The water. Fish live in the wells. The leaves,
A concerned green, are scrawled on the light. Bad
Bindweed and rank ragweed somehow forget to flourish here.
An inexhaustible wardrobe has been placed at the disposal
Of each new occurrence. It can be itself now.
Day is almost reluctant to decline
And slowing down opens out new avenues
That don't infringe on space but are living here with us.
Other dreams came and left while the bank
Of colored verbs and adjectives was shrinking from the light
To nurse in shade their want of a method
But most of all she loved the particles
That transform objects of the same category
Into particular ones, each distinct
Within and apart from its own class.
In all this springing up was no hint
Of a tide, only a pleasant wavering of the air
In which all things seemed present, whether
Just past or soon to come. It was all invitation.
So much the flowers outlined along the night
Alleys when few were visible, yet
Their story sounded louder than the hum
Of bug and stick noises that brought up the rear,
Trundling it along into a new fact of day.
These were meant to be read as any
Salutation before getting down to business,
But they stuck to their guns, and so much

Was their obstinacy in keeping with the rest
(Like long flashes of white birds that refuse to die
When day does) that none knew the warp
Which presented this major movement as a firm
Digression, a plain that slowly becomes a mountain.

So each found himself caught in a net
As a fashion, and all efforts to wriggle free
Involved him further, inexorably, since all
Existed there to be told, shot through
From border to border. Here were stones
That read as patches of sunlight, there was the story
Of the grandparents, of the vigorous young champion
(The lines once given to another, now
Restored to the new speaker), dinners and assemblies,
The light in the old home, the secret way
The rooms fed into each other, but all
Was wariness of time watching itself
For nothing in the complex story grew outside:
The greatness in the moment of telling stayed unresolved
Until its wealth of incident, pain mixed with pleasure,
Faded in the precise moment of bursting
Into bloom, its growth a static lament.

Some stories survived the dynasty of the builders
But their echo was itself locked in, became
Anticipation that was only memory after all,
For the possibilities are limited. It is seen
At the end that the kind and good are rewarded,
That the unjust one is doomed to burn forever
Around his error, sadder and wiser anyway.
Between these extremes the others muddle through
Like us, uncertain but wearing artlessly

Their function of minor characters who must
Be kept in mind. It is we who make this
Jungle and call it space, naming each root,
Each serpent, for the sound of the name
As it clinks dully against our pleasure,
Indifference that is pleasure. And what would they be
Without an audience to restrict the innumerable
Passes and swipes, restored to good humor as it issues
Into the impervious evening air? So in some way
Although the arithmetic is incorrect
The balance is restored because it
Balances, knowing it prevails,
And the man who made the same mistake twice is exonerated.

MELODIC TRAINS

A little girl with scarlet enameled fingernails
Asks me what time it is—evidently that's a toy wristwatch
She's wearing, for fun. And it is fun to wear other
Odd things, like this briar pipe and tweed coat

Like date-colored sierras with the lines of seams
Sketched in and plunging now and then into unfathomable
Valleys that can't be deduced by the shape of the person
Sitting inside it—me, and just as our way is flat across
Dales and gulches, as though our train were a pencil

Guided by a ruler held against a photomural of the Alps
We both come to see distance as something unofficial
And impersonal yet not without its curious justification
Like the time of a stopped watch—right twice a day.

Only the wait in stations is vague and
Dimensionless, like oneself. How do they decide how much

Time to spend in each? One begins to suspect there's no
Rule or that it's applied haphazardly.

Sadness of the faces of children on the platform,
Concern of the grownups for connections, for the chances
Of getting a taxi, since these have no timetable.
You get one if you can find one though in principle

You can always find one, but the segment of chance
In the circle of certainty is what gives these leaning
Tower of Pisa figures their aspect of dogged
Impatience, banking forward into the wind.

In short any stop before the final one creates
Clouds of anxiety, of sad, regretful impatience
With ourselves, our lives, the way we have been dealing
With other people up until now. Why couldn't
We have been more considerate? These figures leaving

The platform or waiting to board the train are my brothers
In a way that really wants to tell me why there is so little
Panic and disorder in the world, and so much unhappiness.
If I were to get down now to stretch, take a few steps

In the wearying and world-weary clouds of steam like great
White apples, might I just through proximity and aping
Of postures and attitudes communicate this concern of mine
To them? That their jagged attitudes correspond to mine,

That their beefing strikes answering silver bells within
My own chest, and that I know, as they do, how the last
Stop is the most anxious one of all, though it means
Getting home at last, to the pleasures and dissatisfactions of home?

It's as though a visible chorus called up the different
Stages of the journey, singing about them and being them:
Not the people in the station, not the child opposite me
With currant fingernails, but the windows, seen through,

Reflecting imperfectly, ruthlessly splitting open the bluish
Vague landscape like a zipper. Each voice has its own
Descending scale to put one in one's place at every stage;
One need never not know where one is

Unless one give up listening, sleeping, approaching a small
Western town that is nothing but a windmill. Then
The great fury of the end can drop as the solo
Voices tell about it, wreathing it somehow with an aura

Of good fortune and colossal welcomes from the mayor and
Citizens' committees tossing their hats into the air.
To hear them singing you'd think it had already happened
And we had focused back on the furniture of the air.

GALWAY KINNELL

Galway Kinnell (b. 1927), born in Providence, Rhode Island, is a leading poet whose books have appeared in print since the early 1950s. He won both the Pulitzer Prize and the National Book Award for his *Selected Poems* (1982). He has continued to turn out excellent writing and published *A New Selected Poems* in 2000. His translations include poetry by François Villon, Rainer Maria Rilke, Yvan Goll, and Yves Bonnefoy. He is also the author of *Black Light* (1966), a novel set in Iran. The volume *Walking Down the Stairs* (1978) contains interviews with Kinnell on poetry.

Kinnell can take the most mundane of subjects, such as eating breakfast by himself in the poem "Oatmeal," and turn it into jubilation. His mind transforms this humdrum moment into a realization about the imagination, but a Zen realization, sparked by laughter. The speaker's fanciful encounter with John Keats seems especially appropriate, since the Romantic poets were champions of the imagination. As Keats wrote in "The Fall of Hyperion," "every man whose soul is not a clod / Hath visions, and would speak, if he had loved / And been well nurtured in his mother tongue." Kinnell's poem also refers to Robert Browning's famous rhetorical question in his poem "Popularity," "What porridge had John Keats?"

When Galway Kinnell reads his poems to an audience, he uses his deep, resonant voice to tug his listeners into the world of his poems. It's a world where human life sometimes faces the most difficult of tests, as in the poem "Parkinson's Disease," about the reversal of roles that takes place when a sick and elderly parent is looked after by a grown child. In Kinnell's poem, the daughter is a loving caregiver, and old age and death are sharp, but cushioned by compassion and intimacy. Kinnell's descriptions can be exquisite and excruciating, as in his portrait of a body worked over by Parkinson's: "His face softens into a kind / of quizzical wince, as if one / of the other animals were working at / getting the knack of the human smile."

In Kinnell's poem "Rapture" a man lazes on his pillow in the morning, admiring his lover getting dressed. He puts the sexy description of the beloved in a spiritual context, from the imagined hordes who have never loved and become the invisible witnesses to this scene, to the use of the word "rapture," with its apocalyptic ripples.

OATMEAL

I eat oatmeal for breakfast.

I make it on the hot plate and put skimmed milk on it.

I eat it alone.

I am aware it is not good to eat oatmeal alone.

Its consistency is such that it is better for your mental health if somebody eats it
    with you.

That is why I often think up an imaginary companion to have breakfast with.

Possibly it is even worse to eat oatmeal with an imaginary companion.

Nevertheless, yesterday morning, I ate my oatmeal with John Keats.

Keats said I was right to invite him: due to its glutinous texture, gluey lumpishness, hint
    of slime, and unusual willingness to disintegrate, oatmeal must never be eaten alone.

He said that in his opinion, however, it is OK to eat it with an imaginary companion,

and that he himself had enjoyed memorable porridges with Edmund Spenser and John
    Milton.

Even if such porridges are not as wholesome as Keats claims, still, you can learn
    something from them.

Yesterday morning, for instance, Keats told me about writing the "Ode to a Nightingale."

He had a heck of a time finishing it—those were his words—"Oi 'ad a 'eck of a toime,"
    he said, more or less, speaking through his porridge.

He wrote it quickly, on scraps of paper, which he then stuck in his pocket,

but when he got home he couldn't figure out the order of the stanzas, and he and a
    friend spread the papers on a table, and they made some sense of them, but he isn't
    sure to this day if they got it right.

He still wonders about the occasional sense of drift between stanzas,

and the way here and there a line will go into the configuration of a Moslem at prayer,
    then raise itself up and peer about, and then lay itself down slightly off the mark,
    causing the poem to move forward with God's reckless wobble.

He said someone told him that later in life Wordsworth heard about the scraps
    of paper on the table and tried shuffling some stanzas of his own but only made
    matters worse.

When breakfast was over, John recited "To Autumn."

He recited it slowly, with much feeling, and he articulated the words lovingly, and his
    odd accent sounded sweet.

He didn't offer the story of writing "To Autumn," I doubt if there is much of one.
But he did say the sight of a just-harvested oat field got him started on it
and two of the lines, "For Summer has o'er-brimmed their clammy cells" and "Thou
  watchest the last oozings hours by hours," came to him while eating oatmeal alone.
I can see him—drawing a spoon through the stuff, gazing into the glimmering furrows,
  muttering—and it occurs to me:
maybe there is no sublime, only the shining of the amnion's tatters.
For supper tonight I am going to have a baked potato left over from lunch.
I am aware that a leftover baked potato is damp, slippery, and simultaneously gummy
  and crumbly,
and therefore I'm going to invite Patrick Kavanagh to join me.

PARKINSON'S DISEASE

While spoon-feeding him with one hand
she holds his hand with her other hand,
or rather lets it rest on top of his,
which is permanently clenched shut.
When he turns his head away, she reaches
around and puts in the spoonful blind.
He will not accept the next morsel
until he has completely chewed this one.
His bright squint tells her he finds
the shrimp she has just put in delicious.
Next to the voice and touch of those we love,
food may be our last pleasure on earth—
a man on death row takes his T-bone
in small bites and swishes around each sip
of the jug wine before swallowing it,
tomorrow it will be too late to jolt
this supper out of him. She strokes
his head very slowly, as if to cheer up
each discomfited hair sticking out

from its root in his stricken brain.
Standing behind him, she presses
her cheek to his, kisses his jowl,
and his eyes seem to stop seeing
and do nothing but emit light.
Could heaven be a time, after we are dead,
of remembering the knowledge
flesh had from flesh? The flesh
of his face is hard, perhaps
from years spent facing down others
until they fell back, and harder
from years of being himself faced down
and falling back, and harder still
from all the while frowning
and beaming and worrying and shouting
and probably letting go in rages.
His face softens into a kind
of quizzical wince, as if one
of the other animals were working at
getting the knack of the human smile.
When picking up a cookie he uses
both thumbtips to grip it
and push it against an index finger
to secure it so that he can lift it.
She takes him then to the bathroom,
where she lowers his pants and removes
the diaper and holds the spout of the bottle
to his old penis until he pisses all he can,
then puts on the fresh diaper and pulls up his pants.
When they come out, she is facing him,
walking backwards in front of him
and holding his hands, pulling him
when he stops, reminding him to step
when he forgets and starts to pitch forward.
She is leading her old father into the future

as far as they can go, and she is walking
him back into her childhood, where she stood
in bare feet on the toes of his shoes
and they foxtrotted on this same rug.
I watch them closely: she could be teaching him
the last steps that one day she may teach me.
At this moment, he glints and shines,
as if it will be only a small dislocation
for him to pass from this paradise into the next.

RAPTURE

I can feel she has got out of bed.
That means it is seven A.M.
I have been lying with eyes shut,
thinking, or possibly dreaming,
of how she might look if, at breakfast,
I spoke about the hidden place in her
which, to me, is like a soprano's tremolo,
and right then, over toast and bramble jelly,
if such things are possible, she came.
I imagine she would show it while trying to conceal it.
I imagine her hair would fall about her face
and she would become apparently downcast,
as she does at a concert when she is moved.
The hypnopompic play passes, and I open my eyes
and there she is, next to the bed,
bending to a low drawer, picking over
various small smooth black, white,
and pink items of underwear. She bends
so low her back runs parallel to the earth,
but there is no sway in it, there is little burden, the day has hardly begun.

The two mounds of muscles for walking, leaping, lovemaking,
lift toward the east—what can I say?
Simile is useless; there is nothing like them on earth.
Her breasts fall full; the nipples
are deep pink in the glare shining up through the iron bars
of the gate under the earth where those who could not love
press, wanting to be born again.
I reach out and take her wrist
and she falls back into bed and at once starts unbuttoning my pajamas.
Later, when I open my eyes, there she is again,
rummaging in the same low drawer.
The clock shows eight. Hmmm.
With huge, silent effort of great,
mounded muscles the earth has been turning.
She takes a piece of silken cloth
from the drawer and stands up. Under the falls
of hair her face has become quiet and downcast,
as if she will be, all day among strangers,
looking down inside herself at our rapture.

GARY SNYDER

Gary Snyder (b. 1930) came of age as a writer during the Beat Generation of the 1950s. He continues to write poems with deep impact, expressing an original worldview that has grown into a global movement.

Snyder was the inspiration for Jack Kerouac's novel *The Dharma Bums* (1958). Born in San Francisco in 1930, Snyder grew up during the Depression on a farm north of Seattle, Washington. He took part in Beat events in the early 1950s, including the legendary Six Gallery reading in San Francisco in 1955. The next year he traveled to Japan, where he spent over a decade studying Zen Buddhism and East Asian languages and literature. Since 1970, he has lived with his family in the foothills of the Sierra Nevada mountains in California. His many honors include the Pulitzer Prize in poetry, the Bollingen Poetry Prize, and the Robert Kirsch Lifetime Achievement Award from the *Los Angeles Times*.

When Snyder teaches poetry at the University of California, Davis, he begins by asking the students: What are the tools of the poet? He then goes over each phoneme, each sound in the English language, to make the students conscious of what their materials are.

This sensitivity to the breath and shapes of spoken language has played a major role in Snyder's work, beginning with his first book, *Riprap & Cold Mountain Poems,* in 1959. Snyder composed *Riprap* when he was working as a fire lookout and a trail crewman with the Forest Service. "Mid-August at Sourdough Mountain Lookout," which opens that book, is a meditation. The speaker pays close attention to surroundings and thoughts, but lets each moment drift through consciousness without clinging to any of the mind's products. The words group themselves around breaths. The simplicity of the description and speech is mirrored in the landscape's clear panorama.

"It Pleases," from the book *Turtle Island* (1974), is an uncharacteristic trip for Snyder to the symbol of power—Washington, D.C. The speaker finds that this representative city is in fact specific, regional—Southern and humid. Just as the self, at the center of the mind, turns out to be empty in Buddhism, the capitol's dome proves not to be the center of society. The poem makes a case that real change happens locally and is not imposed from above.

Snyder's poem "The Bath," also from *Turtle Island,* is a hymn to the closeness and intimacy of family. The sensations of hot and cold in this poem are palpable. The description of the father and mother bathing their child forms a scene that is both ordinary and celestial. In "The Bath," the more physical the body and its world, the more sacred they become.

MID-AUGUST AT SOURDOUGH MOUNTAIN LOOKOUT

Down valley a smoke haze
Three days heat, after five days rain
Pitch glows on the fir-cones
Across rocks and meadows
Swarms of new flies.

I cannot remember things I once read
A few friends, but they are in cities.
Drinking cold snow-water from a tin cup
Looking down for miles
Through high still air.

IT PLEASES

Far above the dome
Of the capitol—
       It's true!
A large bird soars
Against white cloud,
Wings arced,
Sailing easy in this
humid Southern sun-blurred
       breeze—
     the dark-suited policeman
     watches tourist cars—

And the center,
The center of power is nothing!
Nothing here.
Old white stone domes,
Strangely quiet people,

Earth-sky-bird patterns
     idly interlacing

The world does what it pleases.

WASHINGTON, D.C., XI:73

THE BATH

Washing Kai in the sauna,
The kerosene lantern set on a box
    outside the ground-level window,
Lights up the edge of the iron stove and the
    washtub down on the slab
Steaming air and crackle of waterdrops
    brushed by on the pile of rocks on top
He stands in warm water
Soap all over the smooth of his thigh and stomach
    "Gary don't soap my hair!"
    —his eye-sting fear—
    the soapy hand feeling
    through and around the globes and curves of his body
    up in the crotch,
And washing-tickling out the scrotum, little anus,
    his penis curving up and getting hard
    as I pull back skin and try to wash it
Laughing and jumping, flinging arms around,
    I squat all naked too,
                    is this our body?

Sweating and panting in the stove-steam hot-stone
    cedar-planking wooden bucket water-splashing
    kerosene lantern-flicker wind-in-the-pines-out
    sierra forest ridges night—
Masa comes in, letting fresh cool air
    sweep down from the door
    a deep sweet breath
And she tips him over gripping neatly, one knee down
    her hair falling hiding one whole side of
    shoulder, breast, and belly,
Washes deftly Kai's head-hair
    as he gets mad and yells—

The body of my lady, the winding valley spine,
     the space between the thighs I reach through,
     cup her curving vulva arch and hold it from behind,
     a soapy tickle   a hand of grail
The gates of Awe
That open back a turning double-mirror world of
     wombs in wombs, in rings,
     that start in music,
                    is this our body?

The hidden place of seed
The veins net flow across the ribs, that gathers
     milk and peaks up in a nipple—fits
     our mouth—
The sucking milk from this our body sends through
     jolts of light; the son, the father,
     sharing mother's joy
That brings a softness to the flower of the awesome
     open curling lotus gate I cup and kiss
As Kai laughs at his mother's breast he now is weaned
     from, we
     wash each other,
                    this our body

Kai's little scrotum up close to his groin,
     the seed still tucked away, that moved from us to him
In flows that lifted with the same joys forces
     as his nursing Masa later,
     playing with her breast,
Or me within her,
Or him emerging,
                    this is our body:

Clean, and rinsed, and sweating more, we stretch
    out on the redwood benches hearts all beating
Quiet to the simmer of the stove,
    the scent of cedar
And then turn over,
    murmuring gossip of the grasses,
    talking firewood,
Wondering how Gen's napping, how to bring him in
    soon wash him too—
These boys who love their mother
    who loves men, who passes on
    her sons to other women;

The cloud across the sky. The windy pines.
    the trickle gurgle in the swampy meadow

    this is our body.

Fire inside and boiling water on the stove
We sigh and slide ourselves down from the benches
    wrap the babies, step outside,

black night & all the stars.

Pour cold water on the back and thighs
Go in the house—stand steaming by the center fire
Kai scampers on the sheepskin
Gen standing hanging on and shouting,

"Bao! bao! bao! bao! bao!"

This is our body. Drawn up crosslegged by the flames
    drinking icy water
    hugging babies, kissing bellies,

Laughing on the Great Earth

Come out from the bath.

LINDA PASTAN

Poets are often thought of as bohemians or adventurers, but Linda Pastan (b. 1932) breaks the stereotype. She takes family life as her topic. Pastan writes about her world as a wife and a mother with great subtlety, sharply conscious of the day-to-day emotions that pour through a household. She is particularly attuned to changes in life cycles—a couple's anniversary or a child leaving home for college.

Born in New York City, Pastan resides in Maryland, where she has served as the state poet laureate. Her many honors include the Ruth Lilly prize and the Dylan Thomas Award.

Her collection *Carnival Evening: New and Selected Poems, 1968–1998* (1998) spans the first nine books of her career and was a finalist for the National Book Award. In the *Boston Globe*, Liz Rosenberg wrote of this volume, "the accomplishment of *Carnival Evening* is large, large. We can only be grateful for Pastan's sharp eye, her tenderness." In the *New York Times Book Review*, Bruce Bennett wrote of her, "Ms. Pastan's unfailing mastery of her medium holds the darkness firmly in check."

Her poem "Who Is It Accuses Us?" challenges those who view domestic life as being as cushy as a throw pillow. She makes a convincing point that people who put down deep roots have the most at risk. The images of violence, sketched with Pastan's light touch, add to the poem's background of danger. She doesn't ignore the ambivalence of family life but looks it right in the eye and makes those who brave it seem all the more formidable.

"What We Want," also originally from her book *Waiting for My Life* (1981), uses sharp metaphors to depict the subconscious world that attaches to every parent. Both the children in the daylight world and the masked desires in the dream world seem to claim a parent more than she can claim herself. Unlike the nightmare homes of the confessional poets of the 1950s and early 1960s, this environment is strangely comforting and luminous because it has such a strong hold on the mother.

"25th Anniversary" begins as a sophisticated look at how couples sometimes build cases against each other in their minds. Suddenly, Pastan detours the poem to an Etruscan sarcophagus, but she takes the turn smoothly. Ironically, the ancient terra-cotta sculpture of a husband and wife reminds the speaker of her youth, when she and her mate visited Italy together. This thought of the longevity of their marriage gives a sense that their bond is as lasting as the couple intertwined on the lid of the sarcophagus, turning upside down Keats's paradox of eternal separation in "Ode on a Grecian Urn."

WHO IS IT ACCUSES US?

Who is it accuses us of safety,
as if the family were soldiers
instead of hostages,
as if the garden were not mined
with explosive peonies,
as if the most common death
were not by household accident?
We have chosen the dangerous life.
Consider the pale necks of the children
under their colored head scarves,
the skin around the husbands' eyes, flayed
by guilt and promises.
You who risk no more than your own skins
I tell you household gods
are jealous gods.
They will cover your windowsills
with the dust of sunsets;
they will poison your secret wells
with longing.

WHAT WE WANT

What we want
is never simple.
We move among the things
we thought we wanted:
a face, a room, an open book
and these things bear our names—
now they want us.
But what we want appears
in dreams, wearing disguises.
We fall past,
holding out our arms
and in the morning
our arms ache.
We don't remember the dream,
but the dream remembers us.
It is there all day
as an animal is there
under the table,
as the stars are there
even in full sun.

25TH ANNIVERSARY

There is something I want
to tell you beyond love
or gratitude or sex, beyond
irritation or a purer anger.
For years I have hoarded
your small faults the way
I might hoard kindling
towards some future conflagration,
and from the moment you broke
into my life, all out of breath,
I have half expected you
to break back out.
But here we are
like the married couple
from Cerveteri who smile
from their 6th-century sarcophagus
as if they are giving a party.
How young we were in Rome, buying
their portraits on postcards,
thinking that we too
were entangled already
beyond amputation, beyond
even death, as we are
as we are now.

MICHAEL S. HARPER

Michael Harper (b. 1938) is a leading figure in the Black Arts movement that revolutionized American writing beginning in the 1960s. He is the author of over ten volumes of poetry and has co-edited three anthologies of African American literature and edited *The Collected Poems of Sterling Brown* (1980). Harper was the first writer to fill the position of poet laureate of the state of Rhode Island. He has been a university professor and professor of English at Brown University.

Harper's poetry is in constant dialogue with the greats of African American music. He has an encyclopedic knowledge of jazz. Harper has been personal friends with a number of musicians, including that giant of saxophonists and composers, John Coltrane. This personal tie led to the title poem of his collection, *Dear John, Dear Coltrane* (1970), one of two of Harper's books nominated for the National Book Award.

The title poem "Dear John, Dear Coltrane" portrays the musician as ailing but luminous, transmuting even his destruction into grace: "your diseased liver gave / out its purity." The poem is about a life burning down, but radiating incredible heat.

Harper's elegy "For Bud," written for the great jazz pianist Bud Powell who died in his early forties in 1966, explores whether love can grow in the midst of terrible pain. The poem mentions several African American musicians and begins as a question about whether beauty came into bebop the way that marijuana entered saxophonist Charlie Parker or the way trumpeter Dizzy Gillespie goofed on stage. It goes on to ponder whether sweetness can arise amidst the anger of a people brutalized by violence, the way the folksinger and composer Leadbelly survived his experience in chain gangs, his blues infused with the sugar of candied yams. Even the king of hard bop, Bud Powell, deserves the softest rain imaginable.

"If You Don't Force It" is a reflection on a certain mode of jazz improvisation as a way of life. The poem scatters words in sparse couplets, like a Count Basie solo that uses the barest minimum of notes to suggest a melody, "refusing to smother beauty / with too many chords." The power of these choice words and notes allows both the poet and the musician to "put the melody on your heart."

DEAR JOHN, DEAR COLTRANE

a love supreme, a love supreme
a love supreme, a love supreme

Sex fingers toes
in the marketplace
near your father's church
in Hamlet, North Carolina—
witness to this love
in this calm fallow
of these minds,
there is no substitute for pain:
genitals gone or going,
seed burned out,
you tuck the roots in the earth,
turn back, and move
by river through the swamps,
singing: *a love supreme, a love supreme;*
what does it all mean?
Loss, so great each black
woman expects your failure
in mute change, the seed gone.
You plod up into the electric city—
your song now crystal and
the blues. You pick up the horn
with some will and blow
into the freezing night:
a love supreme, a love supreme—

Dawn comes and you cook
up the thick sin 'tween
impotence and death, fuel
the tenor sax cannibal
heart, genitals, and sweat
that makes you clean—
a love supreme, a love supreme—

Why you so black?
cause I am
why you so funky?
cause I am
why you so black?
cause I am
why you so sweet?
cause I am
why you so black?
cause I am
a love supreme, a love supreme:

So sick
you couldn't play *Naima,*
so flat we ached
for song you'd concealed
with your own blood,
your diseased liver gave
out its purity,
the inflated heart
pumps out, the tenor kiss,
tenor love:
a love supreme, a love supreme—
a love supreme, a love supreme—

FOR BUD

Could it be, Bud
that in slow galvanized
fingers beauty seeped
into *bop* like Bird
weed and Diz clowned—
Sugar waltzing
back into dynamite,
sweetest left hook you
ever dug, baby;
could it violate violence
Bud, like Leadbelly's
chaingang chuckle,
the candied yam
twelve string clutch
of all blues:
there's no rain
anywhere, soft
enough for you.

IF YOU DON'T FORCE IT

He's talking about interpolations
riffs that come in the midst

of action, responding to the line,
accommodating the blues

and not neglecting the melody
refusing to smother beauty

with too many chords
to show off is to bungle

the melody with chordal blocks
not building anything to your baby

hiding the melody
like only the young can do

Lester Young would watch the dancers
moving into his vernaculars

with rhythms augmenting the melody
Herschel would set the pace

Pres would follow
Count would comp time

as though you could improve
on stride piano

Ben Webster could do stride
when you get possessed with wild chords

tie your left hand behind your back
then play the melody with one finger

on your right hand:
put the melody on your heart

for Ray Brown

ISHMAEL REED

Part of what makes Ishmael Reed's work so exciting and fun are the myriad literary worlds that converge in his writing. His sources are as diverse as the cowboy novel, the Roman playwright Plautus, science fiction, Voltaire's *Candide,* and literature in Yoruba and Japanese. Ishmael Reed (b. 1938) calls this spicy mixture of styles "gumbo." His work is comic, but his uproarious humor always has a satirical blade. His poetry never strays far from its roots in song. Reed's work is deeply influenced by the culture of the African diaspora in subject and style, and in his writing he celebrates the sanctity of getting down.

Few writers have contributed as extensively to as many genres as Ishmael Reed. He's written plays, poetry, essays, and novels, including the classic *Mumbo Jumbo* (1972). More recent is *The Reed Reader* (2000), a compendium of his work from all these literary forms. His honors include a MacArthur Fellowship and two National Book Award nominations.

Reed grew up in Buffalo, New York, but he has lived on the West Coast for many years. Now retired from his professorship, he was known at the University of California, Berkeley, for his commitment to encouraging young writers.

His poem "On the Fourth of July in Sitka, 1982" takes a hallowed American tradition and shows how the United States has changed. Reed's July 4th in Alaska includes Filipinos, Russians, Inuits, and Canadians. Reed's humor creates an understated critique of rigid and violent forms of patriotism, while celebrating the multicultural fabric of cultures that make up the United States.

"Sky Diving" is a philosophical poem that touches on the precariousness of life and the way fate isolates an individual. Even an experienced sky diver can get a parachute that doesn't open. This accident is contrasted with the stylish and seemingly safe world of a painting by the Harlem Renaissance artist Archibald J. Motley Jr. "Know when to let go," cautions the poet, "Learn how to fall."

In "Loup Garou Means Change Into," Reed uses the French and Cajun word for werewolf, *loup-garou.* West African magic plays a large role in Reed's work, and New Orleans, where French is historically spoken, is the center of that legacy for him. The spirit world can be a source of salvation and groove in Reed's work, but it can also be dangerous. In this poem, the only way to cure the blues is the traditional way that angry gods are appeased in Yoruba religion, by an offering of food.

ON THE FOURTH OF JULY IN SITKA, 1982

On the fourth of July in Sitka
Filipinos sold shish-ka-bob from their
booths in the park
On the fourth of July in Sitka, the children
dressed in deerskin jackets
and coonskin caps
On the fourth of July in Sitka, you
could buy fishpie in the basement of St. Michael's
Church, where the vodka-drunken Russians used to
pray
But the red white and blue cake was not for sale

On the fourth of July in Sitka the people
kicked off shoes and ran through the
streets, pushing beds
On the fourth of July in Sitka, tour buses
with yellow snouts and square heads
delivered tourists to the Shee Atika lodge
where they stared at floats designed by
Sheldon Jackson College and
the Alaska Women in Timber
On the fourth of July in Sitka the
Gajaa Heen dancers performed, wearing their
Klan emblems of Beaver Wolf Killer Whale
Porpoise, and Dog Salmon

On the fourth of July in Sitka the Libertarian
Party announced the winners of its five dollar raffle
1st Prize, a Winchester .300 Magnum
2nd Prize, an Ithaca 12 gauge shotgun
3rd Prize, a Sportsman III knife

On the fourth of July in Sitka the
softball teams were honored at the American
Legion Club and the players drank champagne till dawn
On the fourth of July in Sitka, the night was
speckled with Japanese fireworks
sponsored by Alaska Lumber and Pulp

On the fifth of July in Sitka
a Canadian destroyer brought to Sitka
for the fourth of July in Sitka sailed
through Sitka Sound and out into the
Northern Pacific
All of the men on board stood at
attention, saluting their audience
three bald eagles, two ravens, and me
watching the whole show from Davidoff Hill
the fifth of July in Sitka

SKY DIVING

"It's a good way to live and
A good way to die"
From a Frankenheimer video about
Sky diving
The hero telling why he liked to

> The following noon he leaped
> But his parachute wasn't with him
> He spread out on the field like
> Scrambled eggs

Life is not always
Hi-lifing inside
Archibald Motley's
"Chicken Shack"
You in your derby
Your honey in her beret
Styling before a small vintage
Car

Like too many of us
I am a man who never had much
Use for a real father
And so when I'm heading
For a crash
No one will catch me but
Me

The year is only five days old
Already a comet has glittered out
Its glow sandbagged by
Our brilliance falling off
Like hair from Berkeley's roving
Dogs

Even on Rose Bowl day
An otherwise joyous occasion
A float veered into the crowd
Somebody got bruised over the incident
Like a love affair on second ave.

It's a good lesson to us all
In these downhill days of a
Hard-hearted decade
Jetting through the world
Our tails on fire

You can't always count
On things opening up for you
Know when to let go
Learn how to fall

LOUP GAROU MEANS CHANGE INTO

If Loup Garou means change into
When will I banish mine?
I say, if Loup Garou means change
Into when will I shed mine?
This eager Beast inside of me
Seems never satisfied

I was driving on the Nimitz
Wasn't paying it no mind
I was driving on the Nimitz
Wasn't paying it no mind
Before you could say "Mr. 5 by 5"
I was doin 99

my Cherokee is crazy
Can't drink no more than 4
My Cherokee is crazy
Can't stand no more than 4
By the time I had my 15th one
I was whooping across the floor
I was talking whiskey talking
I was whooping across the floor

Well, I whistled at a Gypsy who was reading at my cards
She was looking at my glad hand when something came
Across the yard started wafting across the kitchen
Started drifting in the room, the black went out her
Eyeballs a cat sprung cross her tomb
I couldn't know what happened till I looked behind the door
Where I saw her cold pale husband
WHO'S BEEN DEAD SINCE 44

They say if you get your 30
You can get your 35
Folks say if you get to 30
You can make it to 35
The only stipulation is you
Leave your Beast outside

Loup Garou the violent one
When will you lay off me
Loup Garou the Evil one
Release my heart my seed
Your storm has come too many times
And yanked me to your sea

I said please Mr. Loup Garou
When will you drop my goat
I said mercy Mr. Loup Garou
Please give me victory
I put out the beans that evening
Next morning I was free

QUINCY TROUPE

Quincy Troupe (b. 1939) doesn't just recite a poem, he dances it. He throws his whole body into reading out loud, bopping with each stressed syllable. He has twice won the Heavyweight Champion of Poetry prize at the World Poetry Bout. His honors also include two American Book Awards. He was California's first poet laureate and formerly taught at the University of California, San Diego.

Child of a professional baseball catcher who played in the Negro Leagues, Troupe loves to write about sports, life in urban America, and African American music. He has published two books on the jazz great Miles Davis: he co-authored *Miles: The Autobiography* (1989) and wrote the memoir *Miles and Me* (2000). Troupe's books of poetry include *Transcircularities: New and Selected Poems* (2002) and *Avalanche* (1996).

In the poem "Following the North Star Boogaloo," Troupe begins by tracing culture back to its primeval origins, before music and language diverged. His diction in the poem remarkably walks this fine line between pure sound and meaning, stepping as deftly as a ballplayer snagging a foul pop-up in front of the opposing dugout. "Following the North Star Boogaloo" is also a plea for a return to the glory days of African American sports, art, and history, before crack and TV drained the ghetto. Don't get thrown by his references to "skateboarding" in the poem. This word is part of Troupe's amazing descriptions of the moves of basketball ("roundball") greats such as Magic Johnson ("Magic"), Michael Jordan ("Air Jordan"), Kenny Anderson ("Kenny"), Julius Erving ("Dr. J"), Reece "Goose" Tatum (of the legendary Harlem Globetrotters), and Oscar Robertson ("The Big O"). No other writer has described basketball as poetically as Troupe.

The late Ted Berrigan once said that poets fall into two categories, fast and slow, depending on how quickly their words reel off as they read. Quincy Troupe is beyond fast, as in "Eye Change Dreams," which starts out in the surreal rush of Times Square station in New York City. Troupe uses the word "eye" instead of the pronoun "I" to suggest his observer's gaze. Then the poet's mind wanders to Gloster, Mississippi (where his wife grew up). His descriptions of nature are as dreamlike as the cityscapes. A tiny mosquito carries the entire poem back to New York. The most unexpected and fun move of all is the ending, where the author recaps his own poem, goofing on it by comparing it to a washed-up starlet. It's an unheard-of way to finish a poem, something only Quincy Troupe could devise.

EYE CHANGE DREAMS

for Joe Overstreet, Corrine Jennings & George Lewis

eye change dreams at 42nd street, times square
as swirling people wearing technicolor attitudes speed
through packed days, carrying speech that machine-guns out
in rhythms equaling movement of averted stares
squares even sashay by quick in flip
mimicking motions, as slick street hustlers roll their eyes around
like marbles searching for hits, lick their chops after clicking onto
some slow-witted hicks dribbling spit down their lips
eating hot dogs paid with fifty-dollar bills
in broad daylight—

                                        yeah, tell me about it, trick—

escalator sidewalks moving everything along
so swiftly everyone thinks it's their own feet carrying
            their bodies, grooving to a different song
                              than say, in gloster, mississippi

where time is a turtle moving after a flood has crawled back
into the space it came out of in the first place
hear no beepers here
in gloster, no portable telephones panicking anywhere
only the constant slow humming glide of bloated mosquitoes
as they slide through air & bank in for fresh blood-kills
                  wind-tongue guiding them into the target
                              wobbling on their zigzag ride above bearded

irises waving sword-shaped leaves in the breeze
as if preparing to do righteous battle with anyone or something
like people living in the big apple (their game faces constantly in place—
& they even wear them into bathrooms, so scared to death they are
of running into some cold-blooded rat there
staking out their own notion of territorial space)

try keeping their fluctuating dreams up to speed
switching up each & every moment, in midtown manhattan,
            manic chameleons
everywhere, here, changing faces at high noon, say,
on 42nd street & 8th avenue, claustrophobic
heat-drenching crowds packed in, in august, locks in on flesh cold
as a triple life sentence served out at comstock—
people here switching up gears, trying to sidestep panic
                        in the middle of slapstick dreams
                                    & in the center of it all

a con man who looks like swifty lazar, the late hollywood agent,
tools around inside a white rolls royce, peddling gimmicks for old
            false-tooth legends,
who look so bizarre in public devoid of heavy makeup—
comic, even—outside of their dream machines, illusions—
tattered memorabilia the con man peddles at some tacky bazaar
inside a rundown building, in a cobwebbed room, where he hawks
            fading photographs of
zsa zsa gabor in her prime, before she started breaking down
in front of our eyes, wearing all that weird graphic white
pancake makeup over her everchanging face-lifts, masking the dreams
we wear ourselves, inside our switching, ballistic imaginations
bewitching us here as we move through times square
popping with the charge of electrical currents

energy eye imagined this poem having when eye first started writing it
then having to deal with how it slowed down midway through,
when eye hit that part about gloster, a third of the way down,
& tried to avoid all those zigzagging mosquitoes
divebombing in for fresh blood-kills—
my direction moving all over the place after that, changing up the focus,
the rhythm, the way my dipstick lines started composing themselves—

at that point in time, they began making it all up
as they went along, as if they were different musicians improvising
this poem—like the swifty lazar look-alike peddling old hollywood
wonders before the fall, before they became toothless legends,
before they became zsa zsa gabor

this sputnik verbal drumstick—a thing to be eaten
after all—promises way more than it could ever deliver
traveling at the speed of complete bullshit, as it were—

a technicolored times-square attitude, without rhyme,
riding in on a broomstick, heartsick & caustic

homesick for that good old big-apple charge

FOLLOWING THE NORTH STAR BOOGALOO

for Miguel Algarin

following the north star boogaloo
the rhythm takes me
back to where music began
to percolate language like coffee in another form
back before frederick douglass laid it down
heavy on abe lincoln
when music was breakdancing, old hottentots
throwing down mean as bojangles ever did
now jump forward through history's dice game
pick up the steps of james brown
michael jackson moonwalking
the old blues talking about yo mama
now fast forward down the lane
pick up the dance of 5 brothers
skateboarding the court
out in the open, one closes the break
after taking it to the hole off the coast to coast

doing a 180 degree phi slamma jamma dunk
before they all high five & glad hand after
stamping their footprints all up in the paint
up in this poet's word dribble
a drummer's paradiddle
word up, yo bro, hip hop, rappers
skateboarding the go go out in the open
court of macking the holy ghost down

hey you, diddle-diddle, voodoo griot, take me
back to when eye was black & hitting proud
out on the slick bop thoroughfares
back before the mean homeboys rolled snarling
duckwaddle down the middle, eyes empty with death
before the alley-oops wore their lives as chips on shoulders
in stratospheric attitudes, hung dip from wall to wall
chained gold, cap bills on heads quaking sideways
muscling up bold masterblasters
checking out reeboks
chillin dead up in the cut "fresh" as "death"
after "mo money," "mo money," "mo money"
check it out bro, pharmaceutical wizards
making 7 figure bank accounts do somersaults, no sweat
it's rolling in so fast for crack ("& it ain't nothing
but a hole in the wall") for homeboys
cash n carry, cold 16 year olds
who cant count nothing but greenbacks
sliding off the screen & roll, they helicopter
after dipping & rolling down the middle
high up above the paint, their footprints walking on space
up over your face hang gliding to the basket, like praying mantises
so fresh they make pootbutts faint slamming
faster than high fiving glory—
180 degrees of schoolboy legends, saints
unfolding in prime time memory

so roll it back, kojak, before magic's knees go permanently
south for the winter, & leave air jordan's footprints
in yo face game as the baddest one in town
before they change up the shake & bake, jam off the sky again with a new
phenom double clutching up there in space, like a ferrari stretching out
flat out burning up german autobahns, changing up the guard quicker
than fear brings down doodoo
but hey, young bro, flash the dice roll back through shit
to when the big O was jackknifing through all them bodies
out on the court, to when goose tatum was shimmying magic
down in the middle, down in the paint
as roy haynes jitterbugged like a magician
hoola hoopin' the ball around him, before fast forwarding to dr. j—Julius Erving!
& did we ever think we'd lose these hoodoo gods
to old age homes for roundball royalty
new age homeboys not even knowing who they are
& do they even know about jonestown, all them
bloated bodies cracking beneath the sun
& did they ever hear about the north carolina
astronaut, david skywalking thompson
jamming out in the open, off the fly
helicoptering to roundball heaven
off the motherfucking coast to coast
before he took the fall for all that shit
he snorted up his nose, before hitting the pipe
that took him right on out like a blown lightbulb—
way back before kenny anderson was even
a glint in his parents pick n roll eyes

before he skateboarded off the juju fake
picked up his dribble, like magic
then rose up in space like hallelujah 4th of july
glory, before dropping a deuce or a trey quick
as a pickpocket off the slide by
sleight of hand trick, eased on by like mojo with his yoyo

pitter patter, now you see me, now you don't, yo bro
whodunit, poor guy got caught in kenny's schoolyard
voodoo, jump back in the alley
say what? did you see that motherfucking bad-boy sky?
past where it all started, somewhere back before
language followed the north star boogaloo
dancing back when they was hamboning the black
bottom for fun, back then in the language
when homeboys picked cotton
played the dozens; "eye hate to talk about yo mama
she was a good old soul, but she got a two-ton pussy
& an iron ass hole, & yo daddy got a dick
big as a motherfucking toothpick!"

say what chu say, say what chu say? say what?

word, when we knew ourselves through songs
through what we saw alive in homeboys eyes
through love, through what it was we were before
commercials told us how to move & groove, who to love
when we did it all & had fun & knew the heroes
new & old & never confused dope for the bomb
back before we fast forwarded to integration
entered the 60s on a bullshit tip
lost ourselves in the fast forwarding
70s & 80s, in the cloning xerox machines
before kenny anderson skateboarded
his prince of a hip hop, roundball game
breakrapping all the way to roundball legend

up north, south of the voodoo connection
north of where we entered from africa

Chana Bloch's poetry is fine-tuned to the nuances of human interaction, joyous or painful. In her book *Mrs. Dumpty* (1998), winner of the Felix Pollak Prize, she extends the possibilities of lyric poetry by achieving what amounts to a novel in verse, using the textured twine of poetry in the intricate knots of the fiction writer. Her poem "The Kiss" is from that book, which traces the story of a marriage and a family. The couple begin with romance and hope, but the union is ultimately shattered by the husband's nervous breakdown.

Bloch's other volumes of poetry include *The Past Keeps Changing* (1992), one of my favorite book titles. Those few words could be a one-line poem. The title also suggests part of Bloch's poetic method: to turn through her memories but to beam on them the knowledge that she has gained over time.

Now retired, Chana Bloch (b. 1940) taught for many years as a professor at Mills College, where she directed the Creative Writing Program.

In addition to her own writing, Chana Bloch is also one of the foremost translators of Hebrew poetry. She has accomplished the difficult feat of bringing into English both the lyricism of the Bible in her sensuous co-translation of the Song of Songs and the excitement of contemporary Israeli poetry in her versions of Yehuda Amichai and Dahlia Ravikovitch. She won the prestigious PEN Translation Award for her work in this area.

It seems appropriate in a book of portraits to include Bloch's poem "What a Poet Does," where the writer takes a turn at capturing the artist. Writers often create a composite when sketching a character, and the speaker of this poem pretends to do that, while using irony to get the better of an artist who has portrayed her less than flatteringly.

Elsewhere Bloch has written sympathetically about her father, but in "The Discipline of Marriage" she explores her mother's feelings. The feminine wiles the speaker affectionately describes are not ends in themselves, but ways the speaker's mother tries to get attention when her own thoughts and feelings don't register in her husband's consciousness.

THE KISS

There was a ghost at our wedding,
the caterer's son,
who drowned that day.

Like every bride I was dressed
in hope so sharp
it tore open
my tight-sewn fear.

You kissed me under the wedding canopy,
a kiss that lasted a few beats longer
than the usual,
and we all laughed.

We were promising: the future
would be like the present,
even better, maybe.
Then your heel came down
on the glass.

We poured champagne
and opened the doors to the garden
and danced
a little drunk, all of us,

as the caterer made the first cut,
one firm stroke, then
dipped his knifeblade
in the water.

WHAT A POET DOES

He showed me the painting he made of me
—at eighty or ninety? Clearly
he didn't mean to flatter.
Now he asks if I'm planning to write
a poem about him. He's smiling,
but under that brushed-on smile
he looks worried.

There's a couple of things he'd prefer to spare
the reading public.
Who wants to be published
stripped to his cotton socks,
with nothing but a fig leaf of metaphor
to keep him decent?

Listen, I promise: I'll change your name.
A poet can do that. And I'll never ask you to pose,
legs crossed at the ankle, eyes bright, cheek nuzzling
your hand—*Don't move!*—so I can get you
just like that. Move all you want, I'll
get you, I've been getting you
all along.

Besides, it's not *you* in the poem—it's you
ground to grist and pigment
with all the others. Don't you know
what a poet can do with a blank
sheet of paper? Words
are the poor man's color. Take a deep breath,
darling. Sit down on that sofa. Relax.
You won't recognize yourself.

THE DISCIPLINE OF MARRIAGE

My mother said what she thought.
If my father looked up from the paper to inquire, mildly,
where the hell anyone would get such a dumb idea,
she'd reply, with a smile like a warning:
"That's how I feel."

Her feelings were larger than his,
full of grievance, of steaming griefs.
She hung up her keys at the door. Diced carrots.
Salted the daily stew.

All day my father depleted his poor stock of words.
Evenings he shrank and fell silent.
The discipline of marriage had taught him
every last thing he knew about silence
and its rewards. After supper, he'd shut his eyes,
set his feet on the hassock and kiss
the evening goodbye.

My mother applied glittery blue to her eyelids.
She had plenty to say. She wanted him
to listen, to say something back! To open
his eyes for once and see her!
Her beaded purse! Her
alligator shoes! On her dressing table
the French perfumes glowed like topaz
in crystal bottles stoppered with milky glass.

FANNY HOWE

Fanny Howe (b. 1940) came of age during the Civil Rights Movement of the 1960s. She worked for the Congress on Racial Equality (CORE), documenting discrimination in housing against African Americans.

When Howe embarked on an interracial marriage with the author Carl Senna, she was already a fiction writer publishing with a major press. The couple had three children and a stormy marriage in racially torn Boston.

In an autobiographical essay, she describes how she began composing poetry during this period of her life: "I wrote poems in bed while I was nursing, or when the sated child was sleeping on my arm. Or I wrote them during potty-training sessions, or while cooking. The focus was always the sentence itself, which comes to me as a long word, a single sound and content unit. The less time I had to concentrate on prolonged prose sections, the more intense each single sentence became. There would be an outburst, then the product would travel around with me, being reduced and amended."

Howe's bursts of charged verse gave shape to the unique structure of her works. She writes suites of poems that are often unpunctuated, usually less than a page. Each poem stands alone but accumulates toward a larger whole.

John Ashbery has written of her poetry, "Fanny Howe's strangely hushed but busy landscape keeps leading us into it until we realize we're lost but wouldn't want to be anywhere else."

Fanny Howe has been a writing instructor at numerous campuses, but has taught in recent years at the University of California, San Diego.

Each section of one of Howe's poem-suites creates a world of its own. Often it fixes on specific states of mind or feelings, seeking to frame them through expression. The excerpts below are from three different sections of her book *Gone* (2003): "The Splinter," "Doubt," and "The Passion." The book begins with a quotation from Charlotte Brontë, and some of the poems seem to refer to the lives of the Brontë family.

The poems range from the carefree ("Once on a summer night") to the obsessive ("See how this being at the neck and bowel") to a novel in miniature ("This angel clung to boats"). The sections may be short in length, but they are often long in insight and power.

from THE SPLINTER

See how this being at the neck and bowel
gives the head and groin a taste of hell

that seeps throughout some nervous systems

all senses battered and enflamed

where the soul drinks disabled

and attacks only a she a she can see
who smiles in dreams between clenched hands

sobbing from wanting to win her pity
her in the born-hating

thing she finds there living

Very pain it came first
through my eyes
they were so compressed
I could still see
forms that will never be
eliminated and illuminations
and words whose imprint
(branded in agony)
still can't be interpreted

from THE PASSION

In the old way the old wood
gathered its shadows and twigs

but they wouldn't burn
They wouldn't burn

because of the ashes and ice
and the snapping

It was the month of red berries
and the brother and sister

held hands and ran
away laughing

III

Once on a summer night
in a humid tunnel

sex was scheduled

but no baby faces
looking up the time

pure lust
like a tulip

budding between our chests

—and it was fun!
—and I would do it again!

She put her hand
inside of his

and they held on
two wings on a bird

Then he let go
willing the sacrifice

to a little nest
at a higher position

"Give me a bucketful of colors
and not this melancholy gray memory"

If a goldfinch can pick up
a bucketful of water

with a tiny string, her mind
can lift her hope again

The knees trembled but she touched the veins
and pulled the skin on that heart-extension

His little wounds, his dirty fingernails,
the beard he wouldn't clean and frayed hems,
the sunset cheeks and sweet skin,
smoke in his hair, himself
naked as a movie screen

Get out of this morass, poverty of spirit

She can't

Who names you but your teacher

His legs were long and thin, his knees bent and feet crossed

I remember him stroking each one automatically

Soon he would be nailed
Agony, he begged

The temptation to suffer is a big quiet one
the kind that is generated by repetition

He got good at sleeping outside the same doors
and staring into the eyes of drivers-by

His empty pockets were stuffed with their glances

Then I'll bear the torch and the needle
I'll carry and marry the ashes

They will be mine

I'll be the main mourner though no one will see me

I'll know why he died and what was the reason

Flowers attract scissors

This angel clung to boats
and pecked at workers on their tits

It pissed and shat on their hair
as well as garden tents

Its song was repetitive

If the air around it wasn't soft
its feathers were

It preferred sugar-liquor to bread
and was Divine Mother's favorite

The mystery of preference
is never solved by acts

MAXINE HONG KINGSTON

Maxine Hong Kingston (b. 1940) grew up in Stockton, California. Kingston taught English and creative writing for many years at the University of California, Berkeley, but is now retired, officially ending a long connection with the campus that began when she enrolled as an undergraduate.

Her books often celebrate people at the bottom of the ladder—laundry workers, peasants, homemakers, farm laborers, even an unemployed college graduate with an English major. Whatever their social class, her characters have stories that fan through the entire range of literary genres. In her book *China Men* (1980), the immigrants who cut the mountains of the Sierra Nevada to build the transcontinental railroads lead lives that are as dimensional and poignant and heroic as any royalty in Elizabethan drama. Her characters, too, are capable of great falls.

She is also an amazing stylist. In Maxine Hong Kingston's writing you can hear ancient rivers of language, just as in James Joyce's refashioning of English you can sense the rumblings of liturgical Latin, Gaelic rebels, and Germanic tribes; and in Allen Ginsberg's verse you can hear prayers dovened by old Jewish men. Kingston writes English through the great linguistic and literary heritage of China, as if we were reading her through translucent calligraphied scrolls.

For her prose, Maxine Hong Kingston has won the National Book Award, the National Book Critics Circle Award, a National Humanities Medal from the National Endowment for the Humanities, and many other honors. Since her prose always has the color and texture of poetry, it's not surprising that she also writes poetry, published in the book *To Be the Poet* (2002). Her poetry is of the moment, Zen and immediate, as in "Birds," where she describes an encounter with a hummingbird in her garden. Her poetry sometimes comes directly out of her journals, as in "Saturday April 8." She records the experiences and thoughts of a mind thirsty for tranquility and epiphany, like a hummingbird seeking nectar.

In "Idea! Four-word poems!" she uses an extremely constricting form with such joy that the constraint becomes a game, a prayer, but never a limitation. She takes this traditional Chinese form and Americanizes it, even incorporating an advertising slogan into her poem.

BIRDS

I'm living in one place so long,
the birds enlace their nests
with my white hair.

I'd like their recognizing me in return.
I play a game with hummingbirds.
I play the hose in jets and spouts,
and the hummer follows the water,
loops and soars, turns and hovers, leaps.
I shorten the arc toward myself,
and the hummer comes to my hands.
It enters the fine spray; it flies in the spray.
It alights on the tomato cage, and waits,
raises a wing, gets a squirt in one armpit,
and the other armpit. It shows its butt
and wiggles its tail. What's that gold thread?
The hummer is spraying me back.

There's a yellow bird that is barely anything
but a reed, a tube of song.
Its beak opens as wide as its throat, its body,
which trembles through and through.
It's a yellow-feathered skinbag of song,
and it sings all day.

Saturday April 8 Swansea, where Dylan Thomas was born on October 27th, the same
    date I was born.

I've never seen tide go out so far.

"The furthest tide in the world."

They're surfers in Swansea. Where's the surf?

Large whole shells bestrew the endless wet land.

So many species of cockles, mussles, clams,
    golden clams, and snails, and oysters,
    jewels I could follow away—until the tide
    turns and runs me over.

I cannot see to the end of it, not a lip of sea.

My life goes out. It goes out. It goes out.

I shouldn't have tanned for 17 years in Hawai'i,
    which left lines and brown spots on my face.
    (The blue a tattoo—I jabbed my temple with a pen.)

Old people fade. The black is gone from my hair,
    and leaving my eyes. My angles lose definition.

I will stay put. The tide will come in and in and in.

Idea!: Four-word poems!
An old Chinese tradition.
Easier, faster than haiku.
To carve on rocks.
To write on doorjambs.
To write on thresholds.
To tattoo on arms.
Anybody can write one.
Form takes no time.
"Father Sky Mother Earth"
"Raid kills bugs dead"—Lew Welch
"Beyond mountains more mountains"—Lazy Old Man, my father
"Across rivers more rivers"—Old Idle Man, my father
Father gone Rabbit moon.
    Giant anthuria Mother's Day
    Sun beams me love.
    Redwood tree one seed.
    Strawberry Creek be free.
    All rivers be free.

The oldest prayer is a four-word poem:

                "May all beings be happy."

Well, that's sayable in four words in Chinese.

                "All beings be happy."
                "All beings be peaceful."
                All beings be kind.
                "All beings be free."

That line about being kind, I made up. A very American four-word poem. Kindness takes going into action.

They sing, they're happy.
We eat our fortune.
Time can. Idea can.
Infinity ribbon circles all.

And there is such a thing as a two-word poem! And five- and seven-word poems. And the ultimate: the one-word poem! "Fook!" "Shou!" Oh, to say it all at once—one resounding word.

My father named me Ting Ting after the four-word poem: "Ting ting doak lup" ("Standing alone as a mountain peak"). Those sounds are pleasant to the Say Yup Chinese ear. Lone travelers—monks, ghosts, lovers, free and independent spirits, poets—meet at the pavilion under the lone pine upon the hill. Stop, listen, burn offerings in the ting.

ROBERT PINSKY

When Robert Pinsky (b. 1940) served as poet laureate of the United States from 1997 to 2000, he launched the Favorite Poem Project. This enormously moving record includes dozens of videotapes of Americans reciting and discussing poems close to their hearts. Many of the videos can be viewed at www.favoritepoem.org.

Robert Pinsky grew up on the New Jersey shore. His books of poems often return to that locale, including the Pulitzer Prize–nominated *The Figured Wheel: New and Collected Poems, 1966–1996* (1996) and *Jersey Rain* (2000). He has also translated *The Inferno of Dante: A New Verse Translation* (1994) and co-translated a book by Czeslaw Milosz. He has published several volumes of essays on poetry, including *The Sounds of Poetry* (1998), nominated for a National Book Critics Circle Award, and *Democracy, Culture, and the Voice of Poetry* (2002).

Pinsky's democratic vision is reflected in his classic poem "Shirt" from his book *The Want Bone* (1990). The sentences are unadorned, trimmed, like the shirt's fabric. The shirt opens a door into the lives of those who sew garments, first the makers of the actual shirt the speaker is holding, then to the young seamstresses who died in the ghastly Triangle Shirtwaist Factory fire in New York City in 1911. The speaker's matter-of-fact admiration for his shirt's craft become a way of understating his fury at the oppression of all those who work for low wages. Pinsky can also be extremely funny as a poet, and "The Shirt" has its moment of needle-sharp humor.

Another poem about an everyday object is "Jar of Pens," part of a series Pinsky is writing. "I set myself the assignment of writing about the next thing I touch," he explained when he read at Berkeley. "The idea is not that subject matter is arbitrary but that the occasion for the poem is not the deepest part of the poem. . . . Is 'Ode to a Nightingale' a 'bird' poem?" he joked. Pinsky uses the tried and true poetic technique of personification to bring these writing implements to life.

Heather McHugh has described Pinsky's work as "abecedarian." She was probably thinking of his "ABC," a remarkable short poem from *Jersey Rain* that contains twenty-six words arranged in alphabetical order. Commenting on this poem, Pinsky quipped, "I do have a tic about the alphabet . . . When I have insomnia I go through the alphabet with names of people I know. . . ." "ABC" begins mournfully, and through the letter R the poem concerns different ways of dying. The poem ends on an uplifting, even ecstatic note, though. "We don't know what is the peak or zenith, Thank God," Pinsky explained. His parting shot about "ABC": "I recommend this poem as very easy to get by heart."

SHIRT

The back, the yoke, the yardage. Lapped seams,
The nearly invisible stitches along the collar
Turned in a sweatshop by Koreans or Malaysians

Gossiping over tea and noodles on their break
Or talking money or politics while one fitted
This armpiece with its overseam to the band

Of cuff I button at my wrist. The presser, the cutter,
The wringer, the mangle. The needle, the union,
The treadle, the bobbin. The code. The infamous blaze

At the Triangle Factory in nineteen-eleven.
One hundred and forty-six died in the flames
On the ninth floor, no hydrants, no fire escapes—

The witness in a building across the street
Who watched how a young man helped a girl to step
up to the windowsill, then held her out

Away from the masonry wall and let her drop.
And then another. As if he were helping them up
To enter a streetcar, and not eternity.

A third before he dropped her put her arms
Around his neck and kissed him. Then he held
Her into space, and dropped her. Almost at once

He stepped to the sill himself, his jacket flared
And fluttered up from his shirt as he came down,
Air filling up the legs of his gray trousers—

Like Hart Crane's Bedlamite, "shrill shirt ballooning."
Wonderful how the pattern matches perfectly
Across the placket and over the twin bar-tacked

Corners of both pockets, like a strict rhyme
Or a major chord. Prints, plaids, checks,
Houndstooth, Tattersall, Madras. The clan tartans

Invented by mill-owners inspired by the hoax of Ossian,
To control their savage Scottish workers, tamed
By a fabricated heraldry: MacGregor,

Bailey, MacMartin. The kilt, devised for workers
To wear among the dusty clattering looms.
Weavers, carders, spinners. The loader,

The docker, the navvy. The planter, the picker, the sorter
Sweating at her machine in a litter of cotton
As slaves in calico headrags sweated in fields:

George Herbert, your descendant is a Black
Lady in South Carolina, her name is Irma
And she inspected my shirt. Its color and fit

And feel and its clean smell have satisfied
Both her and me. We have culled its cost and quality
Down to the buttons of simulated bone,

The buttonholes, the sizing, the facing, the characters
Printed in black on neckband and tail. The shape,
The label, the labor, the color, the shade. The shirt.

JAR OF PENS

Sometimes the sight of them
Huddled in their cylindrical formation
Repels me: humble, erect,
Mute and expectant in their
Rinsed-out honey crock: my quiver
Of detached stingers. (Or, a bouquet
Of lies and intentions unspent.)

Pilots, drones, workers—the Queen is
Cross. Upright lodge
Of the toilworthy—gathered
At attention as though they know
All the ink in the world couldn't
Cover the first syllable
Of one heart's confusion.

This fat fountain pen wishes
In its elastic heart
That I were the farm boy
Whose illiterate father
Rescued it out of the privy
After it fell from the boy's pants:
The man digging in boots
By lanternlight, down in the pit.

Another pen strains to call back
The characters of the five thousand
World languages dead since 1900,
Curlicues, fiddleheads, brushstroke
Splashes and arabesques,
Footprints of extinct species.

The father hosed down his boots
And leaving them in the barn
With his pants and shirt
Came into the kitchen,
Holding the little retrieved
Symbol of symbol-making

O brood of line-scratchers, plastic
Scabbards of the soul, you have
Outlived the sword—talons and
Wingfeathers for the hand.

ABC

Any body can die, evidently. Few
Go happily, irradiating joy,

Knowledge, love. Many
Need oblivion, painkillers,
Quickest respite.

Sweet time unafflicted,
Various world:

X = your zenith.

BILLY COLLINS

Billy Collins's hilarious writing reaches many people who don't often read poetry. As U.S. poet laureate from 2001 to 2003, Collins (b. 1941) started an online poetry jukebox for students, with a new poem for every day of the school year, a project he expanded into the anthology *Poetry 180: A Turning Back to Poetry* (2003).

A resident of Westchester County, New York, Collins was born in New York City. He grew up in the borough of Queens and attended Holy Cross College. He earned his doctorate at the University of California, Riverside. His books include *Sailing Alone Around the Room: New and Selected Poems* (2001). He has also recorded a CD of his poems, *The Best Cigarette* (1997).

Collins's poem "Forgetfulness" treats a serious topic with belly-aching humor. We all worry about losing our memories as we get older, but Collins turns the phenomenon of "literary amnesia" into a romp. His use of metaphor is stunning—"the memories you used to harbor / decided to retire to the southern hemisphere of the brain, / to a little fishing village where there are no phones." He has the ability to take an idea to an absurd and delicious extreme.

"Japan" refers to a famous short poem by Yosa Buson (1716–1783), one of the greatest masters of haiku. The poem has been translated by X. J. Kennedy:

On the one-ton temple bell
a moon-moth, folded into sleep,
sits still.

Collins is so giddy, so in love with the poem, that the reader can't help being swept along. He riffs on the haiku like a jazz musician changing a melody. The three-line stanzas each stand alone as a haiku. Behind Collins's deadpan humor, a moment of depth is waiting.

Collins often writes poems about poetry, but he manages to accomplish this with such self-mockery that he never becomes overly self-conscious. "Nightclub" makes fun of the topics that do and don't appear in poetry and songs. The poem then flows into the speaker's imagination as a cut he is listening to transports him into a nightclub where Johnny Hartman (1923–83) is singing. Collins has said that he tries to do in his poems what every singer knows: start slow and finish strong. In "Nightclub," he does this by walking the proverbial path from the ridiculous to the sublime.

FORGETFULNESS

The name of the author is the first to go
followed obediently by the title, the plot,
the heartbreaking conclusion, the entire novel
which suddenly becomes one you have never read, never even heard of,

as if, one by one, the memories you used to harbor
decided to retire to the southern hemisphere of the brain,
to a little fishing village where there are no phones.

Long ago you kissed the names of the nine Muses good-bye
and watched the quadratic equation pack its bag,
and even now as you memorize the order of the planets,

something else is slipping away, a state flower perhaps,
the address of an uncle, the capital of Paraguay.

Whatever it is you are struggling to remember
it is not poised on the tip of your tongue,
not even lurking in some obscure corner of your spleen.

It has floated away down a dark mythological river
whose name begins with an *L* as far as you can recall,
well on your own way to oblivion where you will join those
who have even forgotten how to swim and how to ride a bicycle.

No wonder you rise in the middle of the night
to look up the date of a famous battle in a book on war.
No wonder the moon in the window seems to have drifted
out of a love poem that you used to know by heart.

JAPAN

Today I pass the time reading
a favorite haiku,
saying the few words over and over.

It feels like eating
the same small, perfect grape
again and again.

I walk through the house reciting it
and leave its letters falling
through the air of every room.

I stand by the big silence of the piano and say it.
I say it in front of a painting of the sea.
I tap out its rhythm on an empty shelf.

I listen to myself saying it,
then I say it without listening,
then I hear it without saying it.

And when the dog looks up at me,
I kneel down on the floor
and whisper it into each of his long white ears.

It's the one about the one-ton
temple bell
with the moth sleeping on its surface,

and every time I say it, I feel the excruciating
pressure of the moth
on the surface of the iron bell.

When I say it at the window,
the bell is the world
and I am the moth resting there.

When I say it into the mirror,
I am the heavy bell
and the moth is life with its papery wings.

And later, when I say it to you in the dark,
you are the bell,
and I am the tongue of the bell, ringing you,

and the moth has flown
from its line
and moves like a hinge in the air above our bed.

NIGHTCLUB

You are so beautiful and I am a fool
to be in love with you
is a theme that keeps coming up
in songs and poems.
There seems to be no room for variation.
I have never heard anyone sing
I am so beautiful
and you are a fool to be in love with me,
even though this notion has surely
crossed the minds of women and men alike.
You are so beautiful, too bad you are a fool
is another one you don't hear.
Or, you are a fool to consider me beautiful.
That one you will never hear, guaranteed.

For no particular reason this afternoon
I am listening to Johnny Hartman
whose dark voice can curl around
the concepts of love, beauty, and foolishness
like no one else's can.
It feels like smoke curling up from a cigarette

someone left burning on a baby grand piano
around three o'clock in the morning;
smoke that billows up into the bright lights
while out there in the darkness
some of the beautiful fools have gathered
around little tables to listen,
some with their eyes closed,
others leaning forward into the music
as if it were holding them up,
or twirling the loose ice in a glass,
slipping by degrees into a rhythmic dream.
Yes, there is all this foolish beauty,
borne beyond midnight,
that has no desire to go home,
especially now when everyone in the room
is watching the large man with the tenor sax
that hangs from his neck like a golden fish.
He moves forward to the edge of the stage
and hands the instrument down to me
and nods that I should play.
So I put the mouthpiece to my lips
and blow into it with all my living breath.
We are all so foolish,
my long bebop solo begins by saying,
so damn foolish
we have become beautiful without even knowing it.

ROBERT HASS

Robert Hass (b. 1941) transformed the role of the U.S. poet laureate when he was appointed to that position from 1995 to 1997. He changed it from a sinecure to the role of activist, tirelessly seeking readers for poetry all over the country, from community centers to Kiwanis Clubs.

Hass is one of the few U.S. writers of our time who has made important contributions in three different literary areas: poetry, criticism, and translation. Hass's highly readable and probing essays in *Twentieth Century Pleasures: Prose on Poetry* (1984) won the National Book Critics Circle Award in Criticism. His translations of Czeslaw Milosz and of Bashō, Buson, and Issa in his collection *The Essential Haiku* (1994) are outstanding. His own poetry has remained consistently strong, including *Field Guide* (1973; chosen as the Yale Younger Poets selection), *Praise* (1979), *Human Wishes* (1989), and *Sun under Wood* (1996).

Born in San Francisco, Hass has brought the terrain and the flora and fauna of the West Coast into American poetry with a biologist's curiosity and a landscape painter's artistry. In "Meditation at Lagunitas" and in the later "Interrupted Meditation," he makes use of his skill in describing nature. He pairs that with an amazing ability to observe and portray human character, as in the "wolfish" bite of the Eastern European intellectual sketched in "Interrupted Meditation."

In "Meditation at Lagunitas," the speaker begins by talking about the contemporary sense of living in a world that tastes less sweet than the past. Even words seem to have lost the strings that tied them to meaning. But a memory of lovemaking, and the specifics of how that experience linked the speaker to his past, turns the poem into praise of the present and the entire physical world.

Hass's poetry surprises in its leaps and juxtapositions, particularly in his more recent work such as "Interrupted Meditation," which brings together history, anecdote, confession, literary observations, and nature poetry. Throughout it all, Hass never loses his compassion for the human condition.

This compassion also surfaces in the poem, "A Story about the Body." The poem is written in prose, maybe in an effort to counter the preciousness of its setting—an artist's colony. The speaker allows the reader to feel the intoxication of the youthful composer's crush but also to judge him as we see, and perhaps understand, his limitations. The final image created by the Japanese painter is almost a visual haiku.

MEDITATION AT LAGUNITAS

All the new thinking is about loss.
In this it resembles all the old thinking.
The idea, for example, that each particular erases
the luminous clarity of a general idea. That the clown-
faced woodpecker probing the dead sculpted trunk
of that black birch is, by his presence,
some tragic falling off from a first world
of undivided light. Or the other notion that,
because there is in this world no one thing
to which the bramble of *blackberry* corresponds,
a word is elegy to what it signifies.
We talked about it late last night and in the voice
of my friend, there was a thin wire of grief, a tone
almost querulous. After a while I understood that,
talking this way, everything dissolves: *justice,*
pine, hair, woman, you and *I.* There was a woman
I made love to and I remembered how, holding
her small shoulders in my hands sometimes,
I felt a violent wonder at her presence
like a thirst for salt, for my childhood river
with its island willows, silly music from the pleasure boat,
muddy places where we caught the little orange-silver fish
called *pumpkinseed.* It hardly had to do with her.
Longing, we say, because desire is full
of endless distances. I must have been the same to her.
But I remember so much, the way her hands dismantled bread,
the thing her father said that hurt her, what
she dreamed. There are moments when the body is as numinous
as words, days that are the good flesh continuing.
Such tenderness, those afternoons and evenings,
saying *blackberry, blackberry, blackberry.*

INTERRUPTED MEDITATION

Little green involute fronds of fern at creekside.
And the sinewy clear water rushing over creekstone
of the palest amber, veined with a darker gold,
thinnest lines of gold rivering through the amber
like—ah, now we come to it. *We were not put on earth,*
the old man said, he was hacking into the crust
of a sourdough half loaf in his vehement, impatient way
with an old horn-handled knife, *to express ourselves.*
I knew he had seen whole cities leveled: also
that there had been a time of shame for him, outskirts
of a ruined town, half Baroque, half Greek Revival,
pediments of Flora and Hygeia from a brief eighteenth-century
health spa boom lying on the streets in broken chunks
and dogs scavenging among them. His one act of courage
then had been to drop pieces of bread or chocolate,
as others did, where a fugitive family of Jews
was rumored to be hiding. *I never raised my voice,*
of course, none of us did. He sliced wedges of cheese
after the bread, spooned out dollops of sour jam
from some Hungarian plum, purple and faintly gingered.
Every day the bits of half-mildewed, dry, hard—
this is my invention—whitened chocolate, dropped furtively
into rubble by the abandoned outbuilding of some suburban
mechanic's shop—but I am sure he said chocolate—
and it comforted no one. *We talked in whispers.*
"Someone is taking them." "Yes," Janos said,
"But it might just be the dogs." He set the table.
Shrugged. Janos was a friend from the university,
who fled east to join a people's liberation army,
died in Siberia somewhere. *"Some of us whispered 'art',"*
he said. *"Some of us 'truth.' A debate with cut vocal chords.*
You have to understand that, for all we knew, the Germans
would be there forever. And if not the Germans, the Russians.

Well, you don't 'have to' understand anything, naturally.
No one knew which way to jump. What we had was language,
you see. Some said art, some said truth. Truth, of course,
was death. Clattered the plates down on the table. *No one,*
no one said 'self-expression.' Well, you had your own forms
of indulgence. Didn't people in the forties say 'man'
instead of 'the self?' I think I said. *I thought 'the self'*
came in in 1949. He laughed. *It's true. Man,*
we said, is the creature who is able to watch himself
eat his own shit from fear. You know what that is?
Melodrama. I tell you, there is no bottom to self-pity.

This comes back to me on the mountainside. Butterflies—
tiny blues with their two-dot wings like quotation marks
or an abandoned pencil sketch of a face. They hover lightly
over lupine blooms, whirr of insects in the three o'clock sun.
What about being? I had asked him. *Isn't language responsible*
to it, all of it, the texture of bread, the hairstyles
of the girls you knew in high school, shoelaces, sunsets,
the smell of tea? Ah, he said, *you've been talking to Milosz.*
To Czeslaw I say this: silence precedes us. We are catching up.
I think he was quoting Jabes whom he liked to read.
Of course, here, gesturing out the window, pines, ragged green
of a winter lawn, the bay, *you can express what you like,*
enumerate the vegetation. And you! you have to, I'm afraid,
since you don't excel at metaphor. A shrewd, quick glance
to see how I have taken this thrust. *You write well, clearly.*
You are an intelligent man. But—finger in the air—
silence is waiting. Milosz believes there is a Word
at the end that explains. There is silence at the end,
and it doesn't explain, it doesn't even ask. He spread chutney
on his bread, meticulously, out to the corners. Something
angry always in his unexpected fits of thoroughness
I liked. Then cheese. Then a lunging, wolfish bite.
Put it this way, I give you, here, now, a magic key.

What does it open? This key I give you, what exactly
does it open? Anything, anything! But what? I found
that what I thought about was the failure of my marriage,
the three or four lost years just at the end and after.
For me there is no key, not even the sum total of our acts.
But you are a poet. You pretend to make poems. And?

She sat on the couch sobbing, her rib cage shaking
from its accumulated abysses of grief and thick sorrow.
I don't love you, she said. The terrible thing is
that I don't think I ever loved you. He thought to himself
fast, to numb it, that she didn't mean it, thought
what he had done to provoke it. It was May.
Also pines, lawn, the bay, a blossoming apricot.
Everyone their own devastation. Each on its own scale.
I don't know what the key opens. I know we die,
and don't know what is at the end. We don't behave well.
And there are monsters out there, and millions of others
to carry out their orders. We live half our lives
in fantasy, and words. This morning I am pretending
to be walking down the mountain in the heat.
A vault of blue sky, traildust, the sweet medicinal
scent of mountain grasses, and at trailside—
I'm a little ashamed that I want to end this poem
singing, but I want to end this poem singing—the wooly
closed-down buds of the sunflower to which, in English,
someone gave the name, sometime, of pearly everlasting.

A STORY ABOUT THE BODY

The young composer, working that summer at an artist's colony, had watched her for a week. She was Japanese, a painter, almost sixty, and he thought he was in love with her. He loved her work, and her work was like the way she moved her body, used her hands, looked at him directly when she made amused and considered answers to his questions. One night, walking back from a concert, they came to her door and she turned to him and said, "I think you would like to have me. I would like that too, but I must tell you that I have had a double mastectomy," and when he didn't understand, "I've lost both my breasts." The radiance that he had carried around in his belly and chest cavity—like music—withered very quickly, and he made himself look at her when he said, "I'm sorry. I don't think I could." He walked back to his own cabin through the pines, and in the morning he found a small blue bowl on the porch outside his door. It looked to be full of rose petals, but he found when he picked it up that the rose petals were on top; the rest of the bowl—she must have swept them from the corners of her studio—was full of dead bees.

LYN HEJINIAN

Lyn Hejinian (b. 1941) is a leading writer of a school often called Language Poetry, after the literary magazine $L=A=N=G=U=A=G=E$, which began in the 1970s. Language poets frequently use a radical version of collage that eliminates the usual thread of literature. The result is a jagged restructuring of words where each reader creates his or her own context for the poem. The intent is to dismantle the standard use of words in order to open the door to new ways of thinking.

Lyn Hejinian, a San Francisco Bay Area native, has authored or co-authored over twenty books. Hejinian is a poet, novelist, translator, and essayist. Her best-known book is a prose work, *My Life*. The magazine *Poetry Flash* has described *My Life* as having "real, almost hypnotic power, obvious intelligence" and called it "astonishingly beautiful." Hejinian teaches in the English Department at the University of California, Berkeley. Her critical writings were assembled in *The Language of Inquiry* (University of California Press, 2000). She is the editor and publisher of Tuumba Press and co-editor of *Poetics Journal*.

Hejinian's "There was once an angel . . ." is part of a highly ambitious work called *The Book of A Thousand Eyes*, a tribute to the character Scheherazade in *1001 Arabian Nights*. "I like this female figure who can educate rulers," she said. "There was once an angel . . ." is a poignant reflection on mortality, with an angel who is as earthy as his neighbor. Hejinian takes apart the story by creating multiple and contradictory morals that almost seem like literary criticism of her own writing.

Hejinian's poem "Chapter 188" is from her book *Oxota: A Short Russian Novel*. Despite the title, the book is actually a collection of poems. She calls them "free sonnets," not in any fixed form. Explaining the book's title, Hejinian wrote, "*Oxota* in Russian means 'the hunt,' but *oxota* can also mean 'desire,' especially erotic desire." The book derives from a period when Hejinian made numerous visits to the former Soviet Union. She describes these trips as surreal journeys where, for instance, "I was told we were going to a certain Misha's house for tea and we ended up in a public building where I was to give a talk on postmodernism."

"Time is filled with beginners" is a section from Hejinian's book-length poem *The Fatalist*. Hejinian wrote these poems in an intriguing way: she collected all the letters, e-mails, and memos she'd written during a two-year period and created an enormous collage from them.

from THE BOOK OF A THOUSAND EYES

There was once an angel who had a neighbor, and this neighbor was ambitious. He wanted more than money or fame, he said; he wanted immortality.

"Why's that?" asked the angel.

The angel had lived an unnaturally long time, but nonetheless he understood some things about nature, and here at the end of a long summer day, he was watering the small garden in front of his house.

"Well," said the neighbor, somewhat portentously but also tentatively—he was a sensitive person but he'd considered this for a long time and he now felt that his thoughts were correct and important—"I don't want my feelings, so very dear and strong and uniquely arising from my life, to go suddenly unfelt, as they will be, when I'm dead."

"So you think you want to be immortal."

"Yes."

"But it is precisely the immortals," said the angel, "who are dead."

Moral: Certain experienced continuums—for example, time, space, the ego—are bridges but without chasms.

Moral: Even when an angel makes you fly, you are the wings.

Moral: An angel's pugnacious twaddle may be as irrefutable as a pistol and in the same way wrong.

Moral: It's not the length of a life but the tension of its parts that lets resound all that it feels.

from OXOTA: A SHORT RUSSIAN NOVEL

Chapter 188

What is the scope of the experience of sex—we talked about that
The crowding it forecasts
A poise pitching
Or the incompetence—it's as if you're trying to find the way around another woman's
 kitchen
Or man's—but that's too much
Proprietors of our own mud and flour
Rain was falling, dividing the light
It was he who was plunging, Masha said, how could I stop
Life always attracts attention
And the trees bristle
The tree tries to remain in one spot with innumerable gradations
So sex just condenses disorientation
Then there's jealousy, that crazy bridge
But do not compare, Arkadii said, living is incomparable

from THE FATALIST

Time is filled with beginners. You are right. Now
each of them is working on something
and it matters. The large increments of life must not go by
unrecognized. That's why my mother's own mother-in-law
was often bawdy. "MEATBALLS!" she would shout
superbly anticipating site-specific specificity in the future
of poetry. Will this work? The long moment is addressed
to the material world's "systems and embodiments" for study
for sentience and for history. Materiality, after all, is about being
a geologist or biologist, bread dough rising
while four boys on skateboards attempt to fly,
spinning to a halt micromillimeters before I watch them, my attention riveted
on getting tangled and forgetting the name of the chair, for example
and the huge young man, he is covered with tattoos
I think. Life is a series of given situations
of which the living have to take note on site
and the storytellers give an account as the wind
tangles the rain or the invaders take over the transmitter. The exchange
of ideas constitutes a challenge to the lyric ego. And so I am reporting
that I was wrong. A real storyteller never asks what story one wants
to hear, not the happy Joel nor the sleepy
Clara nor the dreamy Jane, the seductive Sam, the sullen
Robbie Jones. Nonetheless I have bought a bicycle. I have to remember
to stop. Thank you. I hope you will enjoy it. A bike that is simply locked
but freestanding will be immediately stolen. Of course
there can't be much wrong in helping people get what they want
but creeps and purveyors of negativity
and cruelty are tucked into every institution
and most corners and though my inclination is to vote
in favor of everyone's dearest dreams of advancement I disagree
with the remark that "deathlessness" and "fearlessness" don't work.
I think they do. "Deathlessness" immediately invokes the "breathlessness" we thought
we'd half heard in the panting of deathlessness whose dashing

is life. "Writhing" is self-indulgent however
but the near-rhyme with "writing" is terrific. Don't change *that*. Poetry
can't be *about* flight—that would make flight a perching
instead of a flight. When one thing becomes another
the other is free to become something
else. I remember just where
we were sitting
under the influence of the wind
watching a crow
becoming something else in this case
a crow.
The state of milk in jars takes place
and the state of world affairs
can now change. No cereal manufacturer intentionally includes angels
but marshmallow bits may look angelic in a bowl. Who knows? A poem
full of ruptures could be one from which all kinds of things are flying.

MARILYN HACKER

In the late 1960s and early 1970s, when American poets were bolting from anything that smacked of structure, Marilyn Hacker (b. 1942) began her quest. She started digging through the rubble of formal verse, searching for what was still alive, what remained intact and glistening. Unlike many sonneteers of the past couple of centuries, she avoided ersatz Elizabethan diction and subjects. Instead, she recorded her own contemporary voice and experience in traditional forms, mastering the sonnet, pantoum, villanelle, and ballade with astonishing agility.

The result has been many books of poetry, from *Presentation Piece* in 1974, winner of the National Book Award, to her *Selected Poems* in 1994, to the more recent *Squares and Courtyards* (2000). Whether she writes as a lover, a mother, a woman, a politically engaged citizen, or a breast cancer survivor, Marilyn Hacker always displays a diamond-sharp self-awareness, a sequined intellect, and a wry sense of humor.

Hacker's revival of lyric forms helped inspire an entire movement of poetry, sometimes called the New Formalism, but she has never really embraced it. This is partly, I suspect, because of her interest in the diversity of American poetry. This interest has led her to important work as an editor. For several years, she picked the poems for *The Kenyon Review,* and she has guest-edited issues of *Poetry* and *Ploughshares.*

Her "Sonnet XV" from the "Separations" sequence (1976) is a good example of her early work in traditional structures, where the subject and diction are strikingly contemporary.

Hacker's poem "Rune of the Finland Woman" is a myth woven from the life of a real person she knew, Sára Karig, a gentile who helped save Jewish children during the Holocaust and later spent time in a Stalinist prison camp. The form is Hacker's own invention. She uses variations on the music of the first line in a pattern that evokes braiding hair or weaving textiles.

Hacker lives half the year in Paris, and she writes with great familiarity about French culture. "Graffiti from the Gare Saint-Manqué" is a ballade where she wittily mixes her own life with literary history. The challenges of this form are both the rhyme scheme and having to repeat the same last line in each stanza, as François Villon echoes "But where are the snows of yesteryear?" in his famous poem in this form. The phrase "Gare Saint-Manqué" could be translated "Saint-Notquite Station." The phrase "Coeur mis à nu" in the poem's last stanza means "heart laid bare."

from SEPARATIONS SEQUENCE

XV

And here we are, or rather, here am I;
hungover, headachy, insomniac.
The clock rings four. I turn onto my back.
Four-thirty. Five. Wet traffic whispers by
Thamesward. I've been in London for
twelve hours now. It's already getting light.
I sit up, take my notebook, try to write
ten reasons not to see you anymore.
One: you will hurt me; Two: you will resent
my hurt; Three: but I light a cigarette
and sit against the wall and smoke instead,
thinking of times I've been kicked out of bed
and suffered O. Tired, as the curtains get
pale, I write this, and sleep all morning, spent.

RUNE OF THE FINLAND WOMAN

for Sára Karig

"You are so wise," the reindeer said, "you can bind the
winds of the world in a single strand."

> H. C. Andersen, "The Snow Queen"

She could bind the world's winds in a single strand.
She could find the world's words in a singing wind.
She could lend a weird will to a mottled hand.
She could wind a willed word from a muddled mind.

She could wend the wild woods on a saddled hind.
She could sound a wellspring with a rowan wand.
She could bind the wolf's wounds in a swaddling band.
She could bind a banned book in a silken skin.

She could spend a world war on invaded land.
She could pound the dry roots to a kind of bread.
She could feed a road gang on invented food.
She could find the spare parts of the severed dead.

She could find the stone limbs in a waste of sand.
She could stand the pit cold with a withered lung.
She could handle bad puns in the slang she learned.
She could dandle foundlings in their mother tongue.

She could plait a child's hair with a fishbone comb.
She could tend a coal fire in the Arctic wind.
She could mend an engine with a sewing pin.
She could warm the dark feet of a dying man.

She could drink the stone soup from a doubtful well.
She could breathe the green stink of a trench latrine.
She could drink a queen's share of important wine.
She could think a few things she would never tell.

She could learn the hand code of the deaf and blind.
She could earn the iron keys of the frozen queen.
She could wander uphill with a drunken friend.
She could bind the world's winds in a single strand.

GRAFFITI FROM THE GARE SAINT-MANQUÉ

for Zed Bee

Outside the vineyard is a caravan
of Germans taking pictures in the rain.
The local cheese is Brillat-Savarin.
The local wine is Savigny-les-Beaune.
We learn Burgundies while we have the chance
and lie down under cabbage-rose wallpaper.
It's too much wine and brandy, but I'll taper
off later. Who is watering my plants?
I may go home as wide as Gertrude Stein
—another Jewish Lesbian in France.

Around the sculptured Dukes of Burgundy,
androgynous monastics, faces cowled,
thrust bellies out in marble ecstasy
like child swimmers having their pigtails toweled.
Kids sang last night. A frieze of celebrants
circles the tomb, though students are in school,
while May rain drizzles on the beautiful
headlines confirming François Mitterrand's
election. We have Reagan. Why not be
another Jewish Lesbian in France?

Aspiring Heads of State are literate
here, have favorite poets, can explain
the way structuralists obliterate
a text. They read at night. They're still all men.
Now poppy-studded meadows of Provence
blazon beyond our red sardine-can car.
We hope chairpersons never ask: why are
unblushing deviants abroad on grants?
My project budget listed: Entertain
another Jewish Lesbian in France.

I meant my pithy British village neighbor
who misses old days when sorority
members could always know each other: they wore
short-back-and-sides and a collar and tie.
She did, too. Slavic eyes, all romance
beneath an Eton crop with brilliantined
finger waves, photographed at seventeen
in a dark blazer and a four-in-hand:
a glimpse of salad days that made the day for
another Jewish Lesbian in France.

Then we went on to peanuts and Campari,
she and her friend, my friend and I, and then
somehow it was nine-thirty and a hurry
to car and *carte* and a carafe of wine,
Lapin Sauté or Truite Meunière in Vence.
Convivial quartet of friends and lovers:
had anyone here dreaded any other's
tears, dawn recriminations and demands?
Emphatically not. That must have been
another Jewish Lesbian in France.

It's hard to be almost invisible.
You think you must be almost perfect too.
When your community's not sizable,
it's often a community of two,
and a dissent between communicants
is a commuter pass to the abyss.
Authorities who claim you don't exist
would sometimes find you easy to convince.
(It helps if you can talk about it to
another Jewish Lesbian in France.)

A decorated she-Academician
opines we were thought up by horny males.
No woman of equivalent position
has yet taken the wind out of her sails.
(How would her "lifelong companion" have thanked her?)
Man loving Man's *her* subject, without mention
if what they do is due to her invention
—and if I'd been her mother, I'd have spanked her.
(Perhaps in a suppressed draft *Hadrian*'s
another Jewish Lesbian in France.)

Then the advocates of Feminitude
—with dashes as their only punctuation—
explain that Reason is to be eschewed:
in the Female Subconscious lies salvation.
Suspiciously like Girlish Ignorance,
it seems a rather watery solution.
If I can't dance, it's not my revolution.
If I can't think about it, I won't dance.
So let the ranks of *Psych et Po* include
another Jewish Lesbian in France.

I wish I had been packed off to the nuns
to learn good manners, Attic Greek, and Latin.
(No public Bronx Junior High School fit all that in.)
My angsts could have been casuistic ones.
It's not my feminist inheritance
to eat roots, drink leaf broth, live in a cave,
and not even know how to misbehave
with just one vowel and five consonants.
This patchwork autodidact Anglophone's
another Jewish Lesbian in France,

following Natalie Barney, Alice B.
Toklas, Djuna Barnes, generous Bryher,
Romaine Brooks, Sylvia Beach, H. D.,
Tamara de Lempicka, Janet Flanner.
They made the best use of the circumstance
that blood and stockings often both were bluish;
(they all were white, and only Alice Jewish)
wicked sept/oct/nonagenarians.
Would it have saved Simone Weil's life to be
another Jewish Lesbian in France?

It isn't sex I mean. Sex doesn't save
anyone, except, sometimes, from boredom
(and the underpaid underclass of whoredom
is often bored at work). I have a grave
suspicion ridicule of Continence
or Chastity is one way to disparage
a woman's choice of any job but marriage.
Most of us understand what we renounce.
(This was a lunchtime pep talk I once gave
another Jewish Lesbian in France

depressed by temporary solitude
but thinking coupled bliss was dubious.)
I mean: one way to love a body viewed
as soiled and soiling existential dross
is knowing through your own experience
a like body embodying a soul
to be admirable and lovable.
That is a source that merits nourishment.
Last night despair dressed as self-loathing wooed
another Jewish Lesbian in France.

The sheet was too soft. Unwashed for three weeks,
it smelled like both of us. The sin we are
beset by is despair. I rubbed my cheeks
against the cotton, thought, I wouldn't care
if it were just *my* funk. Despair expands
to fill . . . I willed my arm: extend; hand: stroke
that sullen shoulder. In the time it took
synapse to realize abstract commands,
the shoulder's owner fell asleep. Still there
another Jewish Lesbian in France

stared at the sickle moon above the skylight,
brooding, equally sullen, that alone
is better after all. As close as my right
foot, even my bed stops being my own.
Could I go downstairs quietly, make plans
for myself, not wake her? Who didn't undress,
slept on the couch bundled with loneliness
rather than brave that nuptial expanse
five weeks before. Another contradiction
another Jewish Lesbian in France

may reconcile more gracefully than I.
We're ill equipped to be obliging wives.
The post office and travel agency
are significant others in our lives.
Last summer I left flowers at Saint Anne's
shrine. She had daughters. One who, legends tell,
adrift, woman-companioned, shored (is still
revered) in the Camargue, her holy band's
navigatrix, Mary, calming the sea
—another Jewish Lesbian in France?

It says they lived together forty years,
Mary and Mary and Sarah (who was Black).
Unsaintly ordinary female queers,
we packed up and went separately back.
We'd shared the toad with Gypsy sleeper vans
to join Sarah's procession to the shore.
Our own month-end anabasis was more
ambiguous. Among Americans
my polyglot persona disappears,
another Jewish Lesbian in France.

Coeur mis à nu in sunlight, khaki pants
I've rolled up in a beach towel so ants
and crickets from the leafage won't invade
their sweaty legs: in a loaned hermit glade
pine-redolent of New Hampshire, not France,
I disentangle from the snares I laid.
Liver-lobed mushrooms thicken in the shade,
shrubs unwrap, pinelings thrust through mulch. Noon slants
across my book, my chest, its lemonade
rays sticky as a seven-year-old's hands.

SHARON OLDS

Sharon Olds (b. 1942) picked up the torch of confessional poetry in her early writing. Olds's first two books, *Satan Says* (1980) and *The Dead and the Living* (1984), won The Poetry Center Book Award and the Lamont Poetry Selection, respectively. Her brave poems about the hidden abuse in her family seemed to drive her to write mostly about what she could actually see and feel. Olds became the bard of the body, describing its revelations and failures in poem after poem about lovers, family, and parenting.

Eventually the red-hot anger of her earlier poems began to cool into a transparent clarity, like blown glass. In her book *The Gold Cell* (1987), she writes about her family again in the poem "I Go Back to May 1937." Taking a page out of Delmore Schwartz's story "In Dreams Begin Responsibilities," she imagines herself before her own birth, seeing her parents when they met. Instead of villains, her parents are blundering innocents capable of evil, leaving the gates of their colleges as Adam and Eve were exiled from Eden. Despite what her parents inflicted on each other and their children, the speaker of the poem fervently wants them to meet, bumping their photos together like a child playing house. The headlong emotional pace of the long sentences at the beginning of the poem gives way to realizations, expressed with direct monosyllables at the end. She recognizes that her mission as a writer was born from her parents' mistakes. Olds is known for her "killer endings," and this poem's stunning last line lives up to that reputation.

Also from *The Gold Cell* is "Summer Solstice, New York City," which describes a tense standoff between a potential suicide and the police officers who try to save him. Olds is a master at using metaphors to create a poem underneath the poem that deepens the implications of what occurs on the narrative level. She paints the rescue attempt with images of babies and milk, the officers' treatment of the man suprisingly maternal in this all-male world.

"Necking," from her book *The Wellspring* (1996), takes place in Berkeley, California, where Olds grew up. If another poet had written this, it might have consisted only of comedy and nostalgia. In Olds's hands, the poem has humor but also somber undertones. At the same time it glows with lights and jewels and fire, counterparts to the poem's spiritual incandescence. The teenagers caught in the rising tide of their sexuality are like the child in Wordsworth's "Intimations of Immortality Based on Recollections of Early Childhood." These young people must shuck off their inherent knowledge of eternity to accustom themselves to mundane life.

I GO BACK TO MAY 1937

I see them standing at the formal gates of their colleges,
I see my father strolling out
under the ochre sandstone arch, the
red tiles glinting like bent
plates of blood behind his head, I
see my mother with a few light books at her hip
standing at the pillar made of tiny bricks with the
wrought-iron gate still open behind her, its
sword-tips aglow in the May air,
they are about to graduate, they are about to get married,
they are kids, they are dumb, all they know is they are
innocent, they would never hurt anybody.
I want to go up to them and say Stop,
don't do it—she's the wrong woman,
he's the wrong man, you are going to do things
you cannot imagine you would ever do,
you are going to do bad things to children,
you are going to suffer in ways you have not heard of,
you are going to want to die. I want to go
up to them there in the late May sunlight and say it,
her hungry pretty face turning to me,
her pitiful beautiful untouched body,
his arrogant handsome face turning to me,
his pitiful beautiful untouched body,
but I don't do it. I want to live. I
take them up like the male and female
paper dolls and bang them together
at the hips like chips of flint as if to
strike sparks from them, I say
Do what you are going to do, and I will tell about it.

SUMMER SOLSTICE, NEW YORK CITY

By the end of the longest day of the year he could not stand it,
he went up the iron stairs through the roof of the building
and over the soft, tarry surface
to the edge, put one leg over the complex green tin cornice
and said if they came a step closer that was it.
Then the huge machinery of the earth began to work for his life,
the cops came in their suits blue-grey as the sky on a cloudy evening,
and one put on a bullet-proof vest, a
black shell around his own life,
life of his children's father, in case
the man was armed, and one, slung with a
rope like the sign of his bounden duty,
came up out of a hole in the top of the neighboring building
like the gold hole they say is in the top of the head,
and began to lurk toward the man who wanted to die.
The tallest cop approached him directly,
softly, slowly, talking to him, talking, talking,
while the man's leg hung over the lip of the next world
and the crowd gathered in the street, silent, and the
hairy net with its implacable grid was
unfolded near the curb, and spread out, and
stretched as the sheet is prepared to receive at a birth.
Then they all came a little closer
where he squatted next to his death, his shirt
glowing its milky glow like something
growing in a dish at night in the dark in a lab and then
everything stopped
as his body jerked and he
stepped down from the parapet and went toward them
and they closed on him, I thought they were going to
beat him up, as a mother whose child has been
lost might scream at the child when it's found, they
took him by the arms and held him up and

leaned him against the wall of the chimney and the
tall cop lit a cigarette
in his own mouth, and gave it to him, and
then they all lit cigarettes, and the
red, glowing ends burned like the
tiny campfires we lit at night
back at the beginning of the world.

NECKING

I remember the Arabic numerals on the dashboards,
aquarium green, like the paintbrush tips
the watch-girls licked, licking the radium—
we were there above the Cyclotron,
in the hills, the Rad Lab under us
enclosed in its cyclone fence. The interiors
of the cars were shaped like soft flanks,
the cloth front seats plump as some mothers'
laps. I remember the beauty of the night,
the crisp weightless blackness, the air
that rose up the slope straight from the sea,
from Seal Rock—we slid slowly
along each other. Berkeley, below,
without my glasses, was like a bottom
drawer of smeared light. The rape
and murder of our classmate had happened in these hills,
so the fragrance of the dirt, porous and mineral,
—eucalyptus and redwood humus—
that had buried her body, was there with sex,
and one gleam down there was the doughnut shop
where he had picked her up—as if the intimate
pleasure of eating doughnuts, now,

for all of us, were to bear his mark.
And the easy touch of the four thousand volts,
that was in the car with us
with everything else—the rivets in boys' jeans,
their soldered clothes, the way they carried
the longing of the species, you could not help but pity them
as they set you on stunned fire. I would almost
pass out, my body made of some other
substance, my eyes open in the green darkness
of some other planet. And in some other
car, on some other skirt of the mountain,
a boy I secretly adored. I remember
how it felt, eyes closed, kissing,
streaming through the night, sealed in a capsule
with the wrong person. But the place was right,
mountains on my left hand,
sea on my right, I felt someday I might find him,
proton electron we would hit and stick and
meanwhile there were the stars, and the careful not
looking at or touching the boy's pants,
and my glasses, wings folded, stuck
in a pocket. I can hear the loud snap
when we leaned on them and they broke, we drove down the
hill, the porch-lamp blazed, I would enter
below its blurred gem, it seemed
endless then, the apprenticeship to the mortal.

LINDA McCARRISTON

Linda McCarriston (b. 1943) is a poet of power and great artistry whose reputation has not yet caught up with the stature of her writing. This is partly because she has lived in recent years at the end of a dirt road in Alaska in the company of a horse, a donkey, and various stray dogs and cats. She is not often on the reading circuit that advances a poet's reputation. But this lag in recognition is also because McCarriston's work is so explosive that many critics and anthologists aren't sure how to handle it.

Her second book, *Eva-Mary* (1991), caused an uproar when it was published in 1991. It won the Terrence des Pres Prize for Poetry and was nominated for the National Book Award. Many reviewers lauded the book's frank depiction of domestic violence and sexual abuse in McCarriston's childhood. Others attacked it for being more polemical than emotional. When McCarriston read from this book in public, claiming her experiences with her spellbinding voice, both women and men came up to her afterwards, seeking affirmation and healing for their own experiences of abuse.

McCarriston handles this topic with enormous skill in the poem "For Judge Faolain, Dead Long Enough: A Summons." The poem begins with an ironic tip of the hat to the judge who ignored McCarriston's mother's pleas. The mother is not portrayed as passive but as thwarted by a system that brushed her aside as a working-class woman whose first duty is to obey her abusive husband. McCarriston's craft as a poet emerges in the lines where she describes the family's violent daily life: "you ferried us back down to *the law,* / the black ice eye, the maw, the mako / that circles the kitchen table nightly." She uses striking imagery, alliteration, rhyme, assonance, and classical allusion in tandem to recreate the nightmare that her family faced.

Another poem from *Eva-Mary,* "Le Coursier de Jeanne d'Arc" ("Joan of Arc's Steed"), draws on the poet's lifelong fascination with horses and with the French national heroine. McCarriston's middle name is Joan. Her individual and extremely moving version of this moment in history is not so much about French nationalism or loyalty to a religious hierarchy as it is about a woman sticking to her own truth.

McCarriston's poem "Wrought Figure," from her more recent book *Little River: New and Selected Poems* (2000), is a lighter look at the battle of the sexes. The predominant color of the poem is red, suggesting the bloodied women this man has left in his wake. But his female dinner companion in the late Alaskan summer sun is not intimidated by either his past or her own.

TO JUDGE FAOLAIN, DEAD LONG ENOUGH: A SUMMONS

Your Honor, when my mother stood
before you, with her routine
domestic plea, after weeks
of waiting for speech to return
to her body, with her homemade
forties hairdo, her face purple still
under pancake, her jaw off just a little,
her *holy of holies* healing,
her breasts wrung, her heart
the bursting heart of someone
snagged among rocks deep
in a sharkpool—no, not "someone,"

but a woman there, snagged
with her babies, *by* them,
in one of hope's pedestrian
brutal turns—when, in the tones
of parlors overlooking the harbor,
you admonished that, for the sake
of the family, the wife
must take the husband back to her bed,
what you willed not to see before you
was a woman risen clean to the surface,
a woman who, with one arm flailing,
held up with the other her actual

burdens of flesh. When you clamped
to her leg the chain of *justice,*
you ferried us back down to *the law,*
the black ice eye, the maw, the mako
that circles the kitchen table nightly.
What did you make of the words

she told you, not to have heard her,
not to have seen her there? Almost-
forgiveable ignorance, you were not
the fist, the boot, or the blade,
but the jaded, corrective ear and eye
at the limits of her world. Now

I will you to see her as she was, to ride
your own words back into light: I call
your spirit home again, divesting you
of robe and bench, the fine white hand
and half-lit Irish eye. Tonight, put on
a body in the trailer down the road
where your father, when he can't
get it up, makes love to your mother
with a rifle. Let your name be
Eva-Mary. Let your hour of birth
be dawn. Let your life be long
and common, and your flesh endure.

LE COURSIER DE JEANNE D'ARC

You know that they burned her horse
before her. Though it is not recorded,
you know that they burned her Percheron
first, before her eyes, because you

know that story, so old that story,
the routine story, carried to its
extreme, of the cruelty that can make
of what a woman hears *a silence,*

that can make of what a woman sees
a lie. She had no son for them to burn,
for them to take from her in the world
not of her making and put to its pyre,

so they layered a greater one in front of
where she was staked to her own—
as you have seen her pictured sometimes,
her eyes raised to the sky. But they were

not raised. This is yet one of their lies.
They were not closed. Though her hands
were bound behind her, and her feet were
bound deep in what would become fire,

she watched. Of greenwood stakes
head-high and thicker than a man's waist
they laced the narrow corral that would not
burn until flesh had burned, until

bone was burning, and laid it thick
with tinder—fatted wicks and sulphur,
kindling and logs—and ran a ramp
up to its height from where the gray horse

waited, his dapples making of his flesh
a living metal, layers of life
through which the light shone out
in places as it seems to through the flesh

of certain fish, a light she knew
as purest, coming, like that, from within.
Not flinching, not praying, she looked
the last time on the body she knew

better than the flesh of any man, or child,
or woman, having long since left the lap
of her mother—the chest with its
perfect plates of muscle, the neck

with its perfect, prow-like curve,
the hindquarters'—pistons—powerful cleft
pennoned with the silk of his tail.
Having ridden as they did together

—those places, that hard, that long—
their eyes found easiest that day
the way to each other, their bodies
wedded in a sacrament unmediated

by man. With fire they drove him
up the ramp and off into the pyre
and tossed the flame in with him.
This was the last chance they gave her

to recant her world, in which their power
came not from God. Unmoved, the Men
of God began watching him burn, and better,
watching her watch him burn, hearing

the long mad godlike trumpet of his terror,
his crashing in the wood, the groan
of stakes that held, the silverblack hide,
the pricked ears catching first

like dryest bark, and the eyes.
And she knew, by this agony, that she
might choose to live still, if she would
but make her sign on the parchment

they would lay before her, which now
would include this new truth: that it
did not happen, this death in the circle,
the rearing, plunging, raging, the splendid

armor-colored head raised one last time
above the flames before they took him
—like any game untended on the spit—into
their yellow-green, their blackening red.

WROUGHT FIGURE

As though you were rare, you confessed
at our second candle-lit dinner to your
history: your women. I must confess
each name stung, each one's beauty, gifts
and wit, each one's second language, hair
and eyes, height, even the fights
in which each ended it, or you did.

I'm hard on women, you said. It was
July and night, heavy and fragrant
all around the table set for the
short season out on the porch. Shells
of lobsters, broken, were heaped
on plates, each gruesome body part

a woman scorned. You faced the red
barn, your salt-and-cayenne beard, your
profile inviting the still light my eyes
followed, still wanting you, around and
through the names, the scattered tasty
bits of crustacean. *I love women,*

you said to the barn with a sigh
almost of dread, *especially smart and
pretty ones, Linda,* to the fireflies,
then turned your head to face me, indict
me as victim in the sweet fresh crime.

I took a week, ten days, to think it
through, what you'd said, seeing myself some
time ahead named with the others over
drained shells to some pretty other
woman—and smart—listening. *I'm hard
on men,* I did not confess when you did,
used to not saying so, used to the *used*

in the figure/ground problem of *use.*
Ten days I took to trace the problem
through—figure and ground, ground and
figure, used and user, user and used—
and worked that line back around to its
start, your confession and a circle:
and I love men, pretty and smart, as you are,

and am not rare in this but, as you
confessed, successful, meaning bested by
fewer than I best. Let us dance, then, on
the lawn of what's left of summer, and be
not wary as we dance, the smart and the pretty
in the arms of one another, a woman turned by
a man who loves women, and a man turned
by a woman who loves men.

BILL ZAVATSKY

In addition to being a poet, Bill Zavatsky (b. 1943) has had a distinguished career as a translator and editor. When he edited a poetry magazine called *Roy Rogers,* Zavatsky produced an entire issue of one-line poems. He even carried this process of reduction further, writing a one-word poem: "Pinocerous." Zavatsky was also the founder and publisher of Sun Press. His translations from Spanish (reflecting his pride in his Spanish paternal grandfather) and from French have won him acclaim and the PEN/Book-of-the-Month Club Translation Award.

Zavatsky, a die-hard Manhattanite, was actually born in Bridgeport, Connecticut, son of a gas station owner. One of the first in his family to finish college, he was part of a talented cohort of young writers who went through Columbia University in the 1960s.

In his poems, Zavatsky uses the stand-up-comedy, conversational tone, and references to pop culture often associated with such New York School writers as Frank O'Hara and Kenneth Koch (Koch taught at Columbia when Zavatsky went there). What is distinctive about Zavatsky's work is the fusion of hilarity with biting pathos. This is what makes his poem "Bald" so effective. "Bald," from his book *For Steve Royal and Other Poems* (1985), is a riff on growing older, involving wacky spoofs on middle-aged men, mainly the poet himself. But the poem is also a painful attempt to face the reality of death. In Zavatsky's strange and beautiful universe, this morbid realization only intensifies the humor.

"Live at the Village Vanguard" reflects Zavatsky's deep involvement with music. Starting at age fifteen, Zavatsky played first accordion and then piano at gigs from late-night bars to weddings. He eventually became friends with his idol, the great pianist Bill Evans, even writing a poem for him that appeared on the cover of Evans's last album. "Live at the Village Vanguard" springs from one of the greatest moments in the history of live music recording—Bill Evans's classic sessions with one of the most amazing trios in the annals of jazz. True to his original approach, Zavatsky barely writes about the music in his poem. What he does focus on gives him a surprising stage to discuss the role of art and the artist.

BALD

In the mirror it's plain to see:
soon I'll be bald, like the two faceless men
staring at each other in the word SOON.
Left profile crowding mirror, I can still pretend
it isn't happening—enough tangled skeins
of hair hide the gleam. But from the right,
where the wave lifts, I don't have to push my face
close to see it winking at me—
the mysterious island of my skull,
the dinky coastline of my baby head
swimming back to me at last.
Through the pitiful shrubbery
that dots the beach (I mean my
miserable hairs), it glints. Soon
I'll crawl ashore where all uncles live—
the ones who never grew any hair,
their clown cannibal heads hilarious
in photographs, glaring like chromosomes
from dresser picture frames the way
they always did when I and my cousins
stopped short in a game of tag to stare at them,
trapped under glass in their dumb grown-up world,
a phrenology of how I'd never be. Then
two years ago I saw my head in a three-way mirror
buying a coat: three pink slivers of skin like slices
of pizza radiated from my part. The overhead lighting
shriveled my scalp, scorching my silk purse
to a sow's ass. Soon the morning hairs in the sink
reached out their arms and wailed to me.
Soon the moonlight with its chilly hands
seized my cranium, taking measurements.
Even my wife kept quiet. I was the last to know.
Yes, I'm drifting closer. Closer

to the desert island where I'll live out my days
training to be ever more the skeleton
that's taking over my body pore by pore.
Hair by hair its fingerbone scissors snip me
away, I who in the Sixties fell in love
with my own hair! Who swooned among
battalions of Narcissuses over the ripples
our long tresses made in that mirror
of our generation, the President's face!
I who have always known
that Death is a haircut!
Walking the streets I pause to study my scalp
where it hangs in a butcher shop window,
reflected beside the other meat.
Under my breath I sing the song I'm learning
that goes, "Bald is anonymous . . . bald is goodbye."
I will not grow the hair above my ear
until it's ten feet long, then drape it suavely
over the empty parking lot atop my head
where the forest used to loom, then plaster it down
with goo. No, I don't want a toupee
to fall in my soup, or a hair transplant
driven into my brain with giant needles!
I shoo away the mysterious weave
spun from the dead hair of unfortunate ones,
rich only in what grows from their head.
I reject the compensatory beard—I refuse
to live my life upside-down!
I prepare myself to receive the litanies
chanted by the kids as I enter the classroom:
"Chrome dome, marble head, baldy bean, skin head,
bowling ball brain, reflector head, bubble top. . . ."
I urge them on in the making of metaphor!
I am content to merge with the reflection
of every bald barber who ever adjusted my head.

I am enchanted, so late, to be becoming
someone else—the face in the mirror which,
by the time I claim it, won't even look like me!
I am thrilled to realize that the scythe
of the grim reaper is nothing more
than a cheap plastic comb
you can buy in any drugstore,
and even its teeth fall out.

LIVE AT THE VILLAGE VANGUARD

For forty years now, ever since
the recordings were released, I have wanted
to track down the people who attended
the afternoon and evening performances
of the Bill Evans Trio at the Village Vanguard
in New York City on Sunday, June 25, 1961.
Sometimes I've thought that instead of
the extraordinary music of pianist Bill Evans,
bassist Scott LaFaro, and drummer Paul Motian,
these live recordings featured the audience
that talked, laughed, jabbered, and clinked
their silverware and glasses throughout.

Maybe some of them know that LaFaro
was killed not long afterwards
in a car accident, leaving behind
on those tracks improvised solos
of staggering beauty on the bass violin.
But then everybody knows that these
were "classic" sessions—Evans at one
of his peaks, a trio still unmatched.

Maybe today some of those who were there
put on the CDs (or their scratchy old LPs)
and listen to what they didn't listen to then.
Or maybe they point to their voices
chattering under and around the music,
exclaiming, "Hey, honey—that's *me!*"

One writer claims that he can decipher
some of the dialogue as Evans works his way
through the melody of "Alice in Wonderland":
"I got a new TV—color!" "That brunette
over by the cigarette machine, I think
she has something to say to you. . . ."
"Maris will never top Ruth, but Mantle might."
"The colored bartender waters down the Scotch."
In the introduction to "I Loves You Porgy"
I can hear a guy saying, "Uh, it's something
by Gershwin . . . *Porgy and Bess.*"
Hey, at least they're listening. . . .

What if I could find some of those people
and interview them—*What were you doing
then? Who were you with that night? Why
had you gone to the Village Vanguard? What
did the music of Bill Evans mean to you?* And
there must be some brilliant sound technician
who could "erase" the playing of the musicians
and pull up the table noise and conversation
of the audience. What an interesting recording
that would make!—*Live at the Village Vanguard:
The Audience, Accompanied by the Bill Evans Trio.*

They who yelled for waiters, scraped chairs,
one whose cackle ripped across the music
like a dragged phonograph needle, oh,
I've wanted to find those people and, no,
not murder them; no, not smack their
faces. I've wanted to be the one
to sit them down in my living room
and play for them these recordings
made a few feet from where they sat.
I've wanted them to really *hear*
what they coughed through, for which
they offered smatterings of applause.
I've wanted to see them stiffen and cry out,
"Oh, my God! You mean *that, that* was going on
across the room from my martini?"
"I *missed* the whole damn thing
for that worthless man I spent twenty
of the worst years of my life with!"

Too late. Too late for apologies.
Listen. I'm putting on the first track
now. Hear it if you couldn't hear it then,
wherever you are, whoever you were that day.

ALAN WILLIAMSON

In addition to being a fine poet, Alan Williamson (b. 1944) is a renowned scholar, author of several books of criticism. His studies on literature include *Almost a Girl: Male Writers and Female Identification* (2001) and *Eloquence and Mere Life: Essays on the Art of Poetry* (2001). Williamson has taught at the University of California, Davis, as well as other campuses.

In his fourth volume of poetry, *Res Publica* (1998), Alan Williamson moves from the highly personal focus of his previous book, *Love and the Soul* (1995). This fourth collection looks at an America "heavily thickening to empire," as Robinson Jeffers once put it. *Res Publica* looks back at Williamson's youth in the 1950s and 1960s with a great deal of discernment, seeing the shades of gray that many writers would miss in the high contrasts of those times.

"A Childhood around 1950" opens *Res Publica* by presenting a historic shift in awareness in eighteen lines. The poem shows a world in transition from a pretechnological illusion of stasis to upheaval. It begins with timeless Norman Rockwell images of horses hauling wagons and peddlers going door-to-door. Then Williamson plays the scarier chords of the 1950s—the polio epidemic, fear of atomic radiation, memories of executions that recall the Rosenberg trial. The poem ends with a different attitude toward a world in flux.

His poem "The Minoan Distance," also from *Res Publica,* has a fascinating point of view. The speaker asks the reader to imagine being a citizen of ancient Athens, shortly *after* its Golden Age. But to complicate the story, this Athenian is visiting Crete, the fringe of the empire and the site of the earlier Minoan civilization. The pictures Williamson paints of Crete are deliciously decadent. This outlying Crete seems to have much in common with New Age California—auras, psychics, crystals, "process," and self-help books. The Athenian is drawn to this sensual ambiance, so much less encumbered than Athens, setting up an intriguing conflict of values.

In the poem "Almost at the Horizon" from *Res Publica,* Williamson returns to the sense of constant change he visited in "A Childhood Around 1950." Here the world and society, even literature, are turning away from him, making everything unfamiliar and numb. With sharp details, Williamson masterfully creates a sense that even the ground is continually slipping away as the world rotates on its axis. But "Almost at the Horizon" takes a surprising turn of its own at the end.

A CHILDHOOD AROUND 1950

Sometimes a horse pulled a wagon down the street.
A knife-grinder sometimes knocked at the back door.
Airplanes passed over. Put to bed in the poignant
half-thereness of summer twilights, we followed their long wobble
into Midway, rare and slow as dragonflies.

New kinds of safety. Our parents held their breath,
though sickness, for us, was the vile yellow powders
that burst from the capsules we had to gulp, and couldn't.
The new danger quiet in the milk and air.

The electric chair troubled no one. Good and evil
were stark things, as grainy movies made the dark.
But the city stopped if one of us was stolen,
and found thrown, days later, in a forest preserve.

It was what was. A childhood always is.
Fathers came home at noon and took off their hats.
Later, streetlights . . . But who was that *lamplighter*, in the stories?
And we went on living it, like a wave, that doesn't know
it is at every moment different water.

THE MINOAN DISTANCE

Say you could have come there from Athens, when its empire
started to fade, fleeing the guilts of that, the shortages,
or other things—a wife, the poets
suffering the exactions of their choliambi—
and found it unchanged (unlikelier things have happened,
a palace torched by volcanoes beyond the sea) . . .
—found the wild-beast colors in the porticoes,

and the conversations you imagined, airier, less tightened
on taxes and the weather, less convinced
that fate must bind in tighter with every year . . .
Would it have consoled you?—the constant brightness woven
into everything, the brighter, earlier gods . . .
The children take such an early part in the Mysteries,
and the grown-ups watch them, as if they were the Mystery.
No one despises the rich, or their own greed
for money; no one despises laborers, either.
(There was a painter who stopped for five years and learned the bull-leaping.
When he came back, his colors were somehow bloodier,
as though done from beneath the skin.) The hardest thing
to get used to is the women: how they walk
the streets with their breasts bare, under-cinched with gold;
how even the shrewdest believe the fortune-tellers,
the masseuse who describes the colored auras rising
from each organ as her fingers approach it, drawing the star-map
of their most cosmic fate.

                         And if the middle-aged ones
get still more beautiful, leathery, wise as cats,
explaining you to yourself like the sun
turning on some pretty thing of angled crystal . . .
—You cannot explain to them
that leaving her in Athens, one with its quarrels,
was not a "process," that smiling roller-coaster leaving you
predeterminedly clean at the end, but the slow undying
attrition of an affection that is no longer useful,
but not less real.
In the books they read all day, about how to live,
the greatest sin is depending on, doing too much for, others.

(It is all right to depend entirely on the gods.)
When you're with them, it's the transparent
universe; when it's over,
they'd show their new friend at a party at your mother's,
and think they loved you while they were doing it; and apologize
in a hurt voice, like a caught child, your perspective
too big or small to fit themselves inside it—
not their "needs"; not the great sky where all are shadows . . .
In the end, they prefer their own, who understand this.

ALMOST AT THE HORIZON
For M.

Something in the world
is turning from me. The strange beepers,
like a flock of small birds, that make crossing-lights
safe for the blind. This young man reading us
his story about the goodbye in the morning square,
where nothing can be said because what could be has happened
in a movie already, so he watches their clothes instead
and the other people watching. Something in all this
must feel sexy to him, his short black hair is so carefully
slicked aside, with a little wave. The air
is fresh and cool in the morning, the new buildings
cubic and lucent. Like Hopper, but feelingless.
But perhaps the feeling is just invisible, the way a ship
slipping over the horizon has no hull any more
only masts. Is that how one knows
where one stands on the earth is
slipping east, not to be slowed now? Except
almost at the horizon
your clear eyes.

YUSEF KOMUNYAKAA

Pulitzer Prize winner Yusef Komunyakaa (b. 1947) grew up the oldest of five children, son of a carpenter in Bogalusa, Louisiana, north of Lake Pontchartrain. Komunyakaa's last name arrived with his grandfather, who came to the United States as a stowaway from the West Indies. In the poet's boyhood home, the primary books he encountered were the Bible and the volumes of an encyclopedia that his mother purchased at a supermarket.

In 1969, Komunyakaa enlisted in the U.S. Army and was assigned to Vietnam, where he reported from the front lines and served as managing editor of a military newspaper, *The Southern Cross.*

Initially, Komunyakaa did not write poems explicitly about Vietnam, but fourteen years after his Army duty he published the collection *Dien Cai Dau* (1988), one of the most powerful artistic statements to emerge from that war. It's amazing that Komunyakaa never descends to polemic in the book and that he always rises to poetry, even at his most graphic. The poem "Toys in a Field" depicts Vietnamese children playing in the debris of the war, the expensive equipment now as useless as bones. The children only know how to imitate vultures and soldiers. The poet compares the eerie quiet of their play to rain in the jungle, or to the evening news that was the window onto the war for the North American public. The boy of mixed race at the poem's end has no father left to hug, and only a broken machine gun for a toy.

In Komunyakaa's other books, he often draws on the stories and cadences of the South. His poem "Family Tree" from the book *Copacetic* (1984) is an album of memories, expressing both the "octave of pain" that blacks endured under slavery and Jim Crow, and the unforgettable personalities of his family members. At times the words almost sound like the lyrics of a blues song. Komunyakaa is highly sensitive to the influence of music on literature and has co-edited two anthologies of jazz-rooted poetry, *The Jazz Poetry Anthology* (1991) and *The Second Set: The Jazz Poetry Anthology, Volume 2* (1996).

"Venus's-flytraps" from the book *Magic City* (1992) is a dramatic monologue spoken in the voice of a five-year-old boy. The child tries to make sense of the mysterious adult world, overhearing bits of secrets and confessions. The flowers in the field are both an image of the world beyond his horizon, and an embodiment of the female protection that makes the little boy feel safe in a puzzling and sometimes violent world.

TOYS IN A FIELD

Using gun mounts
for monkey bars,
Vietnamese children
play skin-the-cat,
pulling themselves through—
suspended in doorways
of multimillion-dollar helicopters
abandoned in white-elephant
graveyards. With arms
spread-eagled they imitate
vultures landing in fields.
Their play is silent
as distant rain,
the volume turned down
on the six o'clock news,
except for the boy
with American eyes
who keeps singing
rat-a-tat-tat, hugging
a broken machine gun.

FAMILY TREE

I know better
than a whip
across my back,
her eyes swearing
all the pain. Her father
cut down so young
in this stone garden.
She knows how easy death
first takes root

in the sweet mouth
of a love song.
She knows that long chain
drags in the red dust.
Geechee
bloodholler—
my mother
married at 15,
with my ear pressed
against the drum
of heartbeat.
When my father speaks
of childhood, sunlight
strikes a plowshare.
Across the cotton field
Muddy Waters' bone-song
rings true when my father speaks
of Depression winters
& a wheel within a wheel.
My great-grandmama's name
always turns up
like a twenty-dollar
gold piece.
Born a slave,
how old her hands were.
When my father speaks
of hanging trees
I know
all the old prophets
tied down in the electric chair.
My grandmamas
Mary & Elsie—
Sunday night
Genesis to Revelations

testimonial hard line
neo-auction block
women. Kerosene
lamps & cherry-red
potbellied wood stoves
& chopping cotton for *the man*
from sunup to sundown,
mule-plowing black-metal
blues women grow closer
each year like bent oaks
to the ground. Both still
look you in the eyes
& say, "You gotta eat
a pound of dirt
'fore you can get
to heaven."
Kimberly's ebony eyes
& all I've come to trust.
My daughter's laughter—
a lamp in her mouth.
Uncle Jesse (R.I.P.)
would show up
periodically
out of nowhere.
Perhaps after
a heavy rainstorm
some tin-roof night
after two years
working turpentine camps,
pine scent in his clothes—
shove a wad of greenbacks
into Grandmama Mary's
apron pocket.
A Prince Albert

cigarette between two fingers,
Old Crow on his breath,
that .38 Smith & Wesson
under his overalls jumper,
& the click-click of dice
& bright shuffle of cards
in a game called "coon can"
still in his disposition.
Just a few things he learned at 17
on a Burial Detail
in World War I.
Family tree,
taproot,
genealogy of blues.
We've seen our shadows
like workhorses
limp across ghost fields
& heard the rifle crack.
Blackbirds
blood flowered
in the heart
of the southern sun.
Brass tambourines,
octave of pain
clear as blood on a silent mirror.
Someone close to us
dragged away in dawnlight
here in these iron years.

VENUS'S-FLYTRAPS

I am five,
   Wading out into deep
      Sunny grass,
Unmindful of snakes
   & yellowjackets, out
      To the yellow flowers
Quivering in sluggish heat.
   Don't mess with me
      'Cause I have my Lone Ranger
Six-shooter. I can hurt
   You with questions
      Like silver bullets.
The tall flowers in my dreams are
   Big as the First State Bank,
      & they eat all the people
Except the ones I love.
   They have women's names,
      With mouths like where
Babies come from. I am five.
   I'll dance for you
      If you close your eyes. No
Peeping through your fingers.
   I don't supposed to be
      This close to the tracks.
One afternoon I saw
   What a train did to a cow.
      Sometimes I stand so close
I can see the eyes
   Of men hiding in boxcars.
      Sometimes they wave
& holler for me to get back. I laugh
   When trains make the dogs
      Howl. Their ears hurt.

I also know bees
   Can't live without flowers.
    I wonder why Daddy
Calls Mama honey.
   All the bees in the world
    Live in little white houses
Except the ones in these flowers.
   All sticky & sweet inside.
    I wonder what death tastes like.
Sometimes I toss the butterflies
   Back into the air.
    I wish I knew why
The music in my head
   Makes me scared.
    But I know things
I don't supposed to know.
   I could start walking
    & never stop.
These yellow flowers
   Go on forever.
    Almost to Detroit.
Almost to the sea.
   My mama says I'm a mistake.
    That I made her a bad girl.
My playhouse is underneath
   Our house, & I hear people
    Telling each other secrets.

HEATHER McHUGH

Heather McHugh (b. 1948) is an intellectual poet with a sparkling sense of humor. She twists lines of poetry into puzzles that invite the reader. McHugh loves wordplay and puns. She has written several books of poetry, including *Hinge & Sign: Poems, 1968–1993* (1994), a National Book Award finalist. Her publications also include a highly influential book of criticism, *Broken English: Poetry and Partiality* (1993). Along with her husband, Niko Boris McHugh (whom she refers to simply as "The Bulgarian"), she has translated books by Blaga Dimitrova and by Paul Celan. She has also translated a collection of poems by the wonderful French poet Jean Follain (1903–71) under the title *D'Après Tout* (1981).

Heather McHugh is the author of one of the best ghazals by a writer whose native language is English, "Ghazal of the Better-Unbegun." (For an explanation of the ghazal form, see the biography of Agha Shahid Ali in this volume.) In this poem, she not only adheres to the strict rules of a rigorous form, she plays with the structure and at the same time with her own identity and consciousness. The poem itself becomes a simile for the poem's speaker—appropriate, since the ghazal is a self-referential form. Where the poet has to mention his or her name in the second-to-last line, she addresses herself humorously as "McHugh." The repeated rhyme by the end becomes a tour de force, almost like a Lorenz Hart song lyric.

Her poem "Etymological Dirge" uses the origin of a word as a metaphor for or reflection on the word's current meaning. The relationship between the words and their roots is always unexpected and thought-provoking: "The kin of charity is whore,/the root of charity is dear." The poem is written in quatrain form, ending with an intriguing slant rhyme, "word" and "lord." This nod to an age-old poetic structure works with the poem's subject, the ancient roots of words. The poem is a funeral song, or dirge (a word that, by the way, comes from the Latin *dirige Domine,* "direct, O Lord"), partly because it concerns buried meanings. It draws its epigraph from the hymn "Amazing Grace"!

"The Fence," from her book *A World of Difference* (1981), describes the speaker's crossing from childhood to maturity. Like a love sonnet, the poem has fourteen lines. It tells the story of a first infatuation, more with exuberance and nostalgia than with romance. The beloved hardly appears except as a springboard for the lover's excitement, and she never refers to the lover except bound together in the pronoun "we." The final image is another instance of McHugh's wit, a play on the phallic shape of fence pickets.

GHAZAL OF THE BETTER-UNBEGUN

A book is a suicide postponed.

                    Cioran

Too volatile, am I? too voluble? too much a word-person?
I blame the soup: I'm a primordially
          stirred person.

Two pronouns and a vehicle was Icarus with wings.
The apparatus of his selves made an ab-
          surd person.

The sound I make is sympathy's: sad dogs are tied afar.
But howling I become an ever more un-
          heard person.

I need a hundred more of you to make a likelihood.
The mirror's not convincing—that at-best in-
          ferred person.

As time's revealing gets revolting, I start looking out.
Look in and what you see is one unholy
          blurred person.

The only cure for birth one doesn't love to contemplate.
Better to be an unsung song, an unoc-
          curred person.

McHugh, you'll be the death of me—each self and second studied!
Addressing you like this, I'm halfway to the
          third person.

ETYMOLOGICAL DIRGE

'Twas grace that taught my heart to fear.

Calm comes from burning.
Tall comes from fast.
Comely doesn't come from come.
Person comes from mask.

The kin of charity is whore,
the root of charity is dear.
Incentive has its source in song
and winning in the sufferer.

Afford yourself what you can carry out.
A coward and a coda share a word.
We get our ugliness from fear.
We get our danger from the lord.

THE FENCE

Suddening one day by myself
I took my girlhood off and came
to understand the slugfests
of the forked and haloed boys.

I fell in love, by accident
and by design: its physics
was mishap. Every feather
of our burning wings was fixed

in Fibonacci series; every bush
was script with lash and spine.
It all made sense! My animals
danced, my spirits were artless,

I ran between them,
drumming the uprights of the fence.

NTOZAKE SHANGE

Ntozake Shange (b. 1948) launched the current rage for performance poetry with her play *for colored girls who have considered suicide when the rainbow is enuf.* The most successful use of poetry onstage in the past half century, the play premiered at the Public Theater in New York City in 1975 and went on to a popular run on Broadway the following year. The play is a linked series of dramatic monologues spoken by women wearing a spectrum of different costumes. Shange calls it a "choreopoem" because it combines verse, dance, and acting.

Shange was born in Trenton, New Jersey. When she was eight, her family moved to Saint Louis for five years, but they subsequently returned to New Jersey. Her poetry collections include *A Daughter's Geography* (1983), *Nappy Edges* (1978), and *From Okra to Greens* (1984). She has also written novels and plays.

In her poems, she speaks in a sassy voice, often in black English, using humor, sensuality, political daring, and snippets of Spanish, Portuguese, and French. She frequently abbreviates words or writes them phonetically. Shange avoids capitalization and almost all punctuation except the slash, which she handles as a musical notation to indicate a break as she recites.

Her poem "one" is a highlight of the play *for colored girls.* A sizzling portrait of a woman who entices men, the poem transmits to all five senses. The unnamed character, "the passion flower of southwest los angeles," seems to be the opposite of the housewives and mothers whose windows are shuttered against her. Men are wild about her, but only to possess her. In her bath after her conquests, she is transformed into the women the men neglect her for. She becomes a figure of female vengeance. But this game takes a heavy toll on her personally. The title emphasizes her isolation.

Shange's poem, "We Need a God Who Bleeds Now," proposes nothing less than an expanded concept of divinity. Most of our images of the sacred involve male figures. Shange suggests the image of a woman giving birth. In the poem, Shange makes a fascinating play on the expression "bleeding to death."

The love poem "'If i go all the way without you where would i go?'" does an original spin on the notion of the body as geography. The idea of the beloved as landscape has a long history. In Shange's North American variation on this, she creates images that are fluid and twinkling. It's a valentine of a poem, sexy as only Shange can make it.

from FOR COLORED GIRLS WHO HAVE
CONSIDERED SUICIDE WHEN THE RAINBOW IS ENUF

one

orange butterflies & aqua sequins
ensconsed tween slight bosoms
silk roses dartin from behind her ears
the passion flower of southwest los angeles
meandered down hoover street
past dark shuttered houses where
women from louisiana shelled peas
round 3:00 & sent their sons
whistlin to the store for fatback & black-eyed peas
she glittered in heat
& seemed to be lookin for rides
when she waznt & absolutely
eyed every man who waznt lame white or noddin out
she let her thigh slip from her skirt
crossin the street
she slowed to be examined
& she never looked back to smile
or acknowledge a sincere 'hey mama'
or to meet the eyes of someone
purposely findin sometin to do in
her direction
        she waz sullen
        & the rhinestones etchin the corners of her mouth
        suggested tears
        fresh kisses that had done no good
she always wore her stomach out
lined with small iridescent feathers
the hairs round her navel seemed to dance
& she didnt let on
she knew
from behind her waist waz aching to be held

the pastel ivy drawn on her shoulders
to be brushed with lips & fingers
smellin of honey & jack daniels
                    she waz hot
                    a deliberate coquette
                    who never did without
                    what she wanted
& she wanted to be unforgettable
she wanted to be a memory
a wound   to every man
arragant enough to want her
                    she waz the wrath
                        of women in windows
                            fingerin shades / ol lace curtains
                                camoflagin despair &
                                    stretch marks
so she glittered honestly
delighted she waz desired
& allowed those especially
schemin / tactful suitors
to experience her body & spirit
tearin / so easily blendin with theirs /
& they were so happy
& lay on her lime sheets full & wet
from her tongue   she kissed
them reverently   even ankles
edges of beards . . .

at 4:30 AM
she rose
movin the arms & legs that trapped her
she sighed affirmin the sculptured man
& made herself a bath
of dark musk oil egyptian crystals
& florida water to remove his smell

to wash away the glitter
to watch the butterflies melt into
suds & the rhinestones fall beneath
her buttocks like smooth pebbles
in a missouri creek
layin in water
she became herself
ordinary
brown braided woman
with big legs & full lips
reglar
seriously intendin to finish her
night's work
she quickly walked to her guest
straddled on her pillows & began

        'you'll have to go now / i've
        a lot of work to do / & i cant
        with a man around / here are yr pants /
        there's coffee on the stove / its been
        very nice / but I cant see you again /
        you got what you came for / didnt you'

& she smiled
he wd either mumble curses bout crazy bitches
or sit dumbfounded
while she repeated

        'i cdnt possibly wake up / with
        a strange man in my bed / why
        dont you go home'

she cda been slapped upside the head
or verbally challenged
but she never waz
& the ones who fell prey to the
dazzle of hips painted with
orange blossoms & magnolia scented wrists
had wanted no more

than to lay between her sparklin thighs
& had planned on leavin before dawn
& she had been so divine
devastatingly bizarre the way
her mouth fit round
& now she stood a
reglar colored girl
fulla the same malice
livid indifference as a sistah
worn from supportin a wd be hornplayer
or waitin by the window
                              & they knew
                              & left in a hurry
she wd gather her tinsel &
jewels from the tub
& laugh gayly or vengeful
she stored her silk roses by her bed
& when she finished writin
the account of her exploit in a diary
embroidered with lilies & moonstones
she placed the rose behind her ear
& cried herself to sleep.

WE NEED A GOD WHO BLEEDS NOW

we need a god who bleeds now
a god whose wounds are not
some small male vengeance
some pitiful concession to humility
a desert swept with dryin marrow in honor of the lord

we need a god who bleeds
spreads her lunar vulva & showers us in shades of scarlet
thick & warm like the breath of her
our mothers tearing   to let us   in
this place breaks open
like our mothers bleeding
the planet is heaving   mourning our ignorance
the moon tugs the seas
to hold her / to hold her
embrace swelling hills / i am
not wounded i am bleeding to life

we need a god who bleeds now
whose wounds are not the end of anything

"IF I GO ALL THE WAY WITHOUT YOU
       WHERE WOULD I GO!"
                                        —*The Isley Brothers*

there/to the right of venus
                                close to where yr lion
stalks our horizon/   see/
listen/
glow scarlet/char-scarlet/set my heart down
there/   near you/scaldin *amarillo*/
oh/say/my new day
                                my dawn/
yr fingers trace the rush of my lips/
                            ever so reverent/
                                    ever so hungry/

here/
to the right side of venus/
                                my tongue/
                        tropical lightenin/
rush/now/softly/tween my toes/the seas ebb
& in these sands/i've come back/
                an unpredictible swell
a fresh water lily/in the north atlantic/
when you touch me/   yes
that's how pearls somehow/rip from the white of my
bones
    to yr fingertips/
      incontrovertible hard chicago/
                rococo implications/
& this/   the mississippi delta/tween my thighs
yr second touch/forbids
a thing less/than primordial fluidity/
no/
i lay next to you/
        the undertow at carmel/

the russian river/feelin up stalks of the best/of
humboldt county
& damn it/
        what makes you think/my spine is
yr personal/
san andreas fault?

            shiftin/serene fields break for rain/
til
i open/deep brown moist & black
        cobalt sparklin everywhere/
we are
there/
       where the pacific fondles my furthest
shores/detroit-high-russet/near redwoods/
      i am climbin
          you chase me/from limb to limb/
             pullin/the colored stars/out the
night
                slippin em/over my tongue/
&
i thought i cd get over/
the dangers/of livin
      on the pacific rim/
when i look at you/
i
know/i am riskin my life/
   tossin reason/to the outback of the far
rockaways/
        goin/givin up/everything/with out
protest/
givin up/meteorological episodes
the appalachian mountains/
        handin over/islands from puget

sound/
                    travis county hill country/
givin away/treasures/
i
never
claimed/
        til i felt you/

my own december sunset/teasin cypress/
even campbell street bikers/in downtown oakland/
i stopped resistin/
what won't/be orderly/imagined/legitimate/
yes/yes/
hold me
like/the night grabs wyoming/
& i am more/than i am not/
i cd sing sacred lyrics/to songs i don't know/
my cheek/rubs gainst the nappy black/cacti of yr
chest/
& i am a flood/of supernovas/
if you kiss me like that/i'm browned wetlands
yr lips/invite the moon/to meander/
our mouths open & sing/
yes/
our tongues/
the edge of the earth/

SEKOU SUNDIATA

Sekou Sundiata (b. 1948) records his poems on CDs more often than he publishes them. He performs with a band, the music behind him part jazz, part rock. When he reads solo, his comments between the poems enter into his performance, changing the pace and adding humor to his set. He recites his poems from memory and remarkably quickly, in a deep, resonant voice.

I once asked him the origin of his African name and he replied, "Sekou Sundiata is my nom de guerre." He grew up in housing projects in East Harlem. Sundiata has taught at the New School of Social Research in New York. He appeared in the PBS documentary "The Language of Life," hosted by Bill Moyers. Sundiata also wrote and performed in the theater piece, *The Circle Unbroken Is a Hard Bop* (which includes "Space. A Prose Poem Monologue"). He is also the author of *The Mystery of Love,* a musical theater piece staged at the American Music Theater Festival in 1994.

Many of Sundiata's poems have a repeated section or chorus, such as the "I could wake up in the morning" stanza in "Blink Your Eyes." Another stanza in that poem alludes to Sterling Brown. Sundiata has called Sterling Brown "the dean of African American poetry," and in one of Brown's poem he jokes that "way down South they got laws/can't no Negroes laugh outdoors." Sundiata takes these comic lines and gives them a serious spin about police carrying out racial profiling of African American males. "Blink Your Eyes" is also Sundiata's homage to the rappers who often take his creative writing classes, particularly in its use of rhyme, both straight up and slant.

Like the other poems by Sundiata in this anthology, "Shout Out" appears on his first CD, *The Blue Oneness of Dreams* (1997). The poem is a toast "To what's deep and Deep, to what's down and Down," in all of its varied permutations. A "shout out" is half-way between a greeting and a dedication, often from a DJ to a group of listeners.

In his poems, Sundiata links words in an unbroken flow using a technique called circular breathing. This technique employed by Australian aborigines when they play the didgeridoo has also been adopted by jazz musicians. It has a particularly powerful effect in his work, "Space: A Prose Poem Monologue," which he recites at breakneck speed to simulate the speech of a street person named "Space." Space is half crazy but still sane enough to reflect on the Black Power movement of the 1960s with the honesty and lucidity that only those outside society are allowed.

BLINK YOUR EYES

(Remembering Sterling A. Brown)

I was on my way to see my woman
but the Law said I was on my way
thru a red light red light red light
and if you saw my woman
you could understand.
I was just being a man.
It wasn't about no light
it was about my ride
and if you saw my ride
you could dig that too, you dig?
Sunroof stereo radio black leather
bucket seats sit low you know,
the body's cool, but the tires are worn.
Ride when the hard time come, ride
when they're gone, in other words
the light was green.

I could wake up in the morning
without a warning
and my world could change:
blink you eyes.
All depends, all depends on the skin,
all depends on the skin you're living in

Up to the window comes the Law
with his hand on his gun
what's up? what's happening?
I said I guess
that's when I really broke the law.
He said *a routine, step out the car*
a routine, *assume the position.*
Put your hands up in the air
you know the routine, like you just don't care.

License and registration.
Deep was the night and the light
from the North Star on the car door, déjà vu
we've been through this before,
why did you stop me?
Somebody had to stop you.
I watch the news, you always lose.
You're unreliable, that's undeniable.
This is serious, you could be dangerous.

I could wake up in the morning
without a warning
and my world could change:
blink you eyes.
All depends, all depends on the skin,
all depends on the skin you're living in

New York City, they got laws
can't no bruthas drive outdoors,
in certain neighborhoods, on particular streets
near and around certain types of people.
They got laws.
All depends, all depends on the skin
all depends on the skin you're living in.

SHOUT OUT

Nia, Imani, Kuchajaculia

Here's to the best words in the right place
at the perfect time, to the human mind
blown up & refined
To three hour dinners & long conversations.
To the philosophical ramifications of a beautiful day
To the 12 steppers on the 13th. step
may they never forget the first step
To the increase to the decrease
To the do to the did to the done done
To the lonely
To the broken hearted
To the new blue haiku
Here's to All Or Nothing at All
Here's to the sick & the shut in

Here's to the Was you been, to the Is you in
To what's deep and Deep, to what's down and Down
To the Lost & the Blind & the Almost Found

To the crazy the lazy the bored the ignored
the beginners the sinners the losers the winners
to the smooth and the cool and even to the fools
Here's to your ex-best friend
To the rule benders and the repeat offenders
To the lovers and the troublers
the engaging the enraging
To the healers and the feelers
To the fixers and the tricksters
To a star falling through a dream
To a dream when you know what it means
To the bottom to the root to the bass to the drum

Here's to the Was you been to the Is you in
To what's deep and Deep, to what's down and Down
To the Lost & the Blind & the Almost Found
Here's to somebody within the sound of your voice
this morning
To somebody who can't be within the sound of your voice
tonight
To a low cholesterol pig sandwich smothered in swine
without the pork
To a light buzz in your head & a soundtrack in your mind
going on like a good time
Here's to promises that break by themselves
Here's to the breaks with great promise
To people who don't wait in the car
when you tell them to wait in the car
Here's to the unforgettable

Here's to the Was you been to the Is you in
To what's deep and Deep to what's down and Down
To the Lost & the Blind & the Almost Found

Here's to the hip hoppers, the don't stoppers
heads nodding in the digital glow
of their beloved studios
To the incredible indelible impressions
made by the gazes you gaze in the faces of strangers
to yourself you ask, Is this God straight up
or is it a mask?
Here's to the tribe of the hypercyber
tripping on the virtual-most outpost at the edge on the tip
believing that what they hear is the Mothership drawing near

Here's to the Was you been to the Is you in
to what's deep and Deep to what's down and Down
To the Lost & the Blind & the Almost Found

SPACE. A PROSE POEM MONOLOGUE

From whence we come?
That dark woman of a land only knows so well.
How we tribalize our rest in the West, who can tell?
Was once an X, our knocked over cross to bear
like the flatted fifth note of blue you hear,
the terrible one we wear like a skin color.
The mystery came down once again
crucify the suffer for us to see.
Say X shall be your name
until you raise it and praise it, the Free
you seek before you everywhere like air.
In the beginning In the beginning In the beginning black and shining was our X.

You got the Circle of Blood then you got the Circle of Mind then you got Pi and the Square Root but that's another bop Now the Circle of Blood was what we came here with Tobacco Road Kunte Kente Afrika Bambatta shit like that You can turn your back on the Circle of Blood but you come out something estrange what the philosophy call alienation cause the blood is the transportation system for oxygen and demons and goddesses to get to your brain Neverhowsoneverless you can separate yourself from the Circle but that's another bop

Now the Circle of the Mind that's what we was after The elevation of principle over pigmentation Content of the character not what's on the head but what's-in-the-head approach to the predicament beginning with What's in a Name? Ain't no rose this I know You mean to say a cullud negroistic nigga by any other name would smell the same? I don't think so. We was deep up in the reality: *Nation within a nation looking for a nationality* Call me Money call me Blood Call me B call me the 7th letter in the alphabet G   Griot on the Spot

Boom! Just like that they came through the door like gangbusters habeus corpus magna carta my ass Cordite and tear gas rip your nose open set your eyes on fire What what about the Dreamer? The King Alfred Plan Yeah they sent a negro pig in there alright Malcolm stretched out on the floor and the pig is right there giving him mouth to mouth moving in mysterious ways mysterious ways It was wild pistols shotguns knocking down chairs people stepping on each other rushing to get out the way Black Shining Prince I got your Black Shining Prince all right nobody else got hit no bodyguard mighty funny nobody from the by any means necessary crew not one salaam aleikum not one gotdamn eggs and bacon

> We was nuts from the gitgo insane from the whatnot nuts from the gitgo insane from the whatnot nuts from the gitgo insane from the whatnot nuts from the gitgo insane from the whatnot

Umma tell you like this Marilyn Monroe was butt naked in Bird's hotel room and the parlez vous said Monsieur Parker What is your religion? I'm a devout musician Them Seize the Time/Kujachaculia Bruthas was into white white girls coming and going take the money shoot it up with the sniff and blow too. Umma tell you like this I got the record document And the black ones was so fine they spread they legs like glory haleluja Get this Eat that They was so fine they even came a few times the revolution walking across they sweet snatch with they prone positions being at that time the correct one

So then Nat Turner told me Do the Tighten Up Martha could outsing Diana any gotdamn day The Vandellas Sojourner told me The Vandellas was a tribe of female warriors Do what they say Dance in the Street Why she say that? Sojourner crazy Said it so loud Hoover heard it Dance in the Street Detroit Chicago Washington D.C. Hoover took the record off the radio off the airwaves Too late Beat The Heat Off The Pig

Umma tell you like this not everybody was in was of it Some negroes was there for Electric Church Good Time to the People Then some of us said Freedom and looked it up and Lo and what you know Behold it was flux flux everywhere *Every man in his mind is free* Why you had to be a housewife? Why you had to be a man? Why you had to be in the bourgeoisie? Why you had to be your name? Why you had to play them changes? Why you had to be a woman? Why can't you be free?

We was nuts from the gitgo insane from the whatnot nuts from the gitgo insane from the whatnot nuts from the gitgo insane from the whatnot nuts from the gitgo insane from the whatnot

But I tell you like this It was war The police was stepping in your face and 357 ain't no number to be playing Um saying there was a time when the women got together and said Uh Uh No No dialectical this Unity and Struggle of the antagonistic non-antagonistic contradiction Then they went Upsouth to Canada made peace with the Vietnam Woman came back with earrings and shit made from American war planes talking 'bout See this is how you do it Let the women do it And the bruthas did a dish or two 'til the babies came and the FBI was in effect And who didn't go to jail to the grave to law school laid in the cut selling herb waiting for the fever to go disco But umma tell you like this it was too late too many heard the call too many said Boo! saw the Empire shake too many knew it didn't have to be like this but it was and who knew knew not what to do but still if you was who you knew and Uma tell you like this They got me with some radiowaves, *allnewsallthetime* a frequency can't no acupuncture puncture y'unnerstand? But I know how the go go Go like this Isolate the Seer make the Dream look like a nightmare Fix they tongue so they can't tell they story straight story straight story straight Chemicalize they trauma call it good drugs Put they orisha on a stamp and a tee shirt and sell it back to them Go like this Isolate the Seer say That was then and this is now Take time off line break the bridge Uma tell you like this I like a little good late a night cause I know Life: what it look like what it taste like Life is Round, that what we found Holy Grail can you dig it? And our children ain't right either They wasn't right from the word say go and we wouldn't let them be so They want to know why we got to go to Kwanzaa again? Why can't we just be quiet and watch television? Why you always got to be talking back to the picture? Daddy you ain't right

Let this be my epitaph His heart to the very end was in the left place

We was nuts from the gitgo insane from the whatnot nuts from the gitgo insane from the whatnot nuts from the gitgo insane from the whatnot nuts from the gitgo insane from the whatnot

AGHA SHAHID ALI

In his poems, Agha Shahid Ali (1949–2001) binds together a mastery of form and sound with deep political convictions, a combination familiar to readers of poetry in Urdu, his native language. He grew up in the embattled state of Kashmir, a largely Moslem area incorporated into mostly Hindu India. Among his several books, Ali has translated the work of the greatest Urdu poet of the past 100 years, Faiz Ahmed Faiz, published as *The Rebel's Silhouette: Selected Poems* (1991).

Agha Shahid Ali was a flamboyant and brilliant figure who loved to wear a purple Nehru shirt hand-tailored for him in Kashmir. The seriousness of his view of politics and history never prevented him from relishing a dance or a bit of catty wit.

Before his untimely death from cancer in 2001, Ali gave the English-speaking world an enormous gift—he popularized the ancient ghazal poetic form in our language. Before Ali, the ghazal was known in English mostly through translations of the posthumous poems of the Spanish poet Federico García Lorca, who used the name as a tribute to the Moorish past of his native Andalusia. Unfortunately, Lorca did not learn the ghazal form before attaching the title to some of his poems, with the result that for decades, American writers assumed it just meant a lyric poem.

In fact, the ghazal has a tight structure with a surprisingly contemporary feel to it. Each couplet in the poem stands alone, almost like a cubist sequence of two-line haikus. The fun part comes with the endings of the couplets—each stanza has to end with the same word or combination of words, and the syllable before the repeated pattern has to rhyme. The first stanza is even more of a challenge for the poet, since *both* lines have to end with this rhyming combination. In the poem's second-to-last line, the author has to mention his or her own name, another twist that has a strangely postmodern flavor. The form is featured in Ali's last book, *Call Me Ishmael Tonight: A Book of Ghazals* (2003), and in the anthology he edited, *Ravishing Disunities: Real Ghazals in English* (2000).

Ali's two poems that follow, "In Arabic" and "Stars," are ghazals written or revised when he knew he was suffering from a brain tumor. He had such a passion for perfection that he drastically rewrote "In Arabic" when he was fatally ill, despite the fact that the original version of the poem had already been published and favorably received in his best-known collection, *The Country Without a Post Office* (1997). The many cultures that Ali draws on in "In Arabic" show that peaceful coexistence can be realized, even if it starts in the rhymes of a ghazal.

STARS

When through night's veil they continue to seep, stars
in infant galaxies begin to weep stars.

After the eclipse, there were no cheap stars
How can you be so cheap, stars?

How grateful I am you stay awake with me
till by dawn, like you, I'm ready to sleep, stars!

If God sows sunset embers in you, Shahid,
all night, because of you, the world will reap stars.

IN ARABIC

(with revisions of some couplets of "Arabic")

A language of loss? I have some business in Arabic.
Love letters: calligraphy pitiless in Arabic.

At an exhibit of miniatures, what Kashmiri hairs!
Each paisley inked into a golden tress in Arabic.

This much fuss about a language I don't know? So one day
perfume from a dress may let you digress in Arabic.

A "Guide for the Perplexed" was written—believe me—
by Cordoba's Jew—Maimonides—in Arabic.

Majnoon, by stopped caravans, rips his collars, cries "Laila!"
Pain translated is O! much more—not less—in Arabic.

Writes Shammas: Memory, no longer confused, now is a homeland—
his two languages a Hebrew caress in Arabic.

When Lorca died, they left the balconies open and saw:
On the sea his *qasidas* stitched seamless in Arabic.

In the Veiled One's harem, an adulteress hanged by eunuchs—
So the rank mirrors revealed to Borges in Arabic.

Ah, bisexual Heaven: wide-eyed houris and immortal youths!
To your each desire they say *Yes! O Yes!* in Arabic.

For that excess of sibilance, the last Apocalypse,
so pressing those three forms of S in Arabic.

I too, O Amichai, saw everything, just like you did—
In Death. In Hebrew. And (please let me stress) in Arabic.

They ask me to tell them what *Shahid* means: Listen, listen:
It means "The Beloved" in Persian, "witness" in Arabic.

DAVID ST. JOHN

David St. John's poetry braves the broken glass and hooks in the topics of love and faith, once the givens of poetry. He insists on retaining a critical eye. His project is to bear witness to the human predicament, and to account honestly for his own responses. This makes him an enormously sophisticated observer of passion and of beauty.

Born in 1949 in Fresno, California, St. John has lived for several years in Los Angeles. He has received the Academy Award from the American Academy of Arts and Letters, and the O. B. Hardison, Jr. Poetry Prize. His book *Study for the World's Body: New and Selected Poems* (1994) was a finalist for the National Book Award. Robert Hass wrote of this collection in the *Los Angeles Times Book Review,* "it is go-for-broke gorgeous. It is made of sentences, sweeping through and across the meticulous verse stanzas . . . they are also full, almost past ripeness, of a floating, sometimes painful, sometimes wistful, intense, dark and silvery eroticism that feels as if it comes out of some cross between late nineteenth-century Symbolist lushness—vague and specific at once—and the kind of 60s and 70s European film that talked about eroticism with a wistfulness so intense that it seemed experience and the melancholy recollection of experience were the same thing."

"Desire" is a poem of acute sensuality, from the description of the lover's silky hair to the print on her kimono to the recollection of her tongue during their lovemaking. All the images—the mist, the breath, the strands of hair—seem to flow together. What's intriguing about the physicality in this poem is that, like the fogged-in imagery, it is both sharp and blurred. The sharpness is the vision and recall of the beloved; the blur comes from the paradox that this moment of tremendous desire also isolates the speaker in his desiring, because the present, however vivid, will soon be memory—distant, and therefore alluring.

"Hush" is the title poem of St. John's first volume of poetry. The book was published in 1976, a few years after the breakup of St. John's first marriage. In active imagery, he compares the absence of his young son to a kind of mourning: "Nothing stops it, the crying. Not the clove of moon."

"No Heaven" is also a title poem, this one from St. John's third book of poems (1988). It's literally a feverish poem written while caring for a sick loved one. The hallucinatory daze of a high temperature seems to imbue all the images. The rising of the polluted canal water mimics the peak of the illness. The eerie imagery and the sense of the nearness of death and decay add to the poem's apocalyptic shivers.

DESIRE

There is a small wrought-iron balcony . . .
& at that balcony she stood a moment
Watching a summer fog
Swirl off the river in huge
Drifting pockets as the street lights grew
Alternately muted then wild then to a blurred
Relay of yellow

Her hair was so blond that from a distance
It shone white as spun silk
& as he turned the corner he stopped suddenly
Looking up at the window of the hotel room
Where she stood in her Japanese kimono
Printed with red dragonflies
& a simple bridge

& in that lapse of breath
As the fog both offered & erased her in the night
He could remember every pulse of her tongue
Every pared detail of constancy left
Only to them   as he began
Walking slowly toward the door of the hotel
Carrying the hard loaf of day-old bread
& plums wrapped in newspaper

Already remembering this past he would desire

HUSH

for my son

The way a tired Chippewa woman
Who's lost a child gathers up black feathers,
Black quills & leaves
That she wraps & swaddles in a little bale, a shag
Cocoon she carries with her & speaks to always
As if it were the child,
Until she knows the soul has grown fat & clever,
That the child can find its own way at last;
Well, I go everywhere
Picking the dust out of the dust, scraping the breezes
Up off the floor, & gather them into a doll
Of you, to touch at the nape of the neck, to slip
Under my shirt like a rag—the way
Another man's wallet rides above his heart. As you
Cry out, as if calling to a father you conjure
In the paling light, the voice rises, instead, in me.
Nothing stops it, the crying. Not the clove of moon,
Not the woman raking my back with her words. Our letters
Close. Sometimes, you ask
About the world; sometimes, I answer back. Nights
Return you to me for a while, as sleep returns sleep
To a landscape ravaged
& familiar. The dark watermark of your absence, a hush.

NO HEAVEN

This is the last prayer in the book
Of black prayers   a last
Passionate *yes*

Against bad timing & bad luck

& what else
Could be delivered beyond request
Except: *the living & the dead*

So I'll lay these carved shadow-figures

To rest along the rough rack pallet
Beneath the bed   though
Their shadows still continue   poor pilgrims

Walking the curved white stucco arch
Above our heads   & after
You wake to the scraping of these pine limbs
Against the unlatched windowpane

I'll smooth the delicate line & lace of sweat
That trims your hair's damp open fan
Along the folded pillow

The fever's watermark as it slowly stains
The forehead just as the tides of the canal

Measure these erratic summer rains
Streaking the sheer cement banks & high walls
As the debris of the city

Rises endlessly   & then endlessly falls

& I remember how the light with its simplicity
Frames always the lasting shape
Of your body   (standing)   at the jetty's end

& in the dream: *I'm running toward*

You to drape a silver raincoat   across your
Uncovered shoulders as you turn & the
World flares   & we wait

For an ending that grows irrevocably older
As in every apocalyptic play
& settling on us   upon the jetty   an ash colder

Than   in winter   the iron lattice
Of the cage I grip with both hands as I speak
To the albino mandrill   (at the Historical Zoo)

Not all but some days about the eclipse

Of earth   & flesh   & brick
Though no matter how I've tried   no matter
All of the horrible things I've said

The only response I can ever provoke

Is a few bared teeth as he throws
Back his head   & screams
                                        Is that really
For all of the dead   a child by me
Asked her mother once & then she
Continued   *I mean all of the dead he remembers*
From his monkey dreams

In my dreams the world dies also in white embers

Not ash of course but blown light   drifting
Over the jetty   silently   forever

Yet this morning as I look very
Closely into the dresser mirror I can see
There in my own face

The hard meridian crossed & then re-crossed
    Hope   the new year

& yours is the name I'll say again & again

Until I'm sure this world can't force apart
The simple pulse of heaven
From the elaborate music of the heart

& all I want is for this sickness to have passed

Leaving us the ordinary world
Whole & rising in the dark   *this* world   *this* earth

& walking calmly toward us out of the broken mists

The figure whose passion remains the single
Gift   (yet) who now at last   admits
That we're to be given no heaven

No heaven   but this

JORIE GRAHAM

Jorie Graham (b. 1950) had an unusual childhood, growing up as the daughter of American parents in Rome, while attending French-language schools. Graham did her undergraduate work at the Sorbonne and didn't live in the United States until she attended graduate school. She originally studied film before discovering her true calling as a poet.

Jorie Graham has earned many laurels, including the Pulitzer Prize in poetry and a MacArthur Fellowship. She has directed the poetry program at the premier creative writing graduate school in the United States, the Iowa Writers' Workshop, and has taught at Harvard University.

The critic Helen Vendler has written of her, "This is a poetry of delicate and steady transgression in which the spirit searches the flesh and the flesh the spirit, melting and dissolving the boundaries thought to separate them."

"Salmon," from Graham's book *Erosion* (1983), is probably her best-known work. This gorgeous poem seems to take place simultaneously in several different times, places, and magnifications. Each of these levels mirrors the others. The speaker never actually sees the salmon, only a TV program about them in a motel room. The mother's suicide attempt reflects the salmon's push to mate and die. The speaker's description of witnessing "the primal scene" as a child is surprisingly innocent. Both seeing and traveling constantly recur in the poem, and they intersect in the image of light swimming up the optical nerve. All the motion in the poem slows to a halt with the exhausted couple, leaving the physical world "useless, merely / beautiful."

Her poem "Scirocco" is also from *Erosion*. Explaining the title Jorie Graham has stated, "The scirocco is a hot wind that the Italians say is blown up to them from Africa. . . . Mothers who live in the countryside when the scirocco blows put pebbles in their children's coat pockets when they go out. They say it will hold them down—otherwise the wind will steal their souls away." Like this legend, the short lines of this poem seem to hover between the physical and the metaphysical, between word and breath.

The title poem of her second book, "Erosion," is a hymn to the perishable world. Life is constantly eroding. In contrast to this gradual wearing down, human beings now seem exempt from the process of natural selection and the idea of a higher intelligence outside of time. The speaker's choice is to embrace the winter, the mortal.

SALMON

I watched them once, at dusk, on television, run,
in our motel room half-way through
Nebraska, quick, glittering, past beauty, past
the importance of beauty,
archaic,
not even hungry, not even endangered, driving deeper and deeper
into less. They leapt up falls, ladders,
and rock, tearing and leaping, a gold river
and a blue river traveling
in opposite directions.
They would not stop, resolution of will
and helplessness, as the eye
is helpless
when the image forms itself, upside-down, backward,
driving up into
the mind, and the world
unfastens itself
from the deep ocean of the given. . . . Justice, aspen
leaves, mother attempting
suicide, the white night-flying moth
the ants dismantled bit by bit and carried in
right through the crack
in my wall. . . . How helpless
the still pool is,
upstream,
awaiting the gold blade
of their hurry. Once, indoors, a child,
I watched, at noon, through slatted wooden blinds,
a man and woman, naked, eyes closed,
climb onto each other,
on the terrace floor,
and ride—two gold currents
wrapping round and round each other, fastening,

unfastening. I hardly knew
what I saw. Whatever shadow there was in that world
it was the one each cast
onto the other,
the thin black seam
they seemed to be trying to work away
between them. I held my breath.
As far as I could tell, the work they did
with sweat and light
was good. I'd say
they traveled far in opposite
directions. What is the light
at the end of the day, deep, reddish-gold, bathing the walls,
the corridors, light that is no longer light, no longer clarifies,
illuminates, antique, freed from the body of
the air that carries it. What is it
for the space of time
where it is useless, merely
beautiful? When they were done, they made a distance
one from the other
and slept, outstretched,
on the warm tile
of the terrace floor,
smiling, faces pressed against the stone.

SCIROCCO

In Rome, at 26
      Piazza di Spagna,
at the foot of a long
      flight of
stairs, are rooms
      let to Keats

in 1820,
      where he died. Now
you can visit them,
      the tiny terrace,
the bedroom. The scraps
      of paper

on which he wrote
      lines
are kept behind glass,
      some yellowing,
some xeroxed or
      mimeographed. . . .

Outside his window
      you can hear the scirocco
working
      the invisible.
Every dry leaf of ivy
      is fingered,

refingered. Who is
      the nervous spirit
of this world
      that must go over and over
what it already knows,
      what is it

so hot and dry
      that's looking through us,
by us,
      for its answer?
In the arbor
      on the terrace

the stark hellenic
      forms
of grapes have appeared.
      They'll soften
till weak enough
      to enter

our world, translating
      helplessly
from the beautiful
      to the true. . . .
Whatever the spirit,
      the thickening grapes

are part of its looking,
      and the slow hands
that made this mask
      of Keats
in his other life,
      and the old woman,

the memorial's
      custodian,
sitting on the porch
      beneath the arbor
sorting chick-peas
      from pebbles

into her cast-iron
        pot.
See what her hands
        know—
they are its breath,
        its mother

tongue, dividing,
        discarding.
There is light playing
        over the leaves,
over her face,
        making her

abstract, making
        her quick
and strange. But she
        has no care
for what speckles her,
        changing her,

she is at
        her work. Oh how we want
to be taken
        and changed,
want to be mended
        by what we enter.

Is it thus
        with the world?
Does it wish us
        to mend it,
light and dark,
        green

and flesh? Will it
      be free then?
I think the world
      is a desperate
element. It would have us
      calm it,

receive it. Therefore this
      is what I
must ask you
      to imagine: wind;
the moment
      when the wind

drops; and grapes,
      which are nothing,
which break
      in your hands.

EROSION

I would not want, I think, a higher intelligence, one
simultaneous, cut clean
of sequence. No,
it is our slowness I love, growing slower,
tapping the paintbrush against the visible,
tapping the mind.
We are, ourselves, a mannerism now,
having fallen
out of the chain
of evolution.
So we grow fat with unqualified life.

Today, on this beach
I am history to these fine
pebbles. I run them
through my fingers. Each time
some molecules rub off
evolving into
the invisible. Always
I am trying to feel
the erosion—my grandfather, stiffening
on his bed, learning
to float on time, his mind like bait presented
to the stream ongoing, or you, by my side,
sleep rinsing you always a little less
clean, or daily
the erosion
of the right word, what it shuts,
or the plants coming forth as planned out my window, row
after row, sealed
into here. . . .
I've lined all our wineglasses up on the sill,
a keyboard, a garden. Flowers of the poles.
I'm gifting each with a little less water.
You can tap them
for music.
Outside the window it's starting to snow.
It's going to get colder.
The less full the glass, the truer
the sound.
This is my song
for the North
coming toward us.

MARIE HOWE

Marie Howe (b. 1950) grew up in Rochester, New York, one of nine children. After attending Catholic schools, she graduated from the University of Windsor with a B.A. in English. Howe then worked as a journalist in Rochester; later she taught high school near Boston. Her career as a poet did not begin in earnest until she was twenty-nine. Margaret Atwood chose her first book, *The Good Thief* (1988), for the National Poetry Series. Marie Howe also co-edited *In the Company of My Solitude: American Writing from the AIDS Pandemic* (1995), She has taught at Columbia University and at Sarah Lawrence College.

Marie Howe's second book *What the Living Do* (1998) "has at its heart a series of elegies about a beloved brother," to quote the author. It remains one of the most moving collections of American poetry in recent years. She takes the reader through the illness of a sibling with AIDS, but it is never a depressing set of poems. "Marie Howe has reinvented the elegy as a poem for the living," Mark Doty has written of this book, "these conversational lyrics—open, available—ring with the clarity of struck speech, and their astonishing intensity wakes us to our ordinary crisis . . . *What the Living Do* is an achievement of remarkable power." Her poem "A Certain Light" presents her brother's illness not as a mere subtraction but as a window onto deeper feelings.

The process of watching over her brother exposes the book's speaker to memories and to the present in a way that compels her to experience her own life again at a deeper level. This is the state of mind reflected in the poem "The Kiss," where the sister is finally reawakened to her sensuality after her brother's illness, but with more layers than before. As Rainer Maria Rilke writes at the end of the Fourth Duino Elegy: "that one can contain / death . . . can hold it to one's heart / gently, and not refuse to go on living, / is inexpressible." And yet Howe finds a way to express the sense of continuing after great sorrow.

This new acceptance of her own life in the wake of her brother's trials leads also to the poem "Practicing," a light-hearted and incredibly sexy poem about the speaker's early experiments with making out. The poem is a period piece about how teenage girls were socially conditioned to disregard one another before the change in women's consciousness that began in the late 1960s. But it is also a passionate poem full of wonderful details of finished basements and of how these girls secretly shared a love that was innocent and steamy at the same time.

A CERTAIN LIGHT

He had taken the right pills the night before.
We had counted them out

from the egg carton where they were numbered so there'd be no mistake.
He had taken the morphine and prednisone and amitriptyline

and Florinef and vancomycin and Halcion too quickly
and had thrown up in the bowl Joe brought to the bed—a thin string

of blue spit—then waited a few minutes, to calm himself,
before he took them all again. And had slept through the night

and the morning and was still sleeping at noon—or not sleeping.
He was breathing maybe twice a minute, and we couldn't wake him,

we couldn't wake him until we shook him hard calling, John wake up now
John wake up—Who is the president?

And he couldn't answer.
His doctor told us we'd have to keep him up for hours.

He was all bones and skin, no tissue to absorb the medicine.
He couldn't walk unless two people held him.

And we made him talk about the movies: What was the best moment in
On the Waterfront? What was the music in *Gone with the Wind?*

And for seven hours he answered, if only to please us, mumbling
I like the morphine, sinking, rising, sleeping, rousing,

then only in pain again—but wakened.
So wakened that late that night in one of those still blue moments

that were a kind of paradise, he finally opened his eyes wide,
and the room filled with a certain light we thought we'd never see again.

Look at you two, he said. And we did.
And Joe said, Look at you.   And John said, How do I look?

And Joe said, Handsome.

THE KISS

When he finally put
his mouth on me—on

my shoulder—the world
shifted a little on the tilted

axis of itself. The minutes
since my brother died

stopped marching ahead like
dumb soldiers and

the stars rested.
His mouth on my shoulder and

then on my throat
and the world started up again

for me,
some machine deep inside it

recalibrating,
all the little wheels

slowly reeling and speeding up,
the massive dawn lifting on the other

side of the turning world.
And when his mouth

pressed against my
mouth, I

opened my mouth
and the world's chord

played at once:
a large, ordinary music rising

from a hand neither one of us could see.

PRACTICING

I want to write a love poem for the girls I kissed in seventh grade,
a song for what we did on the floor in the basement

of somebody's parents' house, a hymn for what we didn't say but thought:
That feels good or *I like that,* when we learned how to open each other's mouths

how to move our tongues to make somebody moan. We called it practicing, and
one was the boy, and we paired off—maybe six or eight girls—and turned out

the lights and kissed and kissed until we were stoned on kisses, and lifted our
nightgowns or let the straps drop, and, Now you be the boy:

concrete floor, sleeping bag or couch, playroom, game room, train room, laundry.
Linda's basement was like a boat with booths and portholes

instead of windows. Gloria's father had a bar downstairs with stools that spun,
plush carpeting. We kissed each other's throats.

We sucked each other's breasts, and we left marks, and never spoke of it upstairs
outdoors, in daylight, not once. We did it, and it was

practicing, and slept, sprawled so our legs still locked or crossed, a hand still lost
in someone's hair . . . and we grew up and hardly mentioned who

the first kiss really was—a girl like us, still sticky with moisturizer we'd
shared in the bathroom. I want to write a song

for that thick silence in the dark, and the first pure thrill of unreluctant desire,
just before we made ourselves stop.

BRENDA HILLMAN

The arc of Brenda Hillman's career as a poet has taken her from narrative with a heightened use of description to work that hints at story while examining the process of writing and reading poems. In addition to publishing several books of poetry, she co-edited *The Grand Permission: New Writings on Poetics and Motherhood* (2003) with Patricia Dienstfrey and edited an edition of Emily Dickinson.

Hillman was born in 1951 in Arizona and raised in a Baptist household. Reflecting on the influence of her childhood, she said in an interview, "Baptists . . . espouse the privacy of one's relationship to the constructed universe, which isn't controlled by authority, but which is populated by other spirits." This personal eye on reality infuses her more recent poetry, where she often records sensations and thoughts as they pop up, interrupt, and pull on one another.

Hillman has spent her adult life in California. The landscape of the West Coast plays an important role in her poetry. So does the sociology of California, with its many families that have undergone divorce, as in her poem "A Foghorn" from *Bright Existence* (1993). "A Foghorn" follows families on outings to Point Reyes National Seashore. The natural world of flowers, dairy cows, and whales adds pathos to the plight of these families that have lost the innocence of their nuclear structure. The whales are too far out to sea to hear the human-generated foghorns, and they appear almost too fragile and beautiful to bear, like the wounded lives that go on despite separation.

For several years, Hillman consciously limited herself only to two-word titles for her poems and books. She wrote "The Spark" at the tail end of that period. The poem begins her collection *Loose Sugar* (1997), a finalist for the National Book Critics Circle Award. The poem is in the second person, but the speaker could be talking to herself. She is remembering those luminous moments when sexual energy flared in her life, going back even to conception. Sex appears not as self-contained but as a bright shadow of the holy.

In Hillman's more recent book *Cascadia* (2001), she knots together science, mythology, personal narrative, history, dreams, and literary references. "The Formation of Soils" starts out with geology, but the strata quickly become the floors of the speaker's house. The layers are also historical. All these levels parallel the levels of the speaker's consciousness until the barrier between what is external and internal, real and metaphorical, seems to dissolve like land eroded by rain.

A FOGHORN

On Sundays in mid-winter, when wild iris
put their iridescent blades through the grasses
and yellow lupine wait to flower from their seven-
fingered hands, all the divorced Californians
start out to the Point with their bottled waters
in their fragile foreign cars; they pass the turn-off
for the hopeful murmur of beaches, and pass
the moody grays of cooperative farms, the cattle
with their useful udders the color of wild geranium;
then they park if they can and descend the long steps
by the lighthouse where the tough crimson algae
cling to the broken stones, and when they arrive
at the rail they look past the cormorants, past
the Farallones to the space where the whales should be,
and the split chord of the foghorn calls to them.

The whales are too far to hear it; the whales,
in their secrecy, give off the dull sheen
of Etruscan mirrors. Down the coast they travel,
and the twisted cypresses gather to look: they swim
by L.A., with its nights of shining leather, toward
the temperate waters of Baja where they will mate.
In pictures, they are all smiles: sweet diligence,
or the weak little smile of exhausted history.
Their corrugated sides undulate as they play,
moving in a time both linear and cyclical.
They all swim here: Melville's whale, and Jonah's—
even the hollow plaster whale of Disney—
for this is California. Surely the people crave
some blankness between sightings, but someone
spots one every few minutes: a heart-breaking flash,
the cry goes out—each moment a contained unit—
then the cry passes, brief as a human life.

They say the call is heard in all the great systems.
The sleepy ones have gathered at the shore
to proclaim the glamour of the alien sun,
while in the nearby desert one real solitary
arranges himself on a pile of fronds . . . Come home,
says the disembodied voice to all of them.
But here on the Point the wind is fierce;
it blows the people to the right as they pose
for snapshots under the beehive-shaped, art deco
lantern, and the foghorn calls their two-toned names
until the names sound interchangeable: John-ny! Mar-y!
a major third downward, accent on the second syllable.
The call goes out in reverse, away from them,
over the hugely populated universe as though
it sent their questions out for them:
What shall we be? What shall we do now,
divorced from our lives, and from this century?

And the land splits behind them, the conglomerate cliffs
letting them go, letting the Point slide toward Alaska.
They wait as if at the prow of a fatherless ship,
leaning there; they have waited a long time,
they are so used to waiting, they have waited for
the winning number, or for the changes in someone,
or for the nocturne to rewind itself around the spool—
shouldn't something have pity on them now?
It is late; pelicans and egrets and herons go by,
and the foghorn continues its anthem of names, only
for them, of course, only in this human realm.

THE SPARK

Once you were immortal in the flame.
You were not the fire
but you were in the fire;—

nothing moved except
the way it was already moving;
nothing spoke
except the voice in back of time;—

and when you became your life,
there were those who couldn't,
those who tried to love you and failed
and some who had loved you in the beginning
with the first sexual energy of the world.

Start the memory now,
you who let your life be invented
though not being invented had been more available

and remember those
who lit the abyss. The boys in science fair.
You were probably hall monitor at that time weren't you,
and you admired them;
on their generator, the spark bounced back and forth
like baby lightning
and you saw them run their fingertips
through its danger,
two promising loops stuck up to provide
a home for the sexual light
which was always loose when it wasn't broken,
free joy that didn't go anywhere
but moved between the wires
like a piece of living, in advance—

then later: how much
were you supposed to share?

The boys sat in front of your house at dusk,
the ones who still had parents.
Sometimes they held Marlboros out the car
windows and even
if they didn't, sparks fell from their hands.
Showers of sparks
between nineteen sixty eight and the

hands were sleek
with asking sleek with asking;—

they had those long intramural after
the library type fingers
they would later put in you,—ah.
When? well,
when they had talked you into having a body
they could ask into the depths of

and they rose to meet you
against an ignorance that made you perfect
and you rose to meet them like a waitress of fire—

because: didn't
the spark shine best in the bodies
under the mild shooting stars
on the back-and-forth blanket
from the fathers' cars—
they lay down with you, and when
did you start missing them.
As Sacramento missed its yellow dust 1852.
When did you start missing those
who invented your body with their sparks—

they didn't mind being
plural. They put
their summer stars inside of you,

how nice to have. And then:
the pretty soon. Pretty
soon you were a body,
space, warm
flesh, warm
(this) under
the summer meteors that fell
like lower case i's above
the cave of granite where the white owl slept

without because or why
that first evening of the world. The sparks
of your bodies joined the loud sparks of the sky—

And you carried it, a little flame,
into almost famous cities,
between the ringing of shallow bells,
pretty much like some of that
blue tile work,
walking the bridge of sighs until you found the spark

on quilted bedspreads
in small villages, as if
the not-mattering stitching coming
all 'undone' in the middle
stood for a decade. You barely
burned then;

sex grows rather dim sometimes
doesn't it but it comes back.
Yourself half-gone into those rooms, yourself, a stranger.

You who happened only once:
remember yourself as you are;

when he comes to you
in the revolving dusk,
his full self lighting candles, a little smoke
he sings, the fire
you already own so you can stop
not letting him;

all love is representative
of the beginning of time. When you are loved,
the darkness carries you.
When you are loved, you are golden—

THE FORMATION OF SOILS

For forty million years   a warm, warm rain—

then the sea got up to try to relax.

Vulnerable volcanoes had just melted away.

He worked below, translating the author's imps and downs,
    his ups and demons—;
pines grew skyward though the pines were not.

Thus began long episodes of quiet,

nickel laterites not ready
for the slots.

It took periods of soft showers attacking the dream
under the silt-covered sun,

Osiris washing his fragments,
Leda swimming with her vagabonds.

Everyone is made essentially the same way.

Through notebooks of tight red dirt
Franciscans walked upside down under us:

aluminum oxides,   incidents of magma,

and I had to go down in the earth for something—

Iron sediments spread over the foothills where Caliban
had his flat;

I was wearing the brown sweater when we spoke,
my heart and the one below translating his heart out.

But by that time, what.

Experience had been sent up, at an angle.

BRIGIT PEGEEN KELLY

Brigit Pegeen Kelly's sentence structures are deliberately understated, so the reader is caught by surprise by the strong emotional kick of her poetry. Because of the simplicity of the grammar, the emotional and visual power of her poetry is piercing. She is unflinching in her depiction of mercilessness, but cruelty never has the last word in her poems.

Brigit Pegeen Kelly (b. 1951) won prestigious awards for her first two books of poetry. James Merrill chose her book *To the Place of Trumpets* (1988) for the Yale Younger Poets series in 1987. Her second book, *Song,* was a Lamont Poetry Selection of the Academy of American Poets in 1995.

Born in Palo Alto, California, Kelly has taught at the University of Illinois and in the Warren Wilson College M.F.A. program in writing. Her other honors include a "Discovery" / *The Nation* award, a Pushcart prize, and the Cecil Hemley Award from the Poetry Society of America.

"The Orchard" is the title poem of her third book, *The Orchard* (2004). It begins with a sentence that could almost come out of a reader for children learning their ABCs: "I saw the dog in a dream." Her poems work by accumulation, piling on image after image, like rugs in a shop. The language is straightforward but sometimes lush: "their musky loads / Of blooming and expiring words." Kelly's vision of the world is both impossibly cruel and gorgeous, with the two inextricably entwined. The dog gnawing the remains of a doe in "The Orchard" takes on another significance because of the Garden of Eden–like apple that the speaker finds and the human aspect of the dog. The person witnessing this event becomes implicated in it through her fascination. The dog's appetite for flesh and the viewer's appetite for sensation are gruesome but mesmerizing, and satisfying in disturbing ways.

The mythical level that appears in "The Orchard" is also very close to the surface in "Song," the title poem of her second book. "Song" is a heartbreaking but deeply felt poem. Again the biblical resonances are strong, with a goat's head in a tree seeming like a grotesque echo of the crucifixion. The goat belonged to a little girl, and the gender element in the boys' senseless attack on the animal seems a purposeful comment, as it does with the dog and the doe in "The Orchard."

THE ORCHARD

I saw the dog in a dream. Huge white
Boney creature. Big as a horse. At first
I thought it was a horse. It was feeding
On apples. As a horse might. Though not
With a horse's patience. For it was starving.
Its hipbones were empty bowls. The horse
Wolfed down the apples. Without breathing.
Without looking up. The way a dog wolfs
Down meat. And then it growled. And I saw
That the horse *was* a dog. But the apples
Were still apples. Windfall from the orchard
Above the lake. Pitiful place. The few trees
There grow black and yellow. And the thin grasses
Stagger down to the abandoned north field,
Which floods in winter and then freezes—
Blue ground, marbled with red and white,
Like a slab of meat—and when the far deer
Cross over it, and the birds cross over it,
It is as if the memories held within
The meat were rising from it. Or it is like
Flies crawling. . . . I saw the dog in a dream.
And then, days later, just before dawn,
I climbed to the orchard. And there he was.
The same dog. Chewing on a dead doe.
And it was troubling. I thought I might
Still be dreaming—as was the case
When for many months I could not sleep
And I lost the power to tell the figures
In my dreams from those we call real.
I thought the scene might have been staged
For me. By my mind. Or by someone
Who could read my mind. Someone
Who was having a good laugh

At my expense. Or testing me
In some way I could not understand.
Beneath the black and yellow trees,
The dog's skin seemed abnormally white.
And the blood on his broad muzzle shone
Like wet paint. I closed my eyes. Not because
The ghostly creature was now biting
At the neck of the doe, the way
Those dark creatures who drink blood
And live forever do—since the river
Of blood flows forever, the streams
Of an eternal city, forever running,
Forever carrying their musky loads
Of blooming and expiring words
And figures, a thousand thousand
Yellow lights forever flickering off
And on in the black liquid, gold,
Sweet liquid, fallen—I closed my eyes.
Not out of distaste. But to see if the dog
Would disappear, the way the mist
Had thinned and vanished as I climbed
The hill. But the dog was still there
When I opened them. Staring straight at me.
He lifted his large paw. Placed it
On the doe's chest, and started to rip
At her belly. There was the sound
Of cloth tearing. And what did I do?
I picked up an apple. I wanted to see
If the dog—when the apple struck his side
And he fell—would rise in a second form,
And then a third. As dream figures do.
Dog. To horse. To man. Or I wanted to see
If the apple would pass through the dog
As through a ghost. And if the dog
Like the best of ghosts would turn

And instruct me in my confusion.
Or I wanted to bring the scene down
To size. The way the bright lights
That clank on at the end of the play
Show the mad king to be nothing
But a skinny man holding a costume
Of cloth and paste. I wanted the dog
To be just a stray, gnawing on a bone.
Or maybe I wanted none of these things.
Maybe I wanted what the hunter
Wanted when he struck the doe. Maybe
I wanted a piece of the dog's feasting,
The way the hunter wanted a piece
Of the doe's improbable swiftness.
The gun fires. The smell of burnt powder
Sprays up. A knotted string of birds
Unspools across the white sky. And deep
In running blood a man thrusts his hands.
I wanted something. But I did not throw
The apple. It was a small fruit. The size
Of a child's hand. Black and yellow. Riddled
With worms and misshapen. I put my teeth
To it. I took a bite. Chill flesh. Rank.
The dog kept feeding. I was not bothered
By the blood. The last of the red leaves
Scudded about me. And a few drops fell
From the dark sky. There is blood
Everywhere. The trees shed it. The sky.
There is no end. And isn't it pretty?
We say. Isn't it pretty? Amn't I?
Isn't the starving dog? Isn't the doe?
Even half-eaten? She gave her body
To the dog. The fallen body looked
So heavy. It looked like it weighed
Ten thousand pounds. More than the lake

Or the frozen field. The doe dreamed
Of her death and it came to pass.
She courted the hunter and he shot her.
And she fell. And then the man stood
Over her. A white shadow. Laughing.
And then the dog stood over her. A black
Shadow. Laughing. And the dog came close.
The way a lover might. Had the doe
Been human. And he put his mouth to her.
As a lover might. Had he been human.
And her chastened flesh was a chalice.
And she was peaceful. And there was bliss
In this. And some horror. Around her
The thorns shone black and yellow.
And the fallen fruit lay black and yellow.
And black and yellow are the colors
Of the orchard's hive when it masses
And the queen in a fiery constellation
Is carried to new quarters. The wind
Stirred in the orchard. The dog bit
Into the doe's chest. And the apple
In my hand, against my lips, small,
Misshapen, the size of a child's fist,
Full of worms, turned suddenly warm
And soft. And it was as if, on that hill,
While the dog fed and the lake lay
Frozen, I was holding in my hand,
Against my lips, not a piece of fruit,
Not a piece of bitter, half-eaten fruit,
But the still warm and almost beating
Heart of some holy being—just lifted
From the dead body. And the heart
Was heavy. And wet. And it smelled
As it would smell forever. Of myrrh.
And burning blood. And gold.

SONG

Listen: there was a goat's head hanging by ropes in a tree.
All night it hung there and sang. And those who heard it
Felt a hurt in their hearts and thought they were hearing
The song of a night bird. They sat up in their beds, and then
They lay back down again. In the night wind, the goat's head
Swayed back and forth, and from far off it shone faintly
The way the moonlight shone on the train track miles away
Beside which the goat's headless body lay. Some boys
Had hacked its head off. It was harder work than they had imagined.
The goat cried like a man and struggled hard. But they
Finished the job. They hung the bleeding head by the school
And then ran off into the darkness that seems to hide everything.
The head hung in the tree. The body lay by the tracks.
The head called to the body. The body to the head.
They missed each other. The missing grew large between them,
Until it pulled the heart right out of the body, until
The drawn heart flew toward the head, flew as a bird flies
Back to its cage and the familiar perch from which it trills.
Then the heart sang in the head, softly at first and then louder,
Sang long and low until the morning light came up over
The school and over the tree, and then the singing stopped. . . .
The goat had belonged to a small girl. She named
The goat Broken Thorn Sweet Blackberry, named it after
The night's bush of stars, because the goat's silky hair
Was dark as well water, because it had eyes like wild fruit.
The girl lived near a high railroad track. At night
She heard the trains passing, the sweet sound of the train's horn
Pouring softly over her bed, and each morning she woke
To give the bleating goat his pail of warm milk. She sang
Him songs about girls with ropes and cooks in boats.
She brushed him with a stiff brush. She dreamed daily
That he grew bigger, and he did. She thought her dreaming
Made it so. But one night the girl didn't hear the train's horn,

And the next morning she woke to an empty yard. The goat
Was gone. Everything looked strange. It was as if a storm
Had passed through while she slept, wind and stones, rain
Stripping the branches of fruit. She knew that someone
Had stolen the goat and that he had come to harm. She called
To him. All morning and into the afternoon, she called
And called. She walked and walked. In her chest a bad feeling
Like the feeling of the stones gouging the soft undersides
Of her bare feet. Then somebody found the goat's body
By the high tracks, the flies already filling their soft bottles
At the goat's torn neck. Then somebody found the head
Hanging in a tree by the school. They hurried to take
These things away so that the girl would not see them.
They hurried to raise money to buy the girl another goat.
They hurried to find the boys who had done this, to hear
Them say it was a joke, a joke, it was nothing but a joke. . . .
But listen: here is the point. The boys thought to have
Their fun and be done with it. It was harder work than they
Had imagined, this silly sacrifice, but they finished the job,
Whistling as they washed their large hands in the dark.
What they didn't know was that the goat's head was already
Singing behind them in the tree. What they didn't know
Was that the goat's head would go on singing, just for them,
Long after the ropes were down, and that they would learn to listen,
Pail after pail, stroke after patient stroke. They would
Wake in the night thinking they heard the wind in the trees
Or a night bird, but their hearts beating harder. There
Would be a whistle, a hum, a high murmur, and, at last, a song,
The low song a lost boy sings remembering his mother's call.
Not a cruel song, no, no, not cruel at all. This song
Is sweet. It is sweet. The heart dies of this sweetness.

ROBERT THOMAS

Robert Thomas (b. 1951) typed and filed for twenty years as a legal secretary in San Francisco law firms, working in obscurity to write poems thriving with imagination and daring in their content. Not even most poets knew his name or work.

Then in 2002 his manuscript *Door to Door* was discovered by Yusef Komunyakaa, who selected it for the Poets Out Loud Award. Robert Thomas was flown to New York City and read at Lincoln Center. Since then, his book has been widely and favorably reviewed and he has been awarded a National Endowment for the Arts fellowship.

Laura Kasischke has written of Thomas's book, "The poems in this brilliant and urgent first collection traverse the territory between feverish delirium and remarkable sanity. In *Door to Door,* the lost voices of goddesses as well as salesmen are invoked, and Mozart stands comfortably beside Our Lady of Baby Back Ribs. Robert Thomas is a poet for the 21st century—witty, worried, and ecstatic—and this is a collection that will last."

At a time when most American poets are writing either autobiography or collage, Thomas is taking his own path. His poems are basically fictions, pulled out of the fountain of his imagination. Some are dramatic monologues, some magical realist fantasies, while others are narratives with characters of his own devising.

In Thomas's poetic fictions, though, it's not just the plot that provides the energy. It's the baroque and stunning descriptions and wording, and the surprising responses of the characters to situations. His imagery and phrasing create moments where the paradox of human emotion can glisten.

This paradox is evident in "Ensenada Wedding," where a child prefers to be left alone so his mother can go out dancing. The mother's confession reveals her personality and her vulnerability and becomes a surprising statement on the nature of love.

In "Salamander" the speaker pulls the reader in by beginning in the middle of a thought. This meandering meditation initially doesn't seem to have a focus. Like the speaker, it's a "beautiful mess" waiting for love to enter.

"Repairing the Hubble Telescope" describes a dizzying blend of alienation and enlightenment. In the midst of intoxicating imagery, an astronaut confesses that he found home in the void of space. This discovery seems tremendously liberating, sad and beautiful at the same time.

ENSENADA WEDDING

It was just across the border.
Your father and I had a pitcher of martinis,
the drink back then (I hear it's back), and we competed
with our friends—the best expression
for a dry martini: I want it
so dry a scorpion would feel at home
basking on the olive.

Of course I insisted on separate rooms: in those days
people drank so hard and danced so soft
they hardly thought of sex. But the next morning your father
had on a starched shirt and navy blue tie,
and a coat despite the heat, when he picked me up
for breakfast. He was so tall
we didn't have to wait when he hailed a cab. He took me straight
to *Iglesia de San Juan de la Cruz*. I'd never seen
streets like that: our cab was bigger
than some of those hovels,
and I remember the smell of the meat.

When we got there the church surprised me: hand-painted
stations of the cross, incense, the red candle hung from the rafters
advertising God's presence like a barker—
I almost could have drunk the holy water.
Of course I knew your father
had paid off the priest: he had to—he was divorced.
Enough pesos, the father said, that the church could get a new roof.
He knew right away he shouldn't have mentioned the money
in front of me. I had my hair in a French twist
and wore a milk white suit.

While we waited for the priest to fetch his housecleaner
and her eight-year-old granddaughter to witness,
a cloudburst came out of nowhere; it sounded as if
the whole town were hurling stones against the blue stained glass.
That was the closest I ever felt to him.

Our room overlooked the plaza, children hawking
pinwheels and wooden dolls
for tourists to bring home to their children.
I loved him for the wrong reasons,
and I wish that weren't
the definition of love itself, but it is.
He was so handsome in his captain's uniform,
those medals like candy
brimming over the cut-glass bowl of his heart.

I always knew the latest rage,
the mambo or cha-cha, and I'd stay out
as late as I pleased even after you were born—
that you love. Life is strange. It's always seemed best
in high, high heels, with a gentleman who knows how to dance,
no matter his conduct at home.
He had the maid plait bougainvillea vines around our bed
(even now it sounds strange
to say *our*), a different color for each post:
scarlet, coral, apricot, and mauve.
It was stunning,
though not quite enough for me to bear
someone looking at my body
as anything but the carry-on bag
packed with necessities
it had always been for me. What I remember
is the hotel pool the next morning,
swimming in gardenias.

Your father and I had gone through the war.
Bodies meant something
different then, bodies in the dark. All I wanted,
all I want, is *noise.* All that has ever left me
satisfied is a mariachi band
outside my window, burnished trumpets
blaring like taxi horns, the yellow braids
on the guitarists' jackets
twisting tighter as they cry to me from the loud, crowded street below,
Canta y no llores, Sing don't weep,
which is what I've always done.

SALAMANDER

Of course I burned what I wrote.
What did you expect,
Federal Express?
I rigged up a shack of kindling on the andirons,
stroked and poked.
My father used to call it a salamander, the hook he'd use
to prod logs. That's a good word
for me: the lizard
that lives in the blaze.

Sometimes my words come back to me;
not often. This morning
by the Swannanoa River I noticed water striders skating
helter-skelter
across the river, and for no reason at all
I thought *Fat and sassy*
tongues of flame. And as I crossed the bridge, *your blue*
bloodshot eyes. The problem is: once I think of a scrap,
I remember the whole sweetmeat feast.

I lay down on a dune
where someone had had a picnic, a slew of wings
like new driftwood.
Once I was such a beautiful mess even you
fell in love with me. I was an ear of corn, all my silk tassels
intact, and you, such a husker,
such a waterdog.
You never left a mark
as you held me between your teeth.

REPAIRING THE HUBBLE TELESCOPE

Floating in God's brain
with nothing but a screwdriver
and a box wrench. With my back to the universe,
I saw the gyroscope I'd come to fix
was the size of the red and gold one I got for Christmas
as a child in Phoenix, the one that made me forget
all my other toys forever. It still amazes me
how something at such a skew can spin so hard
it makes the rest of the world
seem out of whack. That's just how it felt
when the air lock opened and I was out there,
as if all my life I'd been listening to Mozart
on a homemade ham radio, music
measured in megahertz, and now I'd been hurled
into the orchestra pit.

Alexie Leonov was the first, not to walk
in space but to bask in it, cook in it—simmering
in those suits, sweat up to our ankles—
Alexie blurted to his partner on the other side
of the solar panel: *Pavel, look at me, these fucking gloves,*
I can't hold the camera, Pavel, I love you,
I don't think I can go back, and in fact
they overshot the target and almost skidded off
earth's atmosphere entirely and spun out
into interstellar ice, but in the end they simply fell in the snow
of the taiga and waited for helicopters
to find them among the fir trees, stumbling from gravity
like bears drunk on a canyon of berries.

I thought for a moment of Alexie, and of Ed White,
the first American to open
eternity's hatch, and then it was time to get to work.
I could just make out Sumatra and the Malay Peninsula,
the Indian Ocean, before I went under the hood.
Even now people ask me about it
but won't believe me. It wasn't the pure, shimmerless
colors, the anarchic perspective, that changed my life—
it was that moment when I felt exactly
as if I were a kid again, on my driveway in Costa Mesa,
sliding on my back under the chassis.
I was home. The enormous gold foil
rectangles looked like the speakers in my den
as they silently absorbed the sun's white noise.

For once I knew what to do, I lost myself,
and now the whole world can see the Cat's Eye,
a dying star, red and gold, spinning,
and the galaxy Lagoon, full of what the astronomers
call wisps and twisters, star embryos
half a light-year long.

Sitting in my den watching CNN,
squeezing a whole lime in my Diet Coke,
I am homesick
for the only place I ever belonged,
alone with the Hourglass Nebula
and the stars they call blue stragglers,
children wandering on a hillside
among crisscrossing deer trails and mist, almost happy it's so late
the search party must be giving up
for the night, the men finishing off the last slug of warmish coffee
from the thermos on the truck's dash,
thinking they know their limits.

JIMMY SANTIAGO BACA

Jimmy Baca's parents divorced and abandoned him at age two in Santa Fe, New Mexico. He was raised by a grandparent till he was sent to an orphanage at age five, which he fled six years later. He then lived on the streets in a culture of substance abuse and was arrested when he was twenty for a drug crime he says he didn't commit. Baca served five years' hard labor. He had never attended school, and it was during his prison term that he taught himself to read and write. Baca (b. 1952) has more than caught up after his difficult beginnings, earning a Ph.D. from the University of New Mexico in 2003 and lecturing at numerous colleges and universities.

Baca, who is of Mexican and Apache descent, sets much of his writing in the Southwest. His poetry is both streetwise and tender. He often writes longer poems, which allow him the freedom to follow a thought or a feeling like a trail that threads through a rocky landscape, often doubling back on itself.

In his readings, he uses the full range of the dynamics of the human voice, from whisper to shout, heightening the emotion of his poetry. He seems to discover his own feelings as he voices them. Baca is an incredibly charismatic and spontaneous performer—at Berkeley, he read a spellbinding long poem to a packed crowd, only to get to the end and find that the last page was missing. He improvised the ending so smoothly that the audience would never have known if he hadn't confessed after finishing.

Baca's books include *C-Train and 13 Mexicans* (2002), and *Martín and Meditations on the South Valley* (1987), which won the American Book Award. He also wrote the script for the 1993 film *Bound by Honor*, directed by Taylor Hackford (released on video as *Blood In, Blood Out*), based on his prison experiences. Baca is the author of a memoir, *A Place to Stand* (2001), and the novel *A Glass of Water*.

His poetry collection *Healing Earthquakes: A Love Story in Poems* (2001) is a rambling book-length meditation on love, hope, history, and parenting, which contains the lines "I have to remember / because you're ready to dismember." He plunges right into the battle of the sexes, depicting a world that is full of extreme, visceral emotion and moments of the most ordinary, moving intimacy.

from HEALING EARTHQUAKES

Thirteen

I have to remember
    because you're ready to dismember
yeah, you just go ahead
    but I'm going to head this problem full on
    because what if our children come up
hating women
    if we don't break this learning to hate ourselves
to hate women
    to hate everything
    you think children aren't going to hurt and hate
you see
    we have to talk us and women
    you see
we're both equal human beings
    shouldn't hide lust or love behind a book
    or a beard or eyeglasses or manners
don't want to hide me
my lust is good,
    could stick your hands into me up to the elbows and never feel
so sweet a goose down on your flesh, woman.
    O, my heart perches eagled on your arm
and I surrender myself to you, woman
    the way land surrenders to high tide
    or winter wool to winter wind
I do
    and more, woman
    my desire to come close to you
is sap-strong bark and cornstalk green
    jointed along the length of our years loving each other
    and I would love to know that you know that way
letting me become more of who I am,
    become more of me, I grow on growing me

emptying our mouths of the silhouettes
behind each word
emptying our bodies of the pain
all weapons
we pile in the middle between us
the way soldiers surrender their rifles
to the resistance.
I wonder how our love could have crumbled.
Remember the first way I made love the way you liked:
a light summer sun-shower
opening the flower seed.

But over the years
the rain passed through climatic changes and turned to hail:
the horses in the field tried to shield themselves from it
they turned right, then left, while each
tried to get in front of the other
to shield themselves from the burning hail
with no way out
the pain bent their forelegs and they collapsed
in the dust.
Both our hearts cringe, twitch, seek escape
and then lie down like that.
Perhaps it is body memory
how I remember my hands gripping Mother's thighs
suckling at her breast
entangled in her hair
clutching her constantly
and how
my body seeks that connection with you.

Now at the window, where I saw the horses go down
        I watch you drive away
angrily, gravel seethes from your spinning tires
        and the umbilical cord snaps.
        The horses went down
        pitilessly at the mercy
        of hail.
Your blue car turns at the stop sign
        and then you're gone.

        Horses were under siege
        tried to fight hail off
        tried to flee
        finally
            capitulated.
        Their surrender so human
        so much strength and dignity
        in the quavering flanks
        in those front legs bending
        the dark crevice of the knees
        finally giving up all hope
        I saw us.

In the garden behind the house, hail shredded the flowers.
But the first year—
        I didn't mind
        cropping vegetable leaves in the garden until my knees bled
        nor stuccoing walls in March wind until my chapped lips cracked and bled
        nor building the adobe fence until my hands bled
I gave thanks
for our life together.

All winter I have been coughing and sleeplessly fighting off bronchial asthma.
I used to love you, woman
     the way a wolf's tongue thrusts up to catch blue-bodied raindrops
     my tongue darted in you.
     We lay in bed and I softly bit your flesh
     a jaguar cub gnawing the steel spindles of his zoo cage.
This has been a particularly hard year for us
friends, wines and books bring little reprieve.
When a coyote howls his male-need call for his mate
with tensile gait, loping buoyantly at the crest of sand dunes, profiled against moon
I see her come
     and I want to howl for you
     but instead I curse—
     what the fuck you want me to do!
     I don't need this shit from you!
O, but I remember the first year
a thousand bees filled
my fingertips with spring
when I touched you
and your nipples were pomegranate seeds
and all summer my lips were red,
your laughter oceaned out
and freed the nets in me
and our bodies moved as wind pushed flames
through brittle grass toward each other!

But what has happened?
I clench my knuckles
     and I want to leave.
We have not held each other warmly in a long time.
This has been a homeless winter.
It has been a bad winter for us.
     I want to leave
     my house, my beliefs, my gods
     and you

and become someone else
in another place and time.
Our teeth are serrated links
of handcuffs
snapping curses to hiss the other shut.
Ice between us cracks, and you cry
and my fear suspends itself from a rib hook
freezing meat in an icehouse.
I pray the ice will hold
to carry me across to a bar
where over whiskey shots
I can complain to another man:

> *Man, I try to make her happy—I quit*
> *trying last night—I turned*
> *and spit out "fuck you!"*
> Accuse me of being insensitive
> of never fulfilling you
> of raping you emotionally
> of not knowing how to make love
> well, the hell with that bullshit!

*   *   *

But I didn't do this male ritual
instead
clouds part out the window and moonlight
spreads on my part of the bed. I stare
at the moon and I can't reach over
and touch you, woman
can't kiss you
can't hold you
can't make love
because my touch draws pain from you
the way a rose picker's hand
brings in only barbs
from green stems.
Yes, the horses fell

and hail shredded the flowers.
These days of hate
play themselves out
a needle that skids across the album
scratching a new song across the old song
of how you hate my hands
hate my eyes
hate my voice
hate my feelings
hate me
hate men.

And after days of hate
    what do we do?
Make love on the floor
my heart sings to the predawn color of your skin
old bells on Andean Peaks in so much solitude and silence
    beating
    I am alive I am alive I am alive
to all the earth and sky
    bells sound in my male dance blood
    I am alive.

* * *

But Grandma taught me when I was a boy how to suck poison
    from a snake bite:
Chew the skin good, chew well, then suck and spit, mijito
increase the hurt, widen the pain
    taste the pain
    the hurt
    touch the darkness
    see and feel the poison in all life
    it is the dark work of life.
Go down into the wound
work your healing by entering the pain
then spit out the poison.

This love is a fish hook
       in my thumb
       can't pull out the barb
       on the other end
       the eye
so I scrape around the hook
in my thumb with my pocketknife blade
widen the hole, increase the pain
all of myself uttered in pain
as I cut the hole rounder
wound blood pours and what I am made of
hurts, I dig deeper and deeper
       work my healing
       then
       extract the hook, clean the wound
       and have learned about myself.

       Men are returning home
       rising
       from their dying
       to live over again
       with their children
men are returning to their children

                              *   *   *

I fix my daughters' swing set, tighten screws on the slide
change diapers sitting on the toilet
       while my other daughter stands in doorway
       next in line on my lap
I move and they follow
I cook and they eat
I sleep and they wake
I sing a new man to them
       they stand in my male shade, I purr my jaguar growl
       they crouch and grunt and leap at my chest
my hands are ripe fruit they nibble

   I sniff
they paw
   we skip and leap across the living room, dancing, yelling
healing myself
   we hug, wrestle
   spin and jump and scamper and land on all fours
   on the carpet
   my children leap and laugh with me
   in our male song, Ahoa, Grandfather!
   Ahoa! Grandmother!

MARY RUEFLE

When Mary Ruefle (b. 1952) was invited to read at Lunch Poems at UC Berkeley, we asked her to send a few items for a display case to publicize the reading. We expected books, broadsides, maybe a page of a manuscript. Instead, we received in the mail a magical package that says a lot about how she works as a writer.

The package was bound with a plastic correction tape from a typewriter, embossed with erased letters. On the wrapping paper she'd scrawled in pen, "If I had my life to live again, I'd be a poet." Included in the package was a photograph that Mary Ruefle had used as a pad to write a poem on, imagining she was a penny for a day, whom she met and where she went.

Also in this package was an illustrated Sunday school primer from the late nineteenth century called *Snowstorm*. Mary Ruefle had taken the book and started to compose her own poem with it, using a blizzard of white-out to delete all but a few words on each page, so that it formed an experimental text, both lyrical and droll.

There was much more, including a traffic ticket from her native Massachusetts, but one thing this package told me about Mary Ruefle's poetry is that the images and moments in her work are not so much part of the string of a narrative as they are like found objects in a Joseph Cornell box, items that seem to speak to one another and combine in surprising ways. She reminds you of someone French, but you're not sure who. Her work is full of a wonderfully quirky humor that suddenly yanks away, revealing points of surprising seriousness.

Her poem "Merengue" from the book *Cold Pluto* (1996) is mostly a series of questions. The questions will be answered differently by each reader or listener of the poem. That in itself is a surprising strategy, since literature is traditionally powered by shared emotions. Ruefle challenges the reader to enjoy not just the expected ecstasies of sex but also the odd moments of life. In reading this poem aloud, Mary Ruefle points out that the merengue is a dance, but it can also be as in lemon meringue, the sweet fluff of baking.

"Suburb of Lost Suffering," which sounds like a parody of a movie title, is a prose poem about being alone. Ruefle's solitude is full of humor, marvels, and pathos.

"Kiss of the Sun" is a play on words and on the idea of the resurrection of the body. Somehow Ruefle is standing there at the end of time with an orange for her friend, and her final gesture is both affirmative and defiant.

MERENGUE

I'm sorry to say it, but fucking
is nothing. To the gods, we look
like dogs. Still, they watch.
Did you lose your wallet?
Did you rip up the photo?
Did you pick up the baby
and kiss its forehead?
Did you drive into a deer?
Did you hack at the grass
as if it could kill you?
Did you ask your mother for milk?
Did you light the candles?
Did you count the buttons on your shirt?
Were you off by one? Did you start again?
Did you learn how to cut a pineapple,
open a coconut?
Did you carry a body once it had died?
For how long and how far?
Did you do the merengue?
Did you wave at the train?
Did you finish the puzzle, or save it for morning?
Did you say something? Would you repeat it?
Did you throw the bottle against the wall?
Did it break? Did you clean it up?
Did you tear down the web? What did you do
with the bug the spider was saving?
Did you dive without clothes into cold water?
Have you been born?
What book will you be reading when you die?
If it's a good one, you won't finish it.
If it's a bad one, what a shame.

SUBURB OF LONG SUFFERING

Fire is my companion, but I do not talk to it, it talks to me. It has white-hot fissures that quiver and rage and complain and sometimes very tender speech towards morning, a low blue word or two. I never tire of listening to my fire. Music is my companion also, but it does not talk to me, I talk to it, I talk to it and it listens without complaint, absorbing whatever I am feeling and I can feel it listening to me. I think it never tires of listening to me. Together, the fire and the music and me, we make a family that, despite its dysfunction, is able to persevere. Yet I have a complaint. When they are in the room together, the fire and the music, they talk to each other and neither do they talk nor listen to me, as for example on a rainy day when the three of us come into the room together to while away the time: the fire and the music begin to converse in soft tones at first, so as not to disturb me I like to think, but soon their conversation grows to such a pitch that between the two of them there seem to be a great many unspoken agreements, while I am left feeling lonelier and lonelier, and end up by the window, a mere eavesdropper in my own home.

KISS OF THE SUN

If, as they say, poetry is a sign of something
among people, then let this be prearranged now,
between us, while we are still peoples: that
at the end of time, which is also the end of poetry
(and wheat and evil and insects and love),
when the entire human race gathers in the flesh,
reconstituted down to the infant's tiniest fold
and littlest nail, I will be standing at the edge
of that fathomless crowd with an orange for you,
reconstituted down to its innermost seed protected
by white thread, in case you are thirsty, which
does not at this time seem like such a wild guess,
and though there will be no poetry between us then,
at the end of time, the geese all gone with the seas,
I hope you will take it, and remember on earth
I did not know how to touch it it was all so raw,
and if by chance there is no edge to the crowd
or anything else so that I am of it,
I will take the orange and toss it as high as I can.

MARK DOTY

Mark Doty (b. 1953) narrates the story of his tumultuous upbringing in the 1960s in his memoir *Firebird* (1999). He was the child of an unhappy marriage between an army engineer and a housewife who longed for the life of an artist, and his family moved from Tennessee to Florida to California to Arizona before he found himself as a writer. Doty is descended from a rascally Mayflower passenger who fought the first duel and filed the first lawsuit in America.

In his many books, Mark Doty has proved himself one of the most sophisticated voices in American poetry, a blend of Tiffany glass and Walt Whitman's earthy longings. His work reflects the glories and grief that the gay community has experienced over the past few decades.

In his poetry, Doty has mastered and refined a difficult technique that can be traced back to Walt Whitman's "When Lilacs Last in the Dooryard Bloom'd." In Whitman's great elegy to Lincoln, he wove together several loosely connected threads. This strategy of taking disconnected threads prominent in the poet's heart and surroundings and braiding them together is one that Doty uses powerfully in his poem "Fog," from his book *My Alexandria* (1993), winner of the National Book Critics Circle Award. "Fog" takes place during the worst days of the AIDS crisis, when Doty lost his lover. In "Fog" the speaker and his partner are being tested for HIV and everything in their lives is drawn into this vortex, from the peonies in the garden with their "blood-color" ruffles to the spooky characters they channel through their Ouija board. These supernatural presences allow for an innocence and transcendence that help the speaker survive crushing news.

Doty's "Crêpe de Chine" from his collection *Atlantis* (1995) is a celebration of drag culture. The poem is a delight prompted by an arrangement of perfume bottles in a drugstore window. In his readings, Doty delivers the poem as if he were belting out a song. Behind this stunning indulgence is a serious aesthetic, a claim that decoration and frills are not only that but a force that can possess and lift us to a higher altitude.

"Fish R Us" from Mark Doty's book *Source* (2001) is an example of his astonishing ability to find unlikely beauty and to capture it in description. The poem portrays something few writers would dream of attempting to put into words, a group of goldfish dumped from a plastic bag into a larger tank in a fish store. Yet in Doty's hands this image of the vitality of life takes on all the glory of Yeats's Byzantium.

FOG

The crested iris by the front gate waves
its blue flags three days, exactly,

then they vanish. The peony buds'
tight wrappings are edged crimson;

when they open, a little blood-color
will ruffle at the heart of the flounced,

unbelievable white. Three weeks after the test,
the vial filled from the crook

of my elbow, I'm seeing blood everywhere:
a casual nick from the garden shears,

a shaving cut and I feel the physical rush
of the welling up, the wine-fountain

dark as Siberian iris. The thin green porcelain
teacup, our homemade Ouija's planchette,

rocks and wobbles every night, spins
and spells. It seems a cloud of spirits

numerous as lilac panicles vie for occupancy—
children grabbing for the telephone,

happy to talk to someone who isn't dead yet?
Everyone wants to speak at once, or at least

these random words appear, incongruous
and exactly spelled: *energy, immunity, kiss.*

Then: *M. has immunity. W. has.*
And that was all. One character, Frank,

distinguishes himself: a boy who lived
in our house in the thirties, loved dogs

and gangster movies, longs for a body,
says he can watch us through the television,

asks us to stand before the screen
and kiss. *God in garden,* he says.

Sitting out on the back porch at twilight,
I'm almost convinced. In this geometry

of paths and raised beds, the green shadows
of delphinium, there's an unseen rustling:

some secret amplitude
seems to open in this orderly space.

Maybe because it contains so much dying,
all these tulip petals thinning

at the base until any wind takes them.
I doubt anyone else would see that, looking in,

and then I realize my garden has no outside, only *is*
subjectively. As blood is utterly without

an outside, can't be seen except out of context,
the wrong color in alien air, no longer itself.

Though it submits to test, two,
to be exact, each done three times,

though not for me, since at their first entry
into my disembodied blood

there was nothing at home there.
For you they entered the blood garden over

and over, like knocking at a door
because you know someone's home. Three times

the Elisa Test, three the Western Blot,
and then the incoherent message. We're

the public health care worker's
nine o'clock appointment,

she is a phantom hand who forms
the letters of your name, and the word

that begins with *P*. I'd lie out
and wait for the god if it weren't

so cold, the blue moon huge
and disruptive above the flowering crab's

foaming collapse. The spirits say *Fog*
when they can't speak clearly

and the letters collide; sometimes
for them there's nothing outside the mist

of their dying. Planchette,
peony, I would think of anything

not to say the word. Maybe the blood
in the flower is a god's. Kiss me,

in front of the screen, please,
the dead are watching.

They haven't had enough yet.
Every new bloom is falling apart.

I would say anything else
in the world, any other word.

CRÊPE DE CHINE

These drugstore windows
—one frame in the mile-long film
of lit-up trash and nothing

fronting the avenue, what Balzac called
"the great poem of display"—
are a tableau of huge bottles

of perfume, unbuyable gallons of scent
for women enormous as the movie screens
of my childhood. Spiritual pharmaceuticals

in their deco bottles,
wide-shouldered, flared,
arrayed in their pastel skylines,

their chrome-topped tiers:
a little Manhattan of tinted alcohols.
Only reading their names

—Mme. Rochas, White Shoulders, Crêpe de Chine—
and I'm hearing the suss of immense stockings,
whispery static of chiffon stoles

on powdered shoulders,
click of compacts, lisp and soft glide
of blush. And I'm thinking of my wig,

my blonde wig, and following the cold sparkle
of pavement I'm wanting not
these shoes but the black clatter

and covenant of heels. Next door
the Italian baker's hung a canopy of garlands
and silver shot, bee lights and silk ivy

high over the sugary excess
of his pastries, and I want
not his product but his display:

I want to wear it,
I want to put the whole big thing
on my head, I want

the tumbling coiffeurs of heaven,
or lacking that, a wig
tiered and stunning as this island.

That's what I want from the city:
to wear it.
That's what drag is: a city

to cover our nakedness,
silk boulevards, sleek avenues
of organza, the budding trees

along the avenue flaunting their haze
of poisonous Caravaggio green . . .
Look how I take the little florists' shops

and twist them into something
for my hair, forced spiky branches
and a thousand tulips. Look, my sleety veil

of urbane rain descends, unrolls
like cinema's dart and flicker, my skirt
in its ravaged sleekness, the shadows

between buildings raked and angled
into these startling pleats,
descending twilight's gabardine

over the little parks and squares
circled by taxis' hot jewels:
my body

made harmonious with downtown.
Look how I rhyme with the skyscraper's
padded sawtooth shoulders,

look at the secret evidence of my slip
frothing like the derelict river
where the piers used to be,

look at my demolished silhouette,
my gone and reconstructed profile,
look at me built and rebuilt,

torn down to make way,
excavated, trumped up, tricked out,
done, darling,

in every sense of the word. Now,
you call me
Evening in Paris, call me Shalimar,

call me Crêpe de Chine.

FISH R US

Clear sac
of coppery eyebrows
suspended in amnion,
not one moving—

A Mars,
composed entirely
of single lips,
each of them gleaming—

this bag of fish
(have they actually
traveled here like *this?*)
bulges while they

acclimate, presumably,
to the new terms
of the big tank
at Fish R Us. Soon

they'll swim out
into separate waters,
but for now they're
shoulder to shoulder

in this clear and
burnished orb, each fry
about the size of this line,
too many lines for any

bronzy antique epic,
a million of them,
a billion incipient citizens
of a goldfish Beijing,

a São Paulo,
a Mexico City.
They seem to have sense
not to move but hang

fire, suspended, held
at just a bit of distance
(a bit is all there is), all
facing outward, eyes

(they can't even blink)
turned toward the skin
of the sac they're in,
this swollen polyethylene.

And though nothing's
actually rippling but their gills,
it's still like looking up
into falling snow,

if all the flakes
were a dull, breathing gold,
as if they were streaming
toward—not us, exactly,

but what they'll be . . .
Perhaps they're small enough
—live sparks, for sale
at a nickel apiece—

that one can actually
see them transpiring:
they want to swim
forward, want to

eat, want to take place.
Who's going to know
or number or even see them all?

They pulse in their golden ball.

Tony Hoagland (b. 1953) writes poetry with a satiric edge. Although satire as a literary genre has a venerable history in European poetry, dating back to the work of Archilochus in ancient Greece, Horace in ancient Rome, and Alexander Pope in eighteenth-century England, satire has not had a major presence in American poetry.

American poetry tends toward a heroic stance that often precludes the squinting of satire. Whether it's the sweeping impulse toward inclusion, or the contrary impulse toward a heroic misanthropy, or brave confessions, American poetry is often underpinned by a sense of great potential. Sometimes this potential is seen as realized, at other times as frustrated. But satire requires a more critical eye, and Tony Hoagland takes that angle of vision.

Hoagland's critical gaze stands him in good stead not only in his creative work but when he writes about poetry. His razor-sharp essays on contemporary writers have appeared in various publications, including the *American Poetry Review* and the *Writers Chronicle.*

Hoagland's poem "Ecology" comes from his book *Donkey Gospel* (1998) (even the title has a satirical ring), winner of the James Laughlin Award of the Academy of American Poets. Hoagland addresses "Ecology" to a friend in an academic hierarchy, trapped like a little fish by the bigger and gaudier species. The comparison Hoagland makes with imperial Rome is jolting—we like to think of ourselves as a society of opportunity—but the analogy fits like Tupperware, both because it recalls satire in Latin poetry and because of the rigidity of university pecking orders.

"Sweet Ruin," the title poem from a book that won the Brittingham Prize in 1992, is a look at a person who smashes a stable home life, seemingly without motive. The poem tells the story of the speaker's father's divorce in memorable detail, with deft use of metaphor. The speaker/son comes to understand what it was that prompted his father to throw away so much that mattered.

Hoagland's poem "America," from his book *What Narcissism Means to Me* (2003), gives a post-9/11 view of the United States. The speaker begins with a highly skeptical portrait of an alienated young man, who sees the American Dream only from a flat, hostile perspective. Then the poem turns inward to the speaker's dream of patricide of a father stuffed with money, and suddenly the skepticism embraces the speaker's own sense of failure at not feeling empathy with those outside the circle of privilege.

ECOLOGY

Mike moved to the city
to begin his life as an adult
and to immerse himself in the cultural milieu

but he wound up being one of those fishes
employed to use their mouths
to vacuum the glass walls of the aquarium,

—hanging around the edges of the party,
fluttering his gills,
trying to get closer to the center of the room

where the big fish flash
their golden fins expansively. . . .
And isn't that the way it goes

when you traffic with power?
There's always someone
with a bigger tail,

more talent, better clothes,
someone whose blue blood
and collegiate chin

or low-cut dress
and cappuccino skin
have something you suspect

to do with their success.
Thus it was in the tiled courts
of the Roman kings:

Flaccus peering enviously
over Tiberion's shoulder
to where Chloe is

dripping her sweet vowels
like a trickle of honey
into the princeling's ear.

The world has always
moved that way,
small fry darting

on the edges of the big
ones ploughing forward,
and you live on what they spill

from the corners of their mouths,
scraps of money and prestige
floating in their wake.
Curse if you want,

but it's just ecology at work,
and you continue
doing what you think is necessary

on a level that is simple, automatic, blessed
in a way that you
no longer see,

even as you wiggle your fins
and lash your tail
with all the skill that you've acquired

to hold your place
among the others,
like miserable Mike, to whom

everything he has
looks like just a snack.
Mike, when you were a kid

you used to have
some imagination.
Now, how will you imagine

your way out of this?

SWEET RUIN

Maybe that is what he was after,
my father, when he arranged, ten years ago,
to be discovered in a mobile home
with a woman named Roxanne, an attractive,
recently divorced masseuse.

He sat there, he said later, in the middle
of a red, imitation-leather sofa,
with his shoes off and a whiskey in his hand,
filling up with a joyful kind of dread—
like a swamp, filling up with night,

—while my mother hammered on the trailer door
with a muddy, pried-up stone,
then smashed the headlights of his car,
drove home,
and locked herself inside.

He paid the piper, was how he put it,
because he wanted to live,
and at the time knew no other way
than to behave like some blind and willful beast,
—to make a huge mistake, like a big leap

into space, as if following
a music that required dissonance
and a plunge into the dark.
That is what he tried to tell me,
the afternoon we talked,

as he reclined in his black chair,
divorced from the people in his story
by ten years and a heavy cloud of smoke.
Trying to explain how a man could come
to a place where he has nothing else to gain

unless he loses everything. So he
louses up his work, his love, his own heart.
He hails disaster like a cab. And years later,
when the storm has descended
and rubbed his face in the mud of himself,

he stands again and looks around,
strangely thankful just to be alive,
oddly jubilant—as if he had been granted
the answer to his riddle,
or as if the question

had been taken back. Perhaps
a wind is freshening the grass,
and he can see now, as for the first time,
the softness of the air between the blades. The pleasure
built into a single bending leaf.

Maybe then he calls it, in a low voice
and only to himself, *Sweet Ruin.*
And maybe only because I am his son,
I can hear just what he means. How
even at this moment, even when the world

seems so perfectly arranged, I feel
a force prepared to take it back.
Like a smudge on the horizon. Like a black spot
on the heart. How one day soon,
I might take this nervous paradise,

bone and muscle of this extraordinary life,
and with one deliberate gesture,
like a man stepping on a stick,
break it into halves. But less gracefully

than that. I think there must be something wrong
with me, or wrong with strength, that I would
break my happiness apart
simply for the pleasure of the sound.
The sound the pieces make. What is wrong

with peace? I couldn't say.
But, sweet ruin, I can hear you.
There is always the desire.
Always the cloud, suddenly present
and willing to oblige.

AMERICA

Then one of the students with blue hair and a tongue stud
Says that America is for him a maximum security prison

Whose walls are made of Radio Shacks and Burger Kings, and MTV episodes
Where you can't tell the show from the commercials,

And as I consider how to express how full of shit I think he is,
He says that even when he's driving to the mall

In his Izuzu Trooper, with a gang of his friends, letting rap music pour over them
Like a boiling jaccuzi full of ballpeen hammers, even then he feels

Buried alive, captured and suffocated in the folds
Of the thick satin quilt of America

And I wonder if this is a legitimate category of pain,
Or whether he is just spin-doctoring a better grade,

And then I remember that when I stabbed my father in the dream last night,
It was not blood but money

That gushed out of him, bright green hundred-dollar bills
Spilling from his wounds, and, this is the funny part,

He gasped, "Thank God—those Ben Franklins were
Clogging up my heart

—And so I perish happily,
Freed from that which kept me from my Liberty"

—Which is when I knew it was a dream, since my dad
Would never speak in rhymed couplets

And I look at the student with his acne and cell phone and phoney ghetto clothes
And I think, "I am asleep in America too,

And I don't know how to wake myself either"
And I remember what Marx said near the end of his life:

"I was listening to the cries of the past,
when I should have been listening to the cries of the future"

But how could he have imagined 100 channels of 24 hour cable
Or what kind of nightmare it might be

When each day you watch rivers of bright merchandise run past you
And you are floating in your pleasure boat upon this river

Even while others are drowning underneath you
And you see their faces twisting in the surface of the waters

And yet it seems to be your own hand
Which turns the volume higher?

HARRYETTE MULLEN

For Harryette Mullen (b. 1953), poetry is a form of play, but the play often has a serious end. Her work has been compared to Lewis Carroll's and Gertrude Stein's. Mullen is also influenced by the work of the European group of writers called OULIPO (Ouvroir de Littérature Potentielle, or Workshop of Potential Literature). But Mullen adds to these formal experiments a distinctly American funk and politics rooted in her beginnings in the Black Arts movement and in her own experience.

Born in Alabama, she grew up in Fort Worth during the struggle for civil rights. In an interview she spoke about her youth: "I remember the colored and white signs on the rest rooms and water fountains, and I remember the first time we tested integration by going to a drive-in restaurant where they refused to serve us, and we left after waiting there for about thirty minutes for our hamburgers that never arrived." After attending the University of Texas at Austin, Mullen went on to earn a Ph.D. at the University of California, Santa Cruz.

Mullen's fourth book, *Muse & Drudge* (1995), is a book-length poem broken into four-line stanzas without punctuation. The poem is a collage of rhythms, rhymes, memories, social commentaries, advertising slogans, history, and elaborate puns. The stanzas roll along like blues lyrics stirred in the stream of consciousness, as in the excerpt, "ain't your fancy . . ."

Mullen's fifth book of poetry, *Sleeping with the Dictionary* (2002), was a finalist for the National Book Award, the National Book Critics Circle Award, and the Los Angeles Times Book Prize in Poetry. The poems are grouped in alphabetical order by title, and each one is a distinct experiment in language.

The prose poem "Kirstenography" from *Sleeping with the Dictionary* is a straight-forward story told in an oblique way. The joy is in reading the piece both ways, as written and in the hidden text. The original text has some hilarious moments: "They were wood in all those paces, and waded to knowledge at Cutie Ostentatious." The coded and the narrative text hug each other, mirroring the two sisters in the poem.

"Why You and I," also from *Sleeping with the Dictionary,* jumps from rhyme to rhyme, often using metaphors from the world of books and writing. Is every sentence in this poem narrated by the same person? Is the "you" in the poem always identical? The poet never makes this clear, but there is a strong sense that the writer is lamenting a lost relationship, one that was defeated by following the rules too closely.

from MUSE & DRUDGE

ain't your fancy
handsome gal
feets too big
my hair don't twirl

from hunger call
on the telephone
asking my oven for
some warm jellyroll

if I can't have love
I'll take sunshine
if I'm too plain for champagne
I'll go float on red wine

what you can do
is what women do
I know you know
what I mean, don't you

arrives early for the date
to tell him she's late
he watches her bio clock balk on seepy time
petals out of rhythm docked for trick crimes

flunked the pregnancy test
mistimed space probe, she aborted
legally blind justice, she miscarried
scorched and salted earth, she's barren

when Aunt Haggie's chirren throws
an all originals ball
the souls ain't got a stray word
for the woman who's wayward

dead to the world
let earth receive her piece
let every dark room repair her heart
let nature and heaven give her release

KIRSTENOGRAPHY
for K. M.

K was burn at the bend of the ear in the mouth of Remember. She was the fecund chill burn
in her famish. She came into the word with a putty smoother, a handsewn farther, and a
yodeler cistern. They were all to gather in a rosy horse on a piety sweet in Alligator Panorama.

When her smoother and farther wrought her chrome from the hose spittle, her cistern
fought the piddle ably was a girly heeded bawl. A bawl that dank silk, booed, burgled, rab-
bled, fried, and tweed in wipers. This was not a bawl that swept in the joy blocks with her
rather joys. This was a giving bawl that wasn't a joy like a fluffed fan mail. Oh no! This
was her grand blue piddle cistern that cold knot talc for a song time, but lonely fried and
braid rather voices that the yodeler one cold knot rubberband.

It shook a few ears until they cold talc to gather, tall yolks, shear sacreds, heave a con-
version or a dish cushion. That was laughter they kissed their handsewn farther who wind
sway to Cheap Cargo, Ill Annoy. Mum and gulls made their mauve to Foreword Text. As
swoon as they cold they boasted fetters in the snail to him and he relied as mulch as he cold.

Their inelegant smoother was a reacher who muddied lard, learned debris, and wept
them upon the prosper pat. Reaching them fright from strong was her per rental doodly.
They threw up and wind soft to mercy rule and hinder guardian, then on to sedimentary,
fecund dairy, and slide rule. They were wood in all those paces, and waded to knowledge at
Cutie Ostentatious.

The smoother and her dodders all learned debris to gather. Evidentially, two quirked as proofs in the loony varsity. K was quirking for the slate of Taxes Hysterical Remission. Laughter a schmaltz fart with a wanky lurk, K fond her Sanity. A proof of reckoned comics. K quirked to learn her nastier debris and latter she rave burps and becalmed herself a smoother.

Now she does her writhing ghostly a tome. Quirks at that muse, um, that's in Chapped Apple Milling Sea. Enduring, she has her Sanity and they becalmed the prod parentheses of Adenoid and Williwaw. They all loved shapely over laughter.

WHY YOU AND I

Who knows why you and I fell off the roster?
Who can figure why you and I never passed muster
on our way out yonder?
Does anyone wonder why you and I lacked
the presence of minding our blunders?
Can anyone see why you and I, no longer intact,
pulled a disappearing act and left with scratch? Our secret pact
required that you and I forget why and where
we lost our place when we went off the books.
Could anyone guess, does anyone know or even care
why you and I can't be found, as hard as we look?
Who'll spell out for us, if we exist,
why you and I missed our turn on the list?
Who can stand to reason why you and I let
our union dissolve to strike the orderly alphabet?

ALEIDA RODRÍGUEZ

Born on a kitchen table in Havana, Aleida Rodríguez (b. 1953) came to the United States at the age of nine through Operation Peter Pan. That program allowed 14,000 unaccompanied children to leave Cuba in the early 1960s after the revolution there. She was separated from her parents for two years before they were able to join her in this country. Rodríguez currently lives in Los Angeles, where she works as an editor, translator, and interpreter.

Aleida Rodríguez's first collection, *Garden of Exile* (1999), won the Kathryn A. Morton Prize in Poetry. Marilyn Hacker wrote, "This is a first book of remarkable range and maturity, which, while revealing its roots, displays the fruit and flower of its branches. The river of Rodríguez's memory is fed by two languages, her perceptions have the acuity of double vision."

Her poem "Torch" from *Garden of Exile* draws its energy from the shimmer of the Hollywood starlet. Rodríguez addresses the poem to an elusive "you" who may be the first person costumed as the second. But this direct address draws the reader into a scrumptious fantasy of a femme fatale. The images are retro and alluring. The internal rhyme in the poem intensifies this sense of looking back to a stylish era. The poem makes a pointed comment on the type of love typified by torch songs.

Rodríguez has written of her poem "Extracted," "The day before 9/11/01, the day before the world changed, I was wandering through my garden, when suddenly this poem started coming—in Spanish, of all things. (I translated it into English the next morning, before turning on the TV.) The Spanish words came in a rush, and in very Cuban-inflected, colloquial Spanish—it just slid out slippery as a baby (well, I guess not so easily, given the torturous months of depression and anguish following my mom's death). But later, after it was written, I realized it was in Spanish because it was for my mother." Rodriguez successfully found equivalents in English for some of the complex wordplay in Spanish. The alliteration of "I desire a wordless world" translates the Spanish "deseo el mundo mudo."

Her poem "Apple" explores the strange reality of poems not penned, steps not taken. "'Apple' was written on a friend's couch in Soho," according to Rodríguez, "where I was staying for ten days while doing readings in New York City. I was reading lots of Adam Zagajewski, whom I adore, and I think the poem's mood is substantially influenced by his work: compressed, musical, idea-filled. I had liked that idea from the [Alan] Lightman book *Einstein's Dreams* (1993) for a long time, and suddenly it clicked into place."

TORCH

Light from a dead star—even at the beginning,
her phone messages sounded like that to you,
her voice snappy as women in thirties films:
the wisecracking gun moll with a heart of gold.
Red gowns in windows made you think of her,
bare shoulders evanescent as dreams for the future.
In her apartment, cigarette smoke monogrammed the air,
wafted like strands of hair into her eyes
when she leaned forward or cocked her head, whiskey in hand.
Then the late-night revelations: childhood
leg braces, the reason for the coquettish way
she stands with one leg crossed over the other.
You love this, being let in behind the curtain,
but then there you are, of course—
you hadn't expected to be pulled into this,
one minute watching comfortably from your seat,
the next, stirring risotto at the stove,
tension rising like granite in your shoulders.
When you turn you hope to god
your flushed cheeks can be blamed on the flame
or the wine. The floor, sinking beneath you,
no longer your lousy linoleum.
You sputter, try to cut angles into your voice,
sharp crags to pull yourself out with—
things like *dame* and *swell* and *packin' beat*—
but, face it, she's running the show.
You feel suddenly weak, like you might drop
to your knees right there in the kitchen
and propose. Is this really you, with the moon
in your eyes? The corny words to torch songs
in your head? Dinah Washington
crooning, *If I were a salad I'd be splashin' my dressing.*
If I were a goose I'd be cooked. . . .

EXTRACTED

For my mother (1926–2000)

When I go out to my garden
all I desire is a world with the mute on,
but then here comes my haughty neighbor, the one
who pronounces words wrong in two languages,
the one who thinks he's too smart to work.
Or when I'm crouched beneath the fig tree, searching
for the darkest, sweetest fig—there suddenly appears
my elderly neighbor,
peering between the coral branches of bougainvillea,
offering me bits of her mind
like appetizers.
And it's not that she doesn't please me—
because I do love to see her
so full of life at 85,
so clearheaded, her eyes shining like the windows
of a house well cared for, like hers,
the one she bought in 1947,
the one that's in her own name and not her husband's.
But when I finally leave my work
abandoned inside, on top of my desk,
I desire a wordless world, desire nothing
more than the silent vines of my mind
feeling into dark places—blood-sweet—
like a tongue exploring the hole left by a tooth that's been extracted.

Translated from the Spanish original by Aleida Rodríguez

APPLE

Just as an object may move in three perpendicular
directions, . . . so an object may participate in three
perpendicular futures.

Alan Lightman, *Einstein's Dreams*

I have not written a new poem
in two years, servant to illness and death.
I have voided my dreams and waking hours
with the drugs of distraction and tedium,
antidotes to hope.
Nevertheless, every day paths branch before me
that I do not take, staying indoors,
avoiding the sun's glare and my own failings.
But accidents happen anyway: my life
calls me away, and on the road
temptation blooms, though I barely recognize it,
retired as I am from longing.
No use pursuing—it's cauterized
shut as youth.
But a ghostly part of me rises,
puts on its smoky coat
and departs through my mouth.
I return home with a sense
of having given up
a child for adoption.
For years I'll calculate its age,
conjure up its face—now, then now.
If I had not left my house,

I may never have understood
how the impossible instructs us,
tangible and sweet
as the apple I am savoring,
or as the never path I almost followed,
no less real for its impossibility.

NYC

CORNELIUS EADY

In his books of poetry, Cornelius Eady (b. 1954) makes strong points about many issues, but he's never dogmatic. He knows how to invite Indignation and Absurdity into the same room and to get them to talk to one another.

His honors include the prestigious Lamont Prize from the Academy of American Poets, which he won for his second collection, *Victims of the Latest Dance Craze* (1986). Eady succeeded June Jordan as director of the Poetry Center at the State University of New York at Stony Brook. More recently he has taught at American University in Washington, D.C. and at Notre Dame.

When he reads his poems out loud, Cornelius Eady uses jazz vocalese, as if a saxophone could speak. His reading style is like Charlie Parker playing a riff or like Eddie Jefferson singing words to the tune of a famous instrumental solo. Eady dramatically raises and lowers the pitch and volume of his voice, changes up cadences, and generally amazes the listener. He particularly uses these techniques when he reads the homages to African American musicians and singers in his book *The Autobiography of a Jukebox,* which includes the poem "Chuck Berry," about the early rock 'n' roll pioneer.

His portrait of Chuck Berry is neither a condensed biography nor a description of a photograph. It's a charm bracelet of impressions, partly of Berry's life and thoughts, but partly of the fans who were waiting for his music to rock their lives.

In his recent poems, Cornelius Eady creates and develops points of view from his imagination, lookouts that provide clear lines of sight into the American mind. His book *Brutal Imagination* (2001) uses a unique lens to focus on the persistence of racism in America. In this collection, Eady sometimes speaks through characters who never existed or no longer exist. He adapted the *Running Man* poems from that book into a music-drama in collaboration with the composer Diedre Murray. *Running Man* was produced on stage in New York and was named a Pulitzer Prize finalist in 1999. Eady's other theatrical collaboration with Murray, *You Don't Miss Your Water,* won an Obie award.

The poem "Running Man" concludes the sequence of that name. It's a biting and lyrical account of being a bright young black male in America.

CHUCK BERRY

Hamburger wizard,
Loose-limbed instigator,
V-8 engine, purring for a storm

The evidence of a tight skirt, viewed from
    the window of a moving city bus,
Yelling her name, a spell, into the glass.
The amazing leap, from nobody to stockholder,
(*Look, Ma, no hands*), piped through a hot amp.

Figure skater on the rim of the invisible class wall,
The strength of the dreamer who wakes up, and it's
    Monday, a week of work, but gets out of bed

The unsung desire of the check-out clerk.
The shops of the sleepy backwater town,
    waiting for the kid to make good,
    to chauffeur home

The twang of the New Jersey turnpike
    in the wee, wee hours.
The myth of the lover as he passes, blameless,
    through the walls.

The fury hidden in the word *almost.*
The fury hidden in the word *please.*

The dream of one's name in lights,
Of sending the posse on the wrong trail,
Shaking the wounded Indian's hand, a brother.

The pulse of a crowd, knowing that the police
Have pushed in the door, dancing regardless

The frenzy of the word *go.*
The frenzy of the word *go.*
The frenzy of the word *go.*

The spark between the thought of the kiss
    and receiving the kiss,
The tension in these words:
    You Can't Dance.

The amazing duck walk.
The understanding that all it's going to take
    is one fast song.

The triumph in these words:
    Bye-bye, New Jersey, as if rising
    from a shallow grave.

The soda-jerk who plots doo-wop songs,
The well-intentioned Business School student
    who does what she's told, suspects
    they're keeping it hid.

Mr. Rock-n-Roll-jump-over
    (or get left behind),
Mr. *Taxes? Who, me?* Money beat,
Money beat, you can't catch me,
    (but they do),

A perpetual well of quarters in the pocket.
The incalculable hit of energy in the voice
    of a 16-year-old as her favorite band
    hits the stage,

And 10,000 pair of eyes look for what they're after:
    More.
And 10,000 voices roar for it:
    More.

And a multitude you wouldn't care to count
    surrounds the joint, waits for their opportunity
    to break in.

RUNNING MAN

I am the running man.
The shadow in the corner
Of your eye,

The reason a grove of trees
Turns sinister in the dark.

Why not
Is my blood,
My story,
My middle name.

God made me pretty.
God made me smart.
God made me black,
Which only proves

God's infinite sense of humor.

Where I come from,
A smart black boy
Is like being a cat
With a duck's bill.

Where I live
The neighbors say
He's so bright
But mean
He's so white

And stare in awe
And pity as
I keep turning
Pages.

Call me a
Useless miracle.

Until my eyes
Fell upon the
Page,
I was just
A drowsy boy.

I admit the words
Tickled my ear
And shook
My tongue
My teeth,

I'm sure it looked
Like violation.

I'm sure it looked like
Anger, slowly
Rinsing over
My body.

I was talking
In another tongue,
The language
That measured
Me and mine
Less,

The civilized tones
Which burned
And noosed
And dusted our roofs
With never enough.

Perhaps my folks withdrew
From the sight
Of me, eyes
Thrilled

As the words
Chose me.

I am the running man.
The chill you feel
Blowing out
A back alley.

When you say *no*
But mean *yes*
You have passed
My doorstep.

I am whispered.
I rise on anger's
Updrafts.

Where in the world
Will he land,
Worried my folks,
This pretty black
Hatchling?
What pushes him up

Will keep him down.

LUIS J. RODRIGUEZ

"By [age] 12 he was a veteran of East L.A. gang warfare, running from rival Sangra gang members and grieving the death of his best friend, who fell through a skylight as the two were being chased by police," reads a *Los Angeles Times* piece on Luis Rodriguez (b. 1954). As a young man, Rodriguez served half a dozen jail sentences for a variety of crimes, ranging from robbery to fire bombing to drive-by shooting. His addictions have included heroin, PCP, and alcohol. He has endured homelessness. Rodriguez's past is the subject of his well-known memoir *Always Running: La Vida Loca, Gang Days in L.A.* (1993).

But Luis Rodriguez survived his gang days, and he has built a life for himself as a poet, prose writer, editor, publisher, and community activist. He is an institution builder, founder of Tia Chucha Press, which has showcased many poets; and of Tia Chucha's Café Cultural in the Northeast San Fernando Valley. Both the press and the café are named for his beloved eccentric aunt who first exposed him to poetry and music. Rodriguez also started Youth Struggling for Survival to help gang members change their lives, and in his spare time, he created the Dos Manos record label.

Rodriguez likes to perform his poems accompanied by a funk band called Seven Rabbit. The backup music is composed by Ernie Perez, and has a danceable 1970s groove. "My Name's Not Rodriguez" is the title song from his first album. In the song, he actually attacks his own last name because of its *conquistador* associations. He prefers to connect with his Indian ancestry, insisting that his real name is "a warrior's saliva on arrow tip, a jaguar's claw, / a woman's enticing contours on volcanic rock."

"Victory, Victoria, My Beautiful Whisper" is a tender poem to his daughter, whom he admits to failing when she was in his care and he was still young and drinking heavily. He offers the poem to her, even though his words "cannot take back the thorns / of falling roses." *Muñeca* is an affectionate term for a pretty girl, though it literally means "doll."

"Meeting the Animal in Washington Square Park" is a character sketch, like one a street artist would draw. The character is the memorable Animal, a boxer and former gang member from Rodriguez's neighborhood in East L.A. Their encounter is rough but sweet. Their contrasting fates and rival gang origins threaten to distance them from one another. Rodriguez is conscious of having become a widely published writer, while his homeboy is living on the streets in New York.

MY NAME'S NOT RODRIGUEZ

My name's not Rodriguez.
It is a sigh of climbing feet,
the lather of gold lust,
the slave masters' religion
with crippled hands gripping greed's tail.
My name's not Rodriguez.
It's an Indian mother's noiseless cry,
a warrior's saliva on arrow tip, a jaguar's claw,
a woman's enticing contours on volcanic rock.
My real name's the ash of memory from burned trees.
It's the three-year-old child wandering in the plain
and shot by U.S. Cavalry in the Sand Creek massacre.
I'm a Geronimo's yell into the canyons of the old ones.
I'm the Comanche scout; the Raramuri shaman
in soiled bandanna running in the wretched rain.
I'm called Rodriguez and my tears leave rivers of salt.
I'm Rodriguez and my skin dries on the bones.
I'm Rodriguez and a diseased laughter enters the pores.
I'm Rodriguez and my father's insanity
blocks every passageway,
scorching the walls of every dwelling.
My name's not Rodriguez; it's a fiber in the wind,
it's what oceans have immersed,
it's what's graceful and sublime over the top of peaks.
what grows red in desert sands.
It's the crawling life, the watery breaths between ledges.
It's taut drum and peyote dance.
It's the brew from fermented heartaches.
Don't call me Rodriguez unless you mean peon and sod carrier,
unless you mean slayer of truths and deep-sixer of hopes.
Unless you mean forget and then die.
My name's the black-hooded 9mm-wielding child in all our alleys.
I'm death row monk. The eight-year-old gum seller

in city bars and taco shops.
I'm unlicensed, uninsured, unregulated, and unforgiven.
I'm free and therefore hungry.
Call me Rodriguez and bleed in shame.
Call me Rodriguez and forget your own name.
Call me Rodriguez and see if I whisper in your ear,
mouth stained with bitter wine.

VICTORY, VICTORIA, MY BEAUTIFUL WHISPER
(*for Andrea Victoria*)

You are the daughter who is sleep's beauty.
You are the woman who birthed my face.
You are a cloud creeping across the shadows,
drenching sorrows into heart-sea's terrain.
Victory, Victoria, my beautiful whisper:
how as a baby you laughed into my neck
when I cried at your leaving
after your mother and I broke up;
how at age three you woke me up from stupid
so I would stop peeing into your toy box
in a stupor of resentment and beer;
and how later, at age five, when I moved in
with another woman who had a daughter about your age,
you asked: "how come *she* gets to live with Daddy?"
        Muñeca, these words cannot traverse the stone
path of our distance; they cannot take back the thorns
of falling roses that greet your awakenings.
These words are from places too wild for hearts to gallop,
too cruel for illusions, too dead for your eternal
gathering of flowers. But here they are, weary offerings
from your appointed father, your anointed man-guide;
make of them your heart's bed.

MEETING THE ANIMAL IN WASHINGTON SQUARE PARK

The acrobats were out in Washington Square Park,
flaying arms and colors: the jokers and break
dancers, the singers and mimes. I pulled out
of a reading at New York City College
and watched a crowd gather around a young man
jumping over 10 garbage cans from a skateboard.
Then out of the side of my eye I saw someone
who didn't seem to belong here, like I didn't
belong. He was a big man, six feet and more,
with tattoos on his arms, back, stomach and neck.
On his abdomen were the words in huge old English
lettering: Hazard. I knew this guy, I knew that place.
I looked closer. It had to be him. It was—Animal!
From East L.A. World heavyweight contender,
the only Chicano from L.A. ever ranked
in the top ten of the division. The one who
went toe-to-toe with Leon Spinks and even
made Muhammad Ali look the other way.
Animal! I yelled. "Who the fuck are you?" he asked,
a quart of beer in his grasp, eyes squinting.
My name's Louie—from East L.A. He brightened. "East L.A.!
Here in Washington Square Park? Man, we everywhere!"
The proverbial "what part of East L.A.?" came next.
But I gave him a shock. From La Gerahty, I said.
That's the mortal enemy of the Big Hazard
gang of the Ramona Gardens Housing Projects.
"I should kill you," Animal replied. If we were in
L.A., I suppose you would—but we in New York City, man.
"I should kill you anyway."
Instead he thrust out his hand with the beer and offered
me a drink. We talked—about what happened since he stopped
boxing. About the time I saw him at the Cleland House
arena looking over some up-and-coming fighters.

How he had been to prison, and later ended up homeless
in New York City, with a couple of kids somewhere.
And there he was, with a mortal enemy from East L.A.,
talking away. I told him how I was now a poet,
doing a reading at City College, and he didn't wince
or looked surprised. Seemed natural. Sure. A poet
from East L.A. That's the way it should be. Poet
and boxer. Drinking beer. Among the homeless,
the tourists and acrobats. Mortal enemies.
When I told him I had to leave, he said "go then,"
but soon shook my hand, East L.A. style, and walked off.
"Maybe, someday, you'll do a poem about me, eh?"
Sure, Animal, that sounds great.
Someday, I'll do a poem about you.

MARILYN CHIN

In her poetry and her life, Marilyn Chin (b. 1955) bridges two cultures. She was born in Hong Kong but raised in Portland, Oregon. Chin made a conscious decision to fold into her American free verse the literary styles of classical Chinese poetry. She also inserts the history, culture, and philosophies of China—and the stories of Chinese immigrants to the United States.

Her credits include co-editing *Dissident Song: A Contemporary Asian American Anthology* (1991) with David Wong Louie and co-translating *The Selected Poems of Ai Qing* (2001) with Eugene Eoyang.

In her own writing Chin sees with dual vision—through the lens of a person who grew up in the United States, and from the viewpoint of someone who feels the resonance of Asian culture in surprising places. In "Urban Love Poem" from the book *The Phoenix Gone, The Terrace Empty* (1994), a gingko in California, where Chin lives, reminds her of the tree's proud Chinese origin, when it was cultivated by an emperor. In the midst of city pollution, the gingko tree seems as displaced and moving as a foreigner lost in an unfamiliar setting. Even in this strange land, though, the poem maintains there is room for gathering jonquils for a lover.

In "Elegy for Chloe Nguyen," Chin describes the two edges of assimilation in America. Her friend Chloe is precocious in every way, walking at five months, speaking three languages as a baby, sexually active before her teenage years. She is a brilliant scholar, fulfilling the expectations of the "model minority" Asian American, but the languages she learns never bolster her soul. Chloe Nguyen seems to fly high but is never grounded in a way that sustains her.

In the poem "Is It Snowing in Guangzhou?," Chin creates new forms. The structure of the poem allows her to respond to her own questions with self-assertion, humor, and doubt, depending on her mood. She wonders how ethnic or how American she can allow herself to be. This dilemma is embodied in her choices about hairstyle—she used to sport a traditional jade pin, but now she colors her hair with henna.

URBAN LOVE POEM

1)

Condominium, stiff bamboo,
refuses to bend in the wind,
squats in the sinking earth
like a thin-hipped dowager.
You arrange the amenities
and we pay the rent. So, please,
don't fall as civilizations fall
in the comfort of night.

2)

Gingko, vomit-eater of the metropolis,
city's oxygen, small men's shadow,
your gentle bark can't protect you now.
One pellicle, another, falls
on the land of your displacement.
Where is the Yellow Emperor who nurtured you?
Where is your birthplace,
the Yangtze, the Pearl?

3)

Hong Kong, San Francisco, San Jose,
the path through the "Golden Mountains"
is a three-tiered freeway. Look up:
it suspends where no prophet can touch.
A quick fix in your veins; a white rush in my mind—
you cry, "Mei Ling, Mei Ling, once
we could've had everything:
the talent, the courage, the wherewithal."

4)
Oh, the small delectables of day:
persimmons from Chinatown,
a stroll through the Tenderloin
with the man I love.

My darling, please, don't be sad.
I've parked my horse
in this gray, gray sunrise
to gather sweet crocuses and jonquils
for you.

ELEGY FOR CHLOE NGUYEN
(1955–1988)

Chloe's father is a professor of linguistics.
Mine runs a quick-you-do-it Laundromat in Chinatown.
If not pretty, at least I'm clean.

Bipedal in five months, trilingual in a year,
at eleven she had her first lover.

Here's a photo of Chloe's mother in the kitchen
making petit fours, petit fours that are very pretty.
Here's my mother picking pears, picking pears
for a self-made millionaire grower.

The night when Chloe died, her father sighed,
"Chloe was my heart; Chloe was my life!"

One day under an earthen black sky
and the breeze brushing our adolescent pinafores,
a star fell—or was it a satellite
exploding into a bonfire at the horizon?
Chloe said, "This is how I want to die,
with a bang and not with a flicker."

Oh, Chloe, eternally sophomore and soporific!
Friend of remote moribund languages!
Chloe read Serbo-Croatian, the Latin of Horace.
She understood Egyptian hieroglyphics, the writing of the tombs.
The tongues of the living, the slangs of the dead—
in learning she had no rival.

Then came the lovers of many languages
to quell her hunger, her despair.
Each night they whispered, "Chloe, you are beautiful."
Then left her with an empty sky in the morning.

Chloe, can you hear me? Is it better in heaven?
Are you happier in hell? This week I don't understand the lesson
being a slow learner—except for the one about survival.
And Death, I know him well . . .

He followed my grandfather as a puff of opium,
my father as a brand new car.
Rowed the boat with my grandmother,
blowing gales into my mother's ear.
Wrapped his arms around my asthmatic sister,
but his comforting never won us over.

Yes, Death is a beautiful man,
and the poor don't need dowries to court him.
His grassy hand, his caliph—you thought you could master.

Chloe, we are finally Americans now. Chloe, we are here!

IS IT SNOWING IN GUANGZHOU?

1)
Is this too dark?
I mean—my new henna.

Is this too pale?
This fresh makeup
that comes off on my pillow.

Is this too coy?
"I part my gauze curtains slowly."

Should I tell you my name?
The familial and the diminuitive.

2)
Is this a metaphor?
"A red-naped insect."

And this?
"A woman walking like a line of ancient waka into the rain."

Is "Black-eyed Susans on a hillock"—
the collective unconscious?

3)
Where is my jade hairpin?
My, aren't you a materialist!

Where is my jade hairpin?
I gave it away; your grandmother will be angry.

Where is my jade hairpin?
If you've borrowed it, please return it!

Then, in turn, I shall return it
back to the Spring and Autumn period
from whence it came.

4)
Is it snowing in Guangzhou?
No, friend, never
in the southernmost province.

Is it snowing in Heilongjiang?
How do I know, I have never been there.

Is it snowing in Beijing?
In that little lane named *Fangfa.*

Note:
fangfa—double entendre, meaning:
1) method, the way of doing things
2) the blossoming of flowers

DIONISIO D. MARTÍNEZ

Dionisio Martínez (b. 1956) is a passionate enthusiast of literature, art, and music. He loves to comb old record stores for vinyl treasures. His eclectic taste in music runs the full range from the acid rock guitar of Jimi Hendrix to the work of the modern Brazilian composer Heitor Villa-Lobos. This love of culture, both refined and popular, figures often in his poems.

Martínez was born in Cuba in 1956. His parents went into exile in 1965 following the Cuban Revolution, and Martínez then lived in Spain and in California. Since 1972, he has resided in Tampa, Florida, where he works as a teacher and consultant. Martínez's first full-length collection, *History as a Second Language* (1993), won the Ohio State University Press / *The Journal* Award in Poetry. In Jorie Graham's introduction to his third book, *Climbing Back* (2001), which she selected for the National Poetry Series, she describes his writing as "heart-breaking, overstuffed, seeping with history, lonelier than imaginable and truly in-the-face of American culture."

In "Bad Alchemy," the title poem of Martínez's second book (1999), the poet brings together a space launching, the death of the speaker's father, the advice on grief of a former lover, and an unforgettable story about lightning. The launch of the space shuttle toward the heavens is linked in the speaker's mind to his father, since it took place the day after his parent died. The shuttle crew is also otherworldly—anonymous because of a news blackout. The speaker's grief is compounded by recollections of his breakup with his lover. In the figure of the man hit by lightning, Martínez masterfully brings together all the disparate elements of the poem.

"Need" creates a moving scene of the relationship between the speaker's parents. Martínez uses a fascinating pun to describe his parents' marriage: "Calling her his love / would have torn all those ambiguous bonds that make / love remotely possible." The word "remotely" is used in two senses here. The speaker's father has a need for distance, but in measuring that distance, the speaker acknowledges his mother's frustration with great sensitivity.

BAD ALCHEMY

You missed it by a day—the shuttle Atlantis
with its secret cargo looking for what's
left of the sky. It was my first sighting
of a night launch, the reds and greens like fallen

stars going home again. My entire block was out,
all of us shielding our eyes as if it were daytime.
One gets used to the days so easily here—
they seem to go on too long, then

vanish overnight. In no time, the fireball
was out of our lives. The neighbor with the best
view says the cape is practically across
the street if you measure the distance as the crow

flies, but all birds look the same to me,
and what do I know about flight?
I'm thinking *navigation* and how little the word
has to do with the sky.

Because the government has imposed a news blackout,
we must imagine the ghost crew navigating;
that is, sailing the rivers of the sky.
A friend recently told me that she noticed

how I've stopped talking about my father.
The day he died, I swore I saw him row
up a shallow river in the sky, a kind of secret
mission. You kept me on the phone for hours,

nearly convinced me that grief
is a town with two roads out. Maybe just
one if you spend the night with the bartender.
Oh, you and your cognac cures. It was always

you and your cognac—even on those nights
at the Chatterbox when the man
at the piano bar didn't show. Even after the money
ran out and the house on Cedar Avenue

began to fall, everything spilling out of our lives
like slow rivers of lightning in the sky.
What do I say now? Be careful with lightning?
I was doomed or blessed to love a woman who

understands the body too well. She tells me about
lightning, how electrical burns leave a mark
when they enter the body and a mark when they leave.
Everything between the two points—the whole crazy

path carved inside us—is instantly scorched.
Like the Midas touch in reverse, I start to think.
Then she tells me how a man, after being hit
by lightning, drove to the hospital calmly,

feeling absolutely no pain. She says he looked
so beautiful—the victim of a perfect
tan—as he walked into the emergency room.
The doctors knew. The doctors had seen

other bodies this beautiful, and they knew
the inevitable end of all beauty,
the bad alchemy that turns bronze to ash.
Once you're burned you're dead, she tells me.

The man didn't know it. He couldn't feel
his insides turning brittle at first.
Gradually, the tan began to harden, the body
began to figure out that it was dead.

One by one, the cells gave up. The doctors
explained the options to the man and to the man's
family, but only the man understood.
They could cut away all the dead tissue,

all the useless parts of the body.
But what would remain? the man wanted to know.
There would be a torso, maybe an arm,
definitely the shoulders and everything above them.

The man imagined himself literally half a man—
maybe much less—yet whole, and decided
he could live like that. You must know
how the will to live is a magnet and suddenly

north is anything that moves. You, with your love
for the fire that loves our bodies to death,
should know well. The man said yes, said
he'd go on regardless of the losses, which became

increasingly insignificant and real.
But while he slept, his family prayed for what
they thought was best, and everyone who had never
been burned nodded, winked, raised a thumb.

NEED

The things you need to live, the people
you love to death—what would you call them tonight

if your life depended on the truth? Let's say a man
breaks into your house, holds

a knife to your throat and makes you call
your wife by her proper name. Suppose you call out

another woman's name. By now all the names
have become one: hers. But you don't know

if you'd be this confident with a knife so close
that the light bouncing off the blade

makes you squint. The Eskimo who shields
his eyes from the sun rising on his white-

on-white world has no all-encompassing word
for snow; instead, he names

each kind of snow as if it bore no relation
to all the other kinds. My father never called

my mother by her name. He even avoided
terms of endearment, fearing that they would gradually

take the place of that name. Calling her his love
would have torn all those ambiguous bonds that make

love remotely possible. My father would start to talk,
assuming that my mother knew she was being addressed.

LI-YOUNG LEE

Li-Young Lee was born in 1957 in Jakarta into an unusual family. His father was Mao Tse-Tung's personal physician and his mother came of Chinese royal ancestry. Lee's family fled political persecution in China, only to find discrimination in their new home in Indonesia. After Lee's father was imprisoned and released, the family moved from Hong Kong to Macao and Japan before coming to the United States.

Li-Young Lee now lives in Chicago with his extended family, including his wife and children. Unlike many poets, who are often ensconced in academia, Li-Young Lee works in a book warehouse.

Lee's second book, *The City in Which I Love You* (1990), was the Lamont Poetry Selection of the Academy of American Poets in 1990. In his next volume, *Book of My Nights* (2001), he shifted from autobiographical material to a more meditative, surreal vision where he approached the craft of writing as a spiritual discipline.

"Tearing the Page" is a wistful look at how children come to grips with time and knowledge. The opening line, "Every wise child is sad," conjures up the mnemonic device used to teach music students the notes on the lines in the treble clef: Every Good Boy Deserves Fudge. The lines in Lee's poem continue the variation on this theme. The language appears unadorned but exciting to unwrap: "Every prince is a member of the grass." The past and the future seem to press down on the child in the poem, and time often has a physical presence, as in the train called The Twentieth Century. (Lee got the idea for this poem when he heard an announcement for this train's departure at Union Station in Chicago.) Part of what the child knows is incomplete, such as how to tie shoes but not how to unknot them. What the child actually knows well—the harmony of his heart and his games and songs—he can't reveal.

"Become Becoming" imagines a time when the dualisms of life are fused. In gorgeous imagery, the poet describes a state of unity between the mortal and the immortal: "Then you can trade places with the wind." Again, childhood seems to be the time when knowledge both pools and divides.

TEARING THE PAGE

Every wise child is sad.

Every prince is a member of the grass.

Each bud opening opens on the unforeseen.

Every wind-strewn flower is God tearing God.

And the stars are leaves
blown across my grandmother's lap.
Or the dew multiplying.

And of time's many hands, who can tell
the bloody from the perfumed,

the one that stitches
from the one that rips.

Every laughing child is forgetful.
Every solitary child rules the universe.

And the child who can't sleep
learns to count, a patient child.

And the child who counts negotiates
between limit and longing,
infinity and subtraction.

Every child who listens
all night to the wind eventually

knows his breathing turns a wheel
pouring time and dream to leave no trace.

Though he can't tell what a minute weighs,
or is an hour too little or too long.

As old as night itself,
he's not old enough in the morning
to heat his milk on the stove.

But he knows about good-byes.
Some of them, anyway.
The good-bye at the door each day, a kiss for a kiss.
The good-bye at bedtime,
stories and songs until it's safe to close his eyes.

And maybe he's even heard about the waiting room
at Union Station, where dust and echoes climb
to the great skylights

accompanied by farewells
of the now-going, to join the distant
farewells of the long gone,

while a voice announces the departure
of the Twentieth Century for all points West.

Yes, every wise child is heart-broken.
A sorrowing pip,

he knows the play
he's called away from each evening
is the beginning and end of order
in a human household.

He's sure his humming to himself
and his rising and falling ball are appointed
by ancient laws his own heart-tides obey.

But he can't tell anybody what he knows.

Old enough to knot his shoelaces,
he's not old enough to unknot them.

Old enough to pray, he doesn't always
know who to pray to.

Old enough to know to close the window
when it storms, old enough to know the rain,
given the chance, would fall on him,

and darken him, and darken him, the way
he himself colors the figures
he draws, pressing so hard he tears the page.

BECOME BECOMING

Wait for evening.
Then you'll be alone.

Wait for the playground to empty.
Then call out those companions from childhood:

The one who pretended to be dead.
The one to whom you told every secret.
The one who made a world of any hiding place.

And don't forget the one who listened
in silence while you wondered:

Is the universe an empty mirror? A flowering tree?
Hourglass, birdcage, quiver of arrows,

mind itself, is the universe the sleep of a woman?
Does she carry inside her,
without her knowing it yet,

the word at the end of the story of time?

Wait for evening.
Then you'll remember the answer.

Wait for that color behind the trees.
That's the color of *Amen.*

All of time began
when you first answered
to the names your mother and father gave you.

Soon those names will travel with the leaves.
Then you can trade places with the wind.

Soon you'll recall that old story beginning
with the great herds of stars at pasture.

And time.   Does time blossom?   Ripen?
Or branch in two directions, seen and unseen?

And what is flesh?   Some pollen?   Perfume?   The very sap?
The bread that rises in a house that fails,
what table fathered it?

Just wait.   Soon you'll remember.   Soon you'll hear
the singing that en-trances the seed
of each fruit that wakes

falling.   Soon
you'll become becoming.

CARL PHILLIPS

Carl Phillips (b. 1959) often writes poetry in long, halting sentences, draped over three-line stanzas. The line breaks slice his ideas into discrete moments of thought. His syntax is unexpected, at times completely unlike everyday speech. His phrases have the intricate and flexible grammar of Latin or ancient Greek, traditions that Phillips knows well; he has co-translated Sophocles' tragedy *Philoctetes* (2003). He is highly conscious of what he has termed "momentum in the act of reading." The elaborate stop-and-go of meaning in his poems allows for subtleties of emotion and an elegance of pace.

Jorie Graham has written of his poems, "Phillips addresses not only passion, but art, history, nature: all in his hands forms of wanting. His rhythms beautifully and powerfully various—sinewy, majestic, casual, adamant—he modulates from honesty to honesty. . . ."

Phillips's volume *From the Devotions* (1998) was nominated for a National Book Award. His collection *Cortège* (1995) was a finalist for the National Book Critics Circle Award and the Lambda Literary Award.

His poem "Loose Hinge," from the book *Rock Harbor* (2002), seems dense, but close reading reveals a network of connections. It begins with an address to an intimate about the body. Paradoxically, it is both the body's endurance and its fragility that make it deserving of love. In another seeming contradiction, constraint raises language to the freedom of song. The mention of song turns the poem to a traditional topic of bards—the hero. Phillips alludes to two: King Arthur pulling the sword from the stone, and Aeneas, whose golden bough allowed him entrance to the Underworld. Heroes turn out to be similar to traitors in the inevitability of their fate. That brings the poem around to betrayal, particularly betrayal in love. Again the poet addresses the intimate, but now his mood is intently emotional. The lover has betrayed his trust. As clearly as mushrooms sprouting after rain, the lover has turned out to be not an exception, but an example of the rule—love is fickle. The poem has come full circle back to the body.

"As a Blow, from the West" relates the speaker's dream. Passion is often called "volcanic," but the volcano this couple lives near is almost extinct. It's surrounded by a fading sea called Friendship. The speaker's final appeal in the poem's last lines can be seen in this light. This poem is also a manifesto. The speaker confesses to being bored by what comes easily to poetry—flowers and names for the moon (this is what the poem's opening lines allude to). What interests him instead is "the illicit."

LOOSE HINGE

Of the body: most,
its resilience, have you
not loved that, its—its

endingness,
that too?
And the unwitting

prayer getting made
between them,
as when we beat at

what is closed,
closed against us, and call
the beating, in time,

song. To have been
among the hands
for which the stone lets go

its sword,
or the tree its gold
crepitating

bough,
what must that
feel like? With what speed

does the hero grow
used to—necessarily—
the world's surrender

until—how
else—how call it
strange, how

not inevitable? Heroes,
in this way at least, resembling
the damned

who are damned
as traitors, some
singing *We could not*

help it, others
Fate,
Circumstance,

X
made me—as if
betrayal required more than

one party, which it
does not.
Admit it: you gave

yourself away. We are
exactly what
we are, as you

suspected, and—
like that—the world
obliging with its fair

examples: rain and,
under it, the yard
an overnight field

of mushrooms,
the wet of them, the yellow-
white of, the

nothing-at-all, outside
themselves, they
stood for. You've been

a seeming
exception only. Hot;
relentless. Yourself the rule.

AS A BLOW, FROM THE WEST

Names for the moon:
Harvest; and Blue; and
Don't Touch Me—

and Do. I dreamed I had
made a home on the side
of a vast, live volcano,

that the rest was water,
that I was one among many of
no distinction: we but

lived there, like so many
birds that, given the chance
not to fly for once in

formation, won't take it, or
cannot, or—or—but
what of choice can a bird know?

Down the volcano's sides,
in the pose of avalanche
except frozen, and so

densely it seemed impossible
they should not strangle
one another—yet they

did not—grew all
the flowers whose names
I'd meant to master;

it was swift, the dream—so
much, still, to catch
up to—though I could not

have known that, of course,
then: isn't it only in
the bracing and first wake of

loss that we guess most cleanly
the speed with which what held us
left us? In the dream, the world

was birdless, lit, yielding, it
seemed safe, which is not to say
you weren't in it. You were, but

changed somewhat, not so much
a man of few words,
more the look of one who

—having entered willfully
some danger, having just returned
from it—chooses instead

of words his body as
the canvas across which to
wordlessly broadcast his coming

through. We lived
in a manner that—if it
didn't suggest an obliviousness

to a very real and always-there
danger—I would call heady;
it was not that. Think,

rather, of the gods: how,
if they do in fact know
everything, they must understand

also they will be eventually
overthrown by a new order,
which is at worst a loss

of power, but not of life,
as the gods know it. I was
not, that is, without

ambition: the illicit, in
particular, I would make it
my business to have studied;

and of that which is gained
easily, to want none
of it. Flowers; names

for the moon. It was
swift, the dream, the body
a wordless and stalled

avalanche that, since forgivable—
if I could—I would forgive, poor
live but flagging, dying now

volcano. And the water
around its sides receding with
a dream's swiftness: everywhere,

soon, sand and sand, a desert that,
because there was no water,
and because they missed it,

the natives had called a sea, and
to the sea had given a name:
Friendship, whose literal

translation in the country of
dream is roughly "that which
all love evolves

down to"—

Until to leave, or
try to—and have drowned

trying—becomes refrain,
the one answer each time
to whatever question:

what was the place called?

what was the house like?

what was it we did inside it?

how is it possible that it cannot be enough to have given
up to you now the dream as—for a time, remember—I did give

my truest self? why won't you take it—if a gift, if yours?

FRANK PAINO

Frank Paino was born in 1960 in Cleveland and grew up in Ohio. Like many artists, he has found refuge working as a staff member at a college.

Paino has two volumes of poetry: *The Rapture of Matter* (1991) and *Out of Eden* (1997). His work from the period when he wrote these books, published under his former name, Frankie Paino, was widely hailed, and was anthologized in *New American Poets of the '90s* (1991) and *Poets for Life* (1989). He won a Pushcart Prize and the Cleveland Arts Prize in Literature.

Roger Weingarten has praised the "almost unbearable beauty" in his poetry. Beckian Fritz Goldberg has said of his writing, "Seductive, edgy, gothic and sublime, these poems haunt the body as much as the soul." And David Wojahn: "By turns fervent, elegiac, and dizzying in their momentum, the poems cast a powerful spell . . . Frankie Paino writes poems as though her life depended on them." Paino's work describes a desperate tug of war between the mortal and the spiritual. What's intriguing about his poems is that the battle is so hard fought, and there is never a clear winner.

In the late 1990s, Paino lost close family members to illness. He also decided to undergo a sex change and to legally switch first names from Frankie to Frank. During this time, Paino stopped writing, and only in recent years has he started creating poems under his new name.

In his poems, Paino likes to portray artists from the past, from Oscar Wilde to Johannes Vermeer. His writing stares down hard moments in these lives and weaves in imagery as lush as a Pre-Raphaelite painting. He also uses his phenomenal gift for description to tear a page from his daily life and turn it into an illuminated manuscript.

In "The Truth" from *Out of Eden,* the speaker tells the story of a father's last hours. The poem explores the tension between faith in the afterlife and the stark reality of watching a loved one die. Despite the realistic approach of the poem, the father's death never becomes ugly or meaningless. It is bathed in emotion, import, and an eerie luminescence.

"Each Bone of the Body," also from *Out of Eden,* is a poem that meanders from medical terminology to a recent affair to biblical story to memories of a Catholic education. All these twine to create a tapestry on the sacred nature of the physical world. As in much of Paino's work, religious imagery and sensuality are linked in a way that heightens both, till the poem rises to a fevered temperature.

THE TRUTH

My father died near evening, having spent
most of the day straining towards that closure.
In the end, I watched the monitor count down
the beats of his heart's surrender, his eyes
fixed on nothing I could see, though I'd like to believe
he was looking *at* something, his own father, say,
coming to show him the path into a different world.

I never knew dying could take such effort, as if Death,
at the last, pulls back his outstretched hand
and we must chase after the shroud of his dark wings.
All day I'd held my father's hand, leaned over
his thin form the way I remember he'd leaned over my bed
when I was a child. I ran my fingers through his fine, black
hair, matching my breath to the respirator's hiss—

as if desire alone could save him. The truth is,
I wanted nothing more than a flat line on the screen,
the steady hum which means the heart has lost its music,
blood going cool and blue in the veins. I wanted
it to be the way that cliché goes, the one which says
we don't die, really, we just go to sleep. But his heart
refused romantic notions, hammering an unsteady beat

hours after I told the doctor to disengage the machine
which kept the pulse constant against his body's will.
I started to write how his muscles, deprived of oxygen,
rippled like the smooth flanks of horses in the home stretch,
that graceful and sure, but it's a lie—the truth is,
the spasms were strong enough to make our own hearts
quicken, our arms strain as his head slipped over the pillow,

his legs quivering, pitiful. I wanted to tell you I saw
a boy, slight and beautiful, leaning against the waiting room
door, his right shoulder transparent, half in, half out
of the dark oak grain, as if he wanted me to see there is a life
beyond the one we know. But that, too, would be a lie.
The truth is, that room was empty except for the boys on t.v.,
the ones in Soweto who doused a man with gasoline, set him

alight, his head engulfed in flame like an infernal nimbus,
fire folding its terrible arms around him as he fell
to the ground, silent as snow. When my father died
the sun was just beginning to set. Friday. High summer.
Though I couldn't see them from the tight, dim room, I knew
cars crowded the streets, everyone anxious to get home where,
perhaps, someone else waited. Or maybe it was just solitude

they rushed toward. I didn't begrudge them such happiness,
but blessed their ignorance as they squinted against the light,
cursed the grass, too long to be ignored, and the mailbox
with its freight of bills, news, catalogues which promised
to satisfy any desire. Standing by my father's bed, I needed
him to live because my own heart was breaking. The truth is,
we never have all we need. I came to understand how my hand

grasping his must have made him hesitate between two
worlds, the way a child learning to swim glances from
a parent's hand to the pool's blue-green shimmer, then back
again, or maybe the way I hope those boys in Soweto paused
before they turned toward their neighbor, small fires
in their palms fingering air. My father moved his head
against his shoulder as if, already, he were looking back

at us from some vast distance. Perhaps Death is more timid than we
imagine, slipping off the soul the way love might begin
with the shy undoing of an evening gown. I held on to my
father's feet—how elegant they were, even then, like the feet
of a Bernini seraph, sleek, cool, too perfect to believe
they'd carried him through the world so long, and finally,
to that bed. I didn't want to hold him back but, if

such a thing is possible, to push his spirit out
through the crown of his head, give him the power to rise
from that body, its twisted spine, thighs thin, hollow, ready
for flight, and the cancer we'd measured in the deliberate
spreading of red, mottled skin like a map being drawn in front
of our eyes. What world, I wonder, did it describe?
We talked about the times my sister and I went with him

after bluegill, grayling, bass—the week in Canada
we didn't catch a thing, the evenings loons would cry
across still water while we sat around a fire,
our faces amber, otherworldly in that light. It must have
been those memories which gave him strength to move
towards that other shore which only the dead can know,
where perhaps he rose from dark waters deep as sleep

and remembered this life as a dream. In his room the monitor
pushed an incandescent line across its screen as if to
underscore mortality. A nurse removed the needles, the tube
which ran like a tap root into the sweet cave of my father's
chest. His mouth, open, filled with the machine's emerald glow,
as if the tongue he now spoke were a language of light. Sometimes
we have nothing to grasp but such implausible fire. Just that.

EACH BONE OF THE BODY

sounds like prayer, sacrum,
sternum, scapula, as if those
who first regarded, then named
them, belonged to an ancient cult
of architects who built temples
which resembled human forms
with limbs outstretched so that
they faced the stars like stars
and offered back this planet's
elements as five spokes
on a spinning wheel.

If each bone of the body *is* holy
it is because it gives shape
to mortal love—bowl of the pelvis
like a cradle, sickles of the hips
like two moons, every angle
open as the mouth to a kiss,
even though we will all be torn
one day from the comfort
of our usual orbits, and broken.

Yesterday, a woman I didn't know
unbuttoned her blouse slow
as the unraveling of a long summer morning,
held the violet silk slightly
apart like those statues of Christ
from my youth with his private
smile red as the hook and eye
of a surgeon's needle, his crimson
nimbus, cold fingers resting
against his quiet stone heart

which was forever on fire, wounded,
crowned with bloody thorns
and worn like false regret, or like
a ghastly pendant hung
at the precise center of his chest.

Once I believed
love was like that. A cruelty
which haunted the empire
of my childhood with the hushed
voices of black-robed nuns
who spoke of Adam's ripped side,
how God drove his fist in
until that first man fell
silent, then snapped off
a single rib which looked, at first,
like the waxing moon until
he crushed it beneath his
heels like dust, mixed in blood
from the season's first kill,
then gave it to the wind for form,
to the man who called that
new shape Eve, though she cared
little for his list of rules
and names, preferred instead slender
throats of irises, pomegranates
with their skins of fire, the orb
of gold at morning, silver-black
at night, and the circular logic
of stars. She was judged to be
too much in love with the sleek
tongues of fallen angels,
the taste of what was sweet and forbidden

and sin. What could she say
except that she loved the heft
of her bones, the way her mouth
had wrapped around the promise
of knowing all there was to know?

In a room whose battered wooden
floor was always covered with
thick curls of white wax, and so
seemed in perpetual winter,
Sister Ignatius would read aloud to us
from a book of martyrs bound
in sanguine leather—those who
were wrapped in sheaves
of wheat, set as torches against
night, whose skin was slipped
off like clothes before love—
stones, arrows, hooks
in the glistening air. Teeth of the lion,
claw of the bear, the wheel
in flames on the hill. Sebastian,
Agnes, Catherine, Paul, all
destined for statues and stained
glass, blood being the coin
and currency of paradise.

Once, I believed faith was a gift
which would help me turn
away from everything that woman,
her open blouse, was trying
to say. Now I think it is a science
of probability, as in
The sun will rise tomorrow or
This woman will stay
with me tonight. And if I'm
wrong, if faith means I must

turn from the truth of her body
beneath mine, the late autumn
hues of her lidded eyes,
then I am content to be damned
to this world, where the sky
will grow heavy with seasons,
wings, or swathes of blue smoke
rising, and rivers at sunset
will burn but not be burning.

All my prayers will be simple,
unspoken, the union of bone
against bone. I will pray
to the body, which never makes
impossible claims of perfection,
and to this world, which promises
this much this morning—
the sound of rain on slate shingles,
the scent of last night's
candle burning down
by white curtains which float
in the mouth of an open window,
and the skin of the woman next to me
which turned to silver
in the moonlight, whose shadow tasted
like the powdered wings of a moth,
an angel, who will wake to this
gift I offer, a branch of forsythia,
its fleet fire bright against
the burnt umber of her hair.

I am telling you this despite
the six o'clock news.
Despite Death who flicks open
the cover of his expensive
watchcase, turns his collar up

against rain, who, after all,
has been mistaken
for that dark child named
Pain with his quick temper,
stamping feet, who stoops
to tie our nerves in knots as if they
are nothing more than
the troublesome laces of high-stitched
boots. I am telling you this
despite Christ's flaming heart,
the wound in Adam's side,
despite martyrs who upset
the general equation, who refused
to flee, but lingered instead
like cheap perfume, then bent
to kiss the cruel angles of strange
and glittering instruments—
morning star, scimitar, stiletto
teeth of the iron lady.

I am telling you this because
it is the only religion
I know to be true, because
the blades of our shoulders are
almost wings, because, whoever
you are, we are alive on this
blue planet, because rain has
overflowed the gutters
and the bruised sky looks only
like itself. Which is enough.
Because this is the only life
we can be certain of. Because
this world, each bone, is holy,
and never, never enough.

ELIZABETH ALEXANDER

Elizabeth Alexander's poetry is hip, edgy, often funny, and always hard-hitting. She speaks frankly about her own experience and her family's, including her childhood in Washington, D.C. Alexander (b. 1962) combines this honesty with historical accuracy and insight, and with panache. She writes from a distinctly personal point of view, but honors her heritage as a woman and as an African American. Her books are an intriguing blend of personal narrative, dreams, and dramatic monologue. She sometimes uses unexpected personae to speak through, including a series of poems in the voice of Muhammad Ali in her *Antebellum Dream Book* (2001). Her work also includes a long poem imagining the thoughts of the early nineteenth-century African woman who was exhibited in Europe as a curiosity, the title piece of her collection *The Venus Hottentot* (1990).

In addition to her books of poems, Elizabeth Alexander has published a collection of essays, *The Black Interior* (2004). She also edited a volume of the work of the poet Melvin Dixon, *Love's Instruments* (1995). Her award-winning teaching has taken her to several campuses, including Yale University.

Her poem "Neonatology" from *Antebellum Dream Book* is a graphic but surprisingly lyrical account of giving birth. In the poem's last section, Alexander focuses on the sudden shift of attention that takes place in birthing from the mother to the newborn. She does justice to the wildness, beauty, and elemental nature of giving birth by comparing it to jazz solos.

"Feminist Poem Number One," also from *Antebellum Dream Book,* deals with the complex emotions of a woman in a committed relationship who is also aware of those pressing against her warm home from the outside. She trumpets the joys of having a husband who treats her royally. She feels deserving, partly because of the grandeur of her African heritage. Paradoxically, her good fortune makes her think of those excluded from safety. She remembers that her grandmother as a child used to roller-skate to Embassy Row to keep track of the rest of the world.

Alexander's earlier collection, *Body of Life* (1996), includes "Affirmative Action Blues (1993)." The poem is a meditation on the Rodney King incident, where a bystander videotaped Los Angeles police officers stopping an unarmed black man in a speeding car and viciously attacking him. In this poem, Alexander links the roots of words to the deep roots of racism that led to Rodney King's bashing.

Giving birth is like jazz, something from silence,
then all of it. Long, elegant boats,
blood-boiling sunshine, human cargo,
a handmade kite—

            Postpartum.
No longer a celebrity, pregnant lady, expectant.
It has happened; you are here,
each dram you drain a step away
from flushed and floating, lush and curled.
Now you are the pink one, the movie star.
It has happened. You are here,

and you sing, mewl, holler, peep,
swallow the light and bubble it back,
shine, contain multitudes, gleam. You

are the new one, the movie star,
and birth is like jazz,
from silence and blood, silence
then everything,

jazz.

FEMINIST POEM NUMBER ONE

Yes I have dreams where I am rescued by men:
my father, brother, husband, no one else.
Last night I dreamed my brother and husband
morphed into each other and rescued me
from a rat-infested apartment. "Run!"
he said, feral scampering at our heels.
And then we went to lunch at the Four Seasons.

What does it mean to be a princess?
"I am what is known as an American Negro,"
my grandmother would say, when "international friends"
would ask her what she was. She'd roller-skate
to Embassy Row and sit on the steps of the embassies
to be certain the rest of the world was there.

What does it mean to be a princess?
My husband drives me at 6 a.m.
to the airport an hour away, drives home,
drives back when I have forgotten my passport.
What does it mean to be a prince? I cook
savory, fragrant meals for my husband
and serve him, if he likes, in front of the TV.
He cooks for me, too. I have a husband.

In the dream we run into Aunt Lucy,
who is waiting for a plane from "Abyssinia"
to bring her lover home. I am the one
married to an Abyssinian, who is already here. I am the one
with the grandmother who wanted to know the world.
I am what is known as an American Negro princess,
married to an African prince,
living in a rat-free apartment in New Haven,
all of it, all of it, under one roof.

AFFIRMATIVE ACTION BLUES (1993)

Right now two black people sit in a jury room
in Southern California trying to persuade
nine white people that what they saw when four white
police officers brought batons back like
they were smashing a beautiful piñata was
"a violation of Rodney King's civil rights,"
just as I am trying to convince my boss not ever
to use the word "niggardly" in my presence again.
He's a bit embarrassed, then asks, but don't you know
the word's etymology? as if that makes it
somehow not the word, as if a word can't batter.
Never again for as long as you live, I tell him,
and righteously. Then I dream of a meeting
with my colleagues where I scream so loud the inside
of my skull bleeds, and my face erupts in scabs.
In the dream I use an office which is overrun
with mice, rats, and round-headed baby otters
who peer at me from exposed water pipes (and somehow
I know these otters are Negroes), and my boss says,
Be grateful, your office is bigger than anyone
else's, and maybe if you kept it clean you wouldn't
have those rats. And meanwhile, black people are dying,
beautiful black men my age, from AIDS. It was amazing
when I learned the root of "venereal disease"
was "Venus," that there was such a thing as a disease
of love. And meanwhile, poor Rodney King can't think straight;
what was knocked into his head was some addled notion
of love his own people make fun of, "Can we all
get along? Please?" You can't hit a lick with a crooked
stick; a straight stick made Rodney King believe he was
not a piñata, that amor vincit omnia.
I know I have been changed by love.
I know that love is not a political agenda, it lacks sustained

analysis, and we can't dance our way out of our constrictions.

I know that the word "niggardly" is "of obscure etymology"
     but probably derived from the French Norman, and that
     Chaucer and Milton and Shakespeare used it. It means
     "stingy," and the root is not the same as "nigger," which
     derives from "negar," meaning black, but they are
     perhaps, perhaps, etymologically related. The two "g"s
     are two teeth gnawing: rodent is from the Latin "rodere"
     which means "to gnaw," as I have said elsewhere.

I know so many things, including the people who love me and the people who do not.

In Tourette's syndrome you say the very thing that you are thinking, and then a word
     is real.

These are words I have heard in the last 24 hours which fascinate me: "vermin," "screed,"
     "carmine," and "niggardly."

I am not a piñata, Rodney King insists. Now can't we all get along?

D. A. POWELL

D. A. Powell was born in 1963 in Albany, Georgia, but moved to California in the mid 1970s. He has taught at Harvard University and at the Iowa Writers Workshop. His honors include the Lyric Poetry Award from the Poetry Society of America, a Pushcart Prize, and the Larry Levis Award from *Prairie Schooner* magazine.

The titles of Powell's first three books all refer to refreshments: *Tea, Lunch,* and *Cocktails.* His first collection, *Tea* (1998), sparkles with references to the disco era and to the freewheeling days when tea dances figured prominently in the gay revolution of the 1970s and 1980s: "I was anybody's favorite song: *dance into my life* [donna summer] I ran with the big boys". The book *Tea* also has an extremely unusual shape. The poems stream across the page, wider than they are tall. Powell avoids capital letters. This structure opens the way for several fragments to occupy the same line, breaking and reforming into new meanings as the reader follows them along. The form conveys well the wide-open lifestyle of the day. The poem titles are just lines from the poems, highlighting the way that certain words and moments seem to stand out or recur with hallucinatory clarity ("tea" is also slang for marijuana).

A poem from *Tea,* "[my neck a toothsome feeding ground. vespered swarms had drunk of me before this new batman]," is subtitled "a song of Robin." Powell humorously recasts this comic strip to expose its gay subtext, painting Robin as a young man kept by an older one. Powell has subtle points to make about the way that power figures into sexual role play: "I must remember to wince when I feel his fangs." The poem's speaker might not be much older than a boy who reads comic books, making the Batman rewrite especially germane.

In his second book, *Lunch* (2000), Powell deals with the AIDS crisis. With singeing irony he recounts the way he learned of his HIV+ diagnosis in the poem "[you don't have syphilis. the doctor says]." When he reads this poem out loud, the audience doesn't laugh at the devastating humor, and can barely keep from crying. This subdued but emotional poem is a textbook on how *not* to tell someone bad medical news.

In the poem "[in the course of travel: strychnine every few hours. some italian art]," the disease has progressed. Symptoms and drug cocktails are the order of the day. Powell's illness has only sharpened his irony. He compares peeing under a maple tree to "a trip on a yacht or dying.com." But that moment also becomes lyrical, another mode that Powell excels at.

[MY NECK A TOOTHSOME FEEDING GROUND.
VESPERED SWARMS HAD DRUNK OF ME BEFORE THIS NEW BATMAN]

a song of Robin

don't be fooled by costumes: I am still an orphan.   I move through his house by stealth.   I thieve
he won't last: when he kisses I'll pull away.   already I know the short attention span of my body

my neck a toothsome feeding ground.   vespered swarms had drunk of me before this new batman

down every dark corridor of gotham I seek my next guardian.   capes fly open: how hunger rushes

when I'm ready to be circled one will circle.   secret cave.   I can make his voice bounce back
boy wonder.   he will believe he is the one hero.   I must remember to wince when I feel his fangs

[YOU DON'T HAVE SYPHILIS. THE DOCTOR SAYS]

you don't have syphilis.   the doctor says
you don't have hepatitis.   he says
you aren't diabetic.   the doctor says

cholesterol level normal.   blood pressure
good.   he says you've got great reflexes
the doctor says these things.   he's the doctor

he says I *do* have a bit of bad news.   he says
just like that: I *do* have a bit of bad news
not a *real* doctor remember: a physician's *assistant*

[IN THE COURSE OF TRAVEL:
STRYCHNINE EVERY FEW HOURS. SOME ITALIAN ART]

in the course of travel: strychnine every few hours.   some italian art
and trees yes pretty but it's the normal routine.   well, "normal routine"

you easterners: your maple trees.   you have your maple trees
                                                                              your nation
and me my eyes bugging late and funny:
                                            scrub compared to the maple trees

every few hours flash fevers.   every few and I'd be small.   a bit nervous
the evening distended as a bad patella: oh my knee.   and I had to pee

virtually every few minutes. someone catches me under the maple trees
taken out of context: like a trip on a yacht or dying.com.
                                                        I would not go

there: among the trees I stood almost grand and well.
                                                with my own nuts

my own birdlike nuts.   my own startled happiness at the slightest breeze

—for Tom Thompson

CREDITS

POEMS

sion of the University of Pittsburgh Press. "Nightclub" from *The Art of Drowning*. Copyright ©
1995 Billy Colllins. Reprinted by permission of the University of Pittsburgh Press. "Forgetful-
ness" from *Questions About Angels*. Copyright © 1991 Billy Collins. Reprinted by permission of
Sterling Lord Literistic and the author.

Mark Doty: "Fish R Us" from *Source*. Copyright © 2001 Mark Doty. Reprinted by permission of
HarperCollins Publishers, Inc. "Crêpe de Chine" from *Atlantis*. Copyright © 1995 Mark Doty.
Reprinted by permission of HarperCollins Publishers, Inc. "Fog" from *My Alexandria*. Copyright
© 1995 Mark Doty. Used with permission of the poet and the University of Illinois Press.

Cornelius Eady: "Running Man." from *Brutal Imagination*. Copyright © 2001 Cornelius Eady. Used
by permission of G.P. Putnam's Sons, a division of Penguin Group (USA) Inc. "Chuck Berry"
from *The Autobiography of a Jukebox*. Copyright © 1997 Cornelius Eady. Reprinted by permission
of Carnegie Mellon University Press and the author.

Jorie Graham: "Salmon," "Scirocco," and "Erosion" from *Erosion*. Copyright © 1983 Jorie Graham.
Reprinted by permission of Princeton University Press and the author.

Marilyn Hacker: "Rune of the Finland Woman" and "Graffiti from the Gare Saint-Manqué" from *Se-
lected Poems: 1965–1990*. Copyright © 1985 Marilyn Hacker. Used by permission of W. W. Norton
& Company, Inc. Sonnet XV from the sequence "Separations" from *Separations*. Copyright © 1972,
1973, 1974, 1975, 1976 Marilyn Hacker. Reprinted by permission of Frances Collin, literary agent.

Michael S. Harper: "Dear John, Dear Coltrane," "If You Don't Force It," and "For Bud" from *Song-
lines in Michaeltree: New and Collected Poems*. Copyright © 2000 Michael S. Harper. Reprinted by per-
mission of the poet and the University of Illinois Press.

Robert Hass: "Interrupted Meditation" from *Sun Under Wood*. Copyright © 1996 Robert Hass.
Reprinted by permission of HarperCollins Publishers, Inc. "Meditation at Lagunitas" from *Praise*.
Copyright © 1979 Robert Hass. Reprinted by permission of HarperCollins Publishers, Inc. "A
Story about the Body" from *Human Wishes*. Copyright © 1989 Robert Hass. Reprinted by per-
mission of HarperCollins Publishers, Inc.

Lyn Hejinian: "Chapter 188" from *Oxota: A Short Russian Novel*. Copyright © 1991 Lyn Hejinian.
Reprinted by permission of The Figures and the author. "There was once an angel . . ." from *The
Book of A Thousand Eyes*. Copyright © 2005 Lyn Hejinian. Reprinted by permission of the author.
"Time is filled with beginners" from *The Fatalist*. Copyright © 2003 Lyn Hejinian. Reprinted by
permission of Omnidawn Publishing and the author.

Brenda Hillman: "The Spark" from *Loose Sugar*. Copyright © 1997 Brenda Hillman. Reprinted by
permission of Wesleyan University Press. "The Formation of Soils" from *Cascadia*. Copyright ©
2001 Brenda Hillman. Reprinted by permission of Wesleyan University Press. "A Foghorn" from
Bright Existence. Copyright © 1993 Brenda Hillman. Reprinted by permission of Wesleyan Uni-
versity Press.

Tony Hoagland: "America" from *What Narcissism Means to Me*. Copyright © 2003 Tony Hoagland.
Reprinted by permission of Graywolf Press. "Ecology" from *Donkey Gospel*. Copyright ©1998
Tony Hoagland. Reprinted with the permission of Graywolf Press. "Sweet Ruin" from *Sweet Ruin*.
Copyright © 1993. Reprinted by permission of the University of Wisconsin Press.

Sharon Olds: "I Go Back to May 1937" and "Summer Solstice, New York City" from *The Gold Cell*. Copyright © 1987 Sharon Olds. Reprinted with permission of Alfred A. Knopf, a division of Random House, Inc. "Necking" from *The Wellspring*. Copyright © 1996 Sharon Olds. Reprinted with permission of Alfred A. Knopf, a division of Random House, Inc.

Frank Paino: "Each Bone of the Body" and "The Truth" from *Out of Eden*. Copyright © 1997 Frank Paino. Reprinted by permission of Cleveland State University Poetry Center and the author.

Linda Pastan: "Who Is It Accuses Us?," "25th Anniversary," and "What We Want" from *Carnival Evening: New and Selected Poems, 1968–1998*. Copyright © 1998 Linda Pastan. Reprinted with permission of W. W. Norton & Company, Inc.

Carl Phillips: "As a Blow, from the West" and "Loose Hinge" from *Rock Harbor*. Copyright © 2001 Carl Phillips. Reprinted by permission of Farrar, Straus and Giroux, LLC.

Robert Pinsky: "ABC" from *Jersey Rain*. Copyright © 2000 Robert Pinsky. Reprinted by permission of Farrar, Straus and Giroux, LLC. "Jar of Pens" from *The Atlantic*. Copyright © Robert Pinsky. Reprinted by permission of the author. "Shirt" from *The Want Bone*. Copyright © 1991 Robert Pinsky. Reprinted by permission of HarperCollins Publishers, Inc.

D. A. Powell: "[my neck a toothsome feeding ground. vespered swarms had drunk of me before this new batman]" from *Tea*. Copyright © 1998 D.A. Powell. Reprinted by permission of Wesleyan University Press. "[you don't have syphilis. the doctor says]" and "[in the course of travel: strychnine every few hours. some italian art]" from *Lunch*. Copyright © 2000 D. A. Powell. Reprinted by permission of Wesleyan University Press.

Ishmael Reed: "On the Fourth of July in Sitka, 1982," "Sky Diving," and "Loup Garou Means Change Into" from *The Reed Reader*. Copyright © 2000 Ishmael Reed. Reprinted by permission of Basic Books, a member of Perseus Books, LLC.

Aleida Rodríguez: "Apple" from *Paterson Literary Review*. Copyright © 2003 Aleida Rodríguez. Reprinted by permission of the author. "Extracted" copyright © 2005 Aleida Rodríguez. Printed by permission of the author. "Torch" from *Garden of Exile*. Copyright © 1999 Aleida Rodríguez. Reprinted by permission of Sarabande Books and the author.

Luis J. Rodriguez: "Meeting the Animal in Washington Square Park" and "Victory, Victoria, My Beautiful Whisper" from *Trochemoche*. Reprinted with permission of Curbstone Press. "My Name's Not Rodriguez" from *My Nature is Hunger*. Copyright © 2005 Luis J. Rodriguez. Reprinted with permission of Curbstone Press.

Mary Ruefle: "Suburb of Long Suffering" originally appeared in *Sentence*. Copyright © 2005 Mary Ruefle. Reprinted by permission of the author. "Kiss of the Sun" originally appeared in *Shade*. Copyright © 2005 Mary Ruefle. Reprinted by permission of the author. "Merengue" from *Cold Pluto*. Copyright © 2001 Mary Ruefle. Reprinted by permission of Carnegie-Mellon University Press and the author.

David St. John: "Hush," "No Heaven," and "Desire" from *Study For the World's Body: Selected Poems*. Copyright © 1994 David St. John. Reprinted by permission of HarperCollins Publishers, Inc.

Ntozake Shange: "One" from *for colored girls who have considered suicide when the rainbow is enuf*. Copyright © 1975, 1976, 1977 Ntozake Shange. Reprinted by permission of Scribner, an imprint of Si-

3, 2003. Recording used by permission of the Media Resources Center, University of California, Berkeley. Recording copyright © 2003 the Regents of the University of California. Used by permission of Carnegie Mellon University and the author. Copyright © 1997 Cornelius Eady.

Jorie Graham: "Scirocco" recorded at The Poetry Center and American Poetry Archives, San Francisco State University, October 22, 1981. Recording used by permission of The Poetry Center and American Poetry Archives, San Francisco State University. Used by permission of Princeton University Press and the author. Copyright © 1983 Jorie Graham.

Michael S. Harper: "If You Don't Force It" recorded at the Lunch Poems Reading Series, UC Berkeley, November 6, 2003. Recording used by permission of the Media Resources Center, University of California, Berkeley. Recording copyright © 2003 the Regents of the University of California. Used by permission of the author and the University of Illinois Press. Copyright © 2000 Michael S. Harper.

Robert Hass: "Interrupted Meditation" recorded at UC Berkeley, March 2005. Recording used by permission of the author. Recording copyright © 2005 Robert Hass. Used by permission of HarperCollins Publishers Inc. Copyright © 1996 Robert Hass.

Brenda Hillman: "The Spark" recorded at the Lunch Poems Reading Series, UC Berkeley, October 3, 2002. Recording used by permission of the Media Resources Center, University of California, Berkeley. Recording copyright © 2002 the Regents of the University of California. Used by permission of Wesleyan University Press. Copyright © 1997 Brenda Hillman.

Marie Howe: "The Kiss" recorded at the Lunch Poems Reading Series, UC Berkeley, April 1, 1999. Recording used by permission of the Media Resources Center, University of California, Berkeley. Recording copyright © 1999 the Regents of the University of California. Used by permission of W. W. Norton & Company, Inc. Copyright © 1997 Marie Howe.

Brigit Pegeen Kelly: excerpt from "The Orchard" recorded at the Lunch Poems Reading Series, UC Berkeley, February 5, 1998. Recording used by permission of the Media Resources Center, University of California, Berkeley. Recording copyright © 1998 the Regents of the University of California. Used by permission of BOA Editions, Ltd. Copyright © 2004 Brigit Pegeen Kelly.

Maxine Hong Kingston: "Idea!: Four-word Poems!" recorded at the Lunch Poems Reading Series, UC Berkeley, February 5, 2004. Recording used by permission of the Media Resources Center, University of California, Berkeley. Recording copyright © 2004 the Regents of the University of California. Used by permission of Harvard University Press. Copyright © 2002 Maxine Hong Kingston.

Galway Kinnell: "Oatmeal" recorded at the Lunch Poems Reading Series, UC Berkeley, April 5, 2001. Recording used by permission of the Media Resources Center, University of California, Berkeley. Recording copyright © 2001 the Regents of the University of California. Used by permission of Alfred A. Knopf, a division of Random House, Inc. Copyright © 1990 Galway Kinnell.

Li-Young Lee: "Tearing the Page" recorded at the Lunch Poems Reading Series, UC Berkeley, November 7, 2002. Recording used by permission of the Media Resources Center, University of California, Berkeley. Recording copyright © 2002 the Regents of the University of California. Used by permission of the author. Copyright © 2005 Li-Young Lee.

Dionisio D. Martínez: "Bad Alchemy" recorded privately by the author, February 2005. Recording used by permission of the author. Recording copyright © 2005 Dionisio D. Martínez. Used by permission of W. W. Norton & Company, Inc. Copyright © 1995 Dionisio D. Martinez.

Linda McCarriston: "Le Coursier de Jeanne d'Arc" recorded privately by the author, April 2005. Recording used by permission of the author. Recording copyright © 2005 Linda McCarriston. Used by permission of Northwestern University Press and the author. Copyright © 1991 Linda McCarriston.

Heather McHugh: "Ghazal of the Better-Unbegun" recorded at the Lunch Poems Reading Series, UC Berkeley, March 4, 1999. Recording used by permission of the Media Resources Center, University of California, Berkeley. Recording copyright © 1999 the Regents of the University of California.

Czeslaw Milosz: "A Song on the End of the World" recorded at the Lunch Poems Reading Series, UC Berkeley, February 3, 2000. Recording used by permission of the Media Resources Center, University of California, Berkeley. Recording copyright © 2000 the Regents of the University of California. Used by permission of HarperCollins Publishers, Inc. Copyright © 1998 Czeslaw Milosz Royalties, Inc.

Harryette Mullen: "ain't your fancy . . ." (excerpt from *Muse & Drudge*) recorded at the Lunch Poems Reading Series, UC Berkeley, October 7, 2004. Recording used by permission of the Media Resources Center, University of California, Berkeley. Recording copyright © 2004 the Regents of the University of California. Used by permission of Singing Horse Press and the author. Copyright © 1995 Harryettte Mullen.

Sharon Olds: "Necking" recorded privately by the author, March 2005. Recording used by permission of the author. Recording copyright © 2005 Sharon Olds. Used by permission of Alfred A. Knopf, a division of Random House, Inc. Copyright © 1996 Sharon Olds.

Frank Paino: "Each Bone of the Body" recorded privately by the author, May 2005. Used by permission of Cleveland State University Poetry Center and the author. Copyright © 1997 Frank Paino.

Linda Pastan: "Who Is It Accuses Us?" recorded privately by the author, December 2004. Recording used by permission of the author. Recording copyright © 2004 Linda Pastan. Used by permission of W. W. Norton & Company, Inc. Copyright © 1998 Linda Pastan.

Robert Pinsky: "ABC" recorded at the Lunch Poems Reading Series, UC Berkeley, February 7, 2002. Recording used by permission of the Media Resources Center, University of California, Berkeley. Recording copyright © 2002 the Regents of the University of California. Used by permission of Farrar, Straus and Giroux, LLC. Copyright © 2000 Robert Pinsky.

Ishmael Reed: "Loup Garou Means Change Into" recorded by the author, UC Berkeley, February 2005. Recording used by permission of the author. Recording copyright © 2005 Ishmael Reed. Used by permission of Basic Books, a member of Perseus Books, LLC. Copyright © 2000 Ishmael Reed.

Luis J. Rodriguez: "My Name's Not Rodriguez" recorded at the Lunch Poems Reading Series, UC Berkeley, March 6, 2003. Recording used by permission of the Media Resources Center, Uni-

INDEX OF TITLES OR FIRST LINES

DESIGNER
Victoria Kuskowski

SOUND ENGINEER FOR COMPACT DISC
José M. Zavaleta

TEXT
11.5/14.5 Venetian

DISPLAY
Univers Condensed, Venetian

COMPOSITOR:
Integrated Composition Systems

PRINTER AND BINDER
Friesens Corporation

PLAYLIST FOR COMPACT DISC

See pages 348–351 for a list of sources and permissions.

1. Czeslaw Milosz, "A Song on the End of the World," recorded at the Lunch Poems Reading Series, UC Berkeley, February 3, 2000. Time: 1:22.
2. Galway Kinnell, "Oatmeal," recorded at the Lunch Poems Reading Series, UC Berkeley, April 5, 2001. Time: 2:58.
3. Gary Snyder, "It Pleases," recorded at the Folger Shakespeare Library, Washington DC, April 1, 1989. Time: 0:42.
4. Linda Pastan, "Who Is It Accuses Us?," recorded privately by the author, December 2004. Time: 0:47.
5. Michael S. Harper, "If You Don't Force It," recorded at the Lunch Poems Reading Series, UC Berkeley, November 6, 2003. Time: 1:10.
6. Ishmael Reed, "Loup Garou Means Change Into," recorded by the author, UC Berkeley, February 2005. Time: 1:16.
7. Quincy Troupe, excerpt from "Eye Change Dreams," recorded at UC Berkeley, April 2005. Time: 0:42.
8. Maxine Hong Kingston, "Idea!: Four-word Poems!," recorded at the Lunch Poems Reading Series, UC Berkeley, February 5, 2004. Time: 4:14.
9. Robert Pinsky, "ABC," recorded at the Lunch Poems Reading Series, UC Berkeley, February 7, 2002. Time: 0:37.
10. Billy Collins, "Japan," recorded at the Lunch Poems Reading Series, UC Berkeley, December 2, 2004. Time: 1:35.
11. Robert Hass, "Interrupted Meditation," recorded at UC Berkeley, March 2005. Time: 6:53.
12. Sharon Olds, "Necking," recorded privately by the author, March 2005. Time: 2:52.
13. Linda McCarriston, "Le Coursier de Jeanne d'Arc," recorded privately by the author, April 2005. Time: 4:06.
14. Bill Zavatsky, "Live at the Village Vanguard," recorded privately by the author, February 2005. Time: 3:43.
15. Heather McHugh, "Ghazal of the Better-Unbegun," recorded at the Lunch Poems Reading Series, UC Berkeley, March 4, 1999. Time: 1:24.
16. Ntozake Shange, "one" (excerpt from *for colored girls who have considered suicide when the rainbow is enuf*), recorded at The Poetry Center and American Poetry Archives, San Francisco State University, November 17, 1976. Time: 3:50.
17. Sekou Sundiata, "Blink Your Eyes," recorded at The Poetry Center and American Poetry Archives, San Francisco State University, February 6, 1997. Time: 2:14.
18. Jorie Graham, "Scirocco," recorded at The Poetry Center and American Poetry Archives, San Francisco State University, October 22, 1981. Time: 3:11.

19. Marie Howe, "The Kiss," recorded at the Lunch Poems Reading Series, UC Berkeley, April 1, 1999. Time: 1:14.

20. Brenda Hillman, "The Spark," recorded at the Lunch Poems Reading Series, UC Berkeley, October 3, 2002. Time: 1:39.

21. Brigit Pegeen Kelly, excerpt from "The Orchard," recorded at the Lunch Poems Reading Series, UC Berkeley, February 5, 1998. Time: 2:50.

22. Jimmy Santiago Baca, "I have to remember / because you're ready to dismember" (excerpt from *Healing Earthquakes*), recorded at the Lunch Poems Reading Series, UC Berkeley, October 1, 1998. Time: 4:20.

23. Mary Ruefle, "Merengue," recorded at the Lunch Poems Reading Series, UC Berkeley, December 5, 2002. Time: 1:06.

24. Mark Doty, "Crêpe de Chine," recorded at the Lunch Poems Reading Series, UC Berkeley, October 3, 1996. Time: 3:32.

25. Harryette Mullen, "ain't your fancy . . ." (excerpt from *Muse & Drudge*), recorded at the Lunch Poems Reading Series, UC Berkeley, October 7, 2004. Time: 1:23.

26. Cornelius Eady, "Chuck Berry," recorded at the Lunch Poems Reading Series, UC Berkeley, April 3, 2003. Time: 2:27.

27. Luis J. Rodriguez, "My Name's Not Rodriguez," recorded at the Lunch Poems Reading Series, UC Berkeley, March 6, 2003. Time: 1:53.

28. Dionisio D. Martínez, "Bad Alchemy," recorded privately by the author, February 2005. Time: 4:23.

29. Li-Young Lee, "Tearing the Page," recorded at the Lunch Poems Reading Series, UC Berkeley, November 7, 2002. Time: 3:36.

30. Frank Paino, "Each Bone of the Body," recorded privately by the author, May 2005. Time: 6:28.